To Joan and Henry Leistner
of Toronto –

I enjoyed guiding you through
Confederate Charleston today –

Best Wishes

Jack Thomson
May 6, 2004
Mills House

CHARLESTON AT WAR

THE PHOTOGRAPHIC RECORD

1860 – 1865

by
Jack Thomson

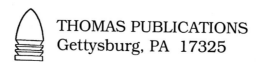

THOMAS PUBLICATIONS
Gettysburg, PA 17325

CHARLESTON AT WAR

THE PHOTOGRAPHIC RECORD

1860 – 1865

Copyright © 2000 Jack Thomson

Printed and bound in the United States of America

Published by   THOMAS PUBLICATIONS
                P.O. Box 3031
                Gettysburg, Pa. 17325

ISBN-1-57747-052-4   Hardbound
ISBN-0-57747-094-X   Softbound

Cover design by Ryan C. Stouch

THOMAS PUBLICATIONS publishes books about the American
Colonial era, the Revolutionary War, the Civil War, and other important topics. For a complete list of titles, please visit our web site at
www.thomaspublications.com or write to us at the address listed
above.

To the Charleston artists of 1860-1 and the visitors of early 1865, who in pursuit of an honest dollar, created a photographic record of a Confederate city, unequaled to any other city of that war.

And to my wife of only six years, Mary Peters, who gently but firmly encouraged me to complete this record of these early photographer's work.

CONTENTS

viii *Charleston At War*

ACKNOWLEDGMENTS

This book is possible because many institutions and collectors have preserved early photographs of Charleston. The Library of Congress and the National Archives have supplied many prints of original glass negatives and original collodion prints. Michael Winey and Randy Hackenburg of the U. S. Army Military History Institute, Carlisle, Pa. have, with little support, cared for the wonderful Civil War image collection of the Massachusetts Commandery, Military Order of the Loyal Legion. These are three sources that must be used by any student of photography of this war.

Abbreviations for the photographic sources used are:

Beaufort	Public Library, Beaufort, S. C.
Chas Mus	Charleston Museum, S. C.
Greyscale	Greyscale Fine Photography Center
L. C.	Library of Congress
N. A.	National Archives
SCHS	South Carolina Historical Society
Val. Mus.	Valentine Museum, Richmond, Va.
West Point	U. S. Military College Library, West Point, N. Y.

Private collectors who have shared their images with me are John Bennett, Ray Davenport, Greyscale Fine Photography Center, George Lathan, Charlie Peery, M. D., all of Charleston; Gil Barrett, of Laurel, Md., Jeffrey Krause of Gardinier, N. Y., Joseph Matthison, and Cal Packard of Mansfield, Ohio.

Other institutions that assisted in my research are:

Atlanta Historical Society
Avery Institute for African-American Studies, Charleston
Boston Public Library
Chicago Historical Society
George Eastman House, Rochester, N. Y.
Louisiana State University Library
Notre Dame University Library
Franklin D. Roosevelt Home, Hyde Park, N. Y.
South Caroliniana Library, Columbia, S. C.
University of N.C., Chapel Hill, N. C.
University of S.C., Columbia, S. C.
White House of the Confederacy, Richmond, Va.

A major thank you to William A. Frassanito of Gettysburg, pioneer in then-and-now photography, who encouraged me to include every wartime image of Charleston in this work, including the USS *Ironsides* combat photo. He generously shared his time and inspiration, led me to my publisher, and gave me the title for this book.

Many more have shared their research and insights:

Anna Blythe, tour guide and historian
Richard N. Coté, professional writer
Beverly Donald, Magnolia Cemetery Director
Jack Dugan, Military Historian
Anne Fox, Manigault Mansion
Grayscale Fine Photography Center, Charleston
Faye Halfacre, Circular Congregational Church
Rick Hatcher, Ft. Sumter National Park
Les Jensen, uniforms
Fritz Kirsch, modern wet-plate photographer
Juanita Leisch, women's clothing
Ralph Livingstone, Lt. Henry Belfield papers
Renee Marshall, Historic Charleston Foundation
Randolph Martz, architect
Lenette Maxwell
John Meffert, architectural historian
Ruth Miller, Charleston tour guide and author
Peggy Moseley, Charleston County Tax Auditor
Ann Peterson, Beaufort Nat'l Military Cemetery
Jim and Harriet Pratt, maps
Karen Prewitt, historic interiors
Debbie Rhoad, maps
Dr. Randy Sparks, College of Charleston
Jane Yates, Citadel Archives
June Wells, United Daughters of the Confederacy
Peter Wilkerson, S. C. Historical Society
Dr. Curtis Worthington, Waring Historical Lib.

This writer wants to remember some people he met as a youth, who had a brush with history: Mrs. Pierrepont of Miami, who as a girl cheered when Jefferson Davis stopped at her Georgia railroad station; Charlie Smith of Bartow, Fla., a former Texas slave cowboy; and Private John Salling of Slant, Va., next to last surviving Confederate Veteran.

Finally, this book could not have been written without the encouragement and computer expertise of Jim and Kathy Nicholson and it would not have been completed but for editorial advice, hand-holding, and the eye for a good phrase from my mentor Dr. Caroline Hunt of the College of Charleston.

TIMELINE

April 23-30, 1860   Democratic National Convention, held in Charleston
Nov. 6, 1860   Lincoln elected President
Nov. 9, 1860   Gov. Gist posts S. C. militia outside Charleston Arsenal
Dec. 20, 1860   S. C. secedes from the Union
Dec. 26, 1860   Major Robert Anderson concentrates his men into Fort Sumter

Jan. 9, 1861   Star of the West supply ship to Fort Sumter, turned back by Citadel guns.
March 3, 1861   Beauregard commands C. S. Military in Charleston
April 14, 1861   Ft. Sumter fired upon
May 11, 1861   Blockade of Charleston harbor begins, by steam-frigate *Niagara*
Nov. 7, 1861   Hilton Head & Beaufort fall to Federal Navy
Nov. 7, 1861   Brigadier General Robert E. Lee commands S. C., Ga., & East Florida
Dec. 11, 1861   Great Charleston Fire

March, 1862   Maj. Gen. John C. Pemberton commands
May 13, 1862   Negro pilot Robert Smalls takes supply ship *Planter* to Union fleet
June 16, 1862   Battle of Secessionville, on James Island
Sept. 15, 1862   Beauregard welcomed back to Charleston

Jan. 31, 1863   CSS *Palmetto State* and *Chicora* scatter Union blockading fleet
Mar. 28, 1863   Federals land on Folly Beach, ten miles from Charleston
July 10, 1863   Federals land on Morris Island, nine miles from Charleston
July 18, 1863   Federals assault Battery Wagner, seven miles from Charleston
mid-Aug., 1863   Two 12.75" Blakely rifled cannon run blockade into Wilmington, N. C.
Aug. 17, 1863   Bombardment of Fort Sumter begins
Aug. 21, 1863   Bombardment of Charleston begins
Aug. 29, 1863   First Blakely arrives in Charleston
Sept. 11, 1863   First Blakely burst during test firing
Sept. 8, 1863   USS *New Ironsides* & 5 or more monitors help grounded Weehawken
Oct. 5, 1863   CSS *David* rams USS *New Ironsides*
Nov. 2-6, 1863   President Jefferson Davis visits Charleston

Feb. 17, 1864   Hunley sinks USS *Housatonic*
Apr. 20, 1864   Gen. Sam Jones commands
Sept. 1, 1864   Atlanta falls to Sherman
Dec. 22, 1864   Savannah falls to Sherman

Feb. 17, 1865   Last blockade runner, *G. T. Watson*, leaves from flaming dock
Feb. 18, 1865   Charleston evacuated
end Feb. 1865   First northern photographer shoots King Street at the Bend
April 9, 1865   Robert E. Lee surrenders in Virginia
April 15, 1865   Brigadier-General Anderson raises his original flag over Fort Sumter
April 15, 1865   Lincoln assassinated
April, 1865   By Order, Charleston mourns Lincoln's death
April 19, 1865   Joseph E. Johnston surrenders in North Carolina

1876   Union occupation of Charleston withdrawn

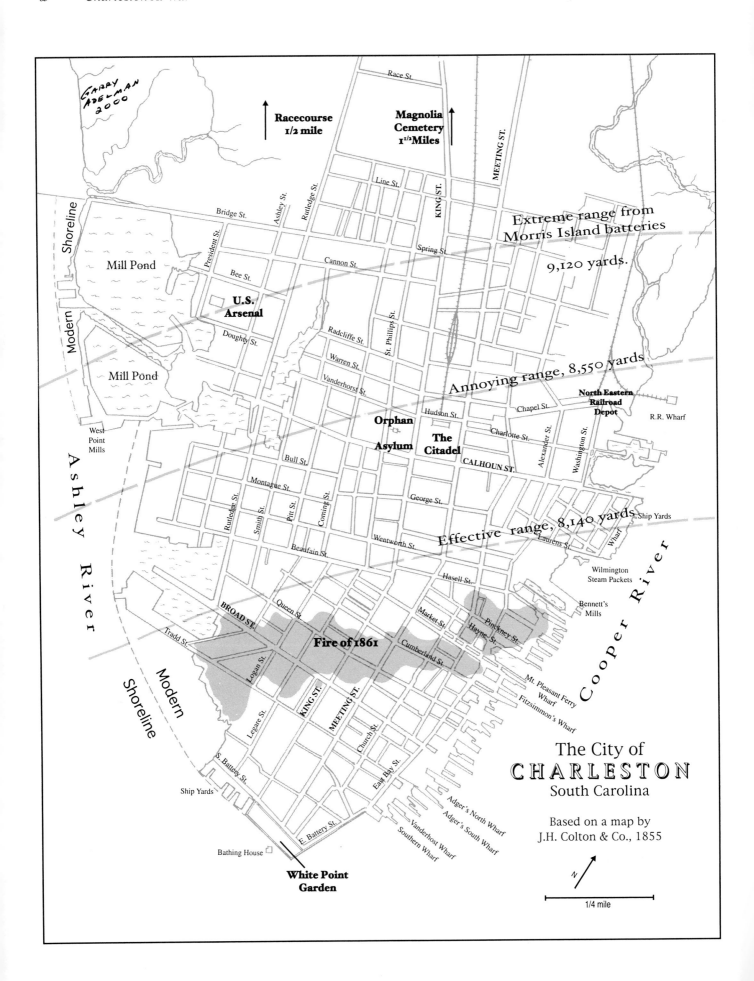

GARRY ADELMAN 2000

Race St.

Racecourse 1/2 mile

Magnolia Cemetery 1¹/²Miles

MEETING ST.

Line St.

KING ST.

Shoreline

Bridge St.

Ashley St.

Rutledge St.

Spring St.

Extreme range from Morris Island batteries 9,120 yards.

Mill Pond

President St.

Bee St.

Cannon St.

U.S. Arsenal

Modern

Doughty St.

Radcliffe St.

St. Phillips St.

Mill Pond

Warren St.

Vanderhorst St.

Annoying range, 8,550 yards

Chapel St.

North Eastern Railroad Depot

West Point Mills

Hudson St.

Charlotte St.

Alexander St.

Washington St.

R.R. Wharf

Orphan Asylum

The Citadel

CALHOUN ST.

Ashley River

Bull St.

Montague St.

George St.

Rutledge St.

Smith St.

Pitt St.

Coming St.

Wentworth St.

Effective range, 8,140 yards

Ship Yards

Laurens St.

Wharf

Beaufain St.

Hasell St.

Wilmington Steam Packets

Cooper River

Bennett's Mills

Tradd St.

BROAD ST.

Queen St.

Market St.

Pinckney St.

Hayne St.

Fire of 1861

Cumberland St.

Modern Shoreline

Logan St.

KING ST.

MEETING ST.

Church St.

Mt. Pleasant Ferry Wharf

Fitzsimmon's Wharf

Legare St.

East Bay St.

The City of CHARLESTON South Carolina

S. Battery St.

Ship Yards

Adger's North Wharf

Adger's South Wharf

Based on a map by J.H. Colton & Co., 1855

E. Battery St.

Vanderhost Wharf

Southern Wharf

Bathing House

N

White Point Garden

1/4 mile

INTRODUCTION

This book will show a Southern city as it appeared during the American Civil War and, to a great extent, still appears today. Nowhere in America is history so beautifully preserved as in the streets of Charleston, South Carolina.

Charleston is presented through a series of wartime images, matched by modern-day photographs of the same sites. Commentaries show how scenes have changed (or not changed). Information about the photographers and how they worked, with particular attention to how each image was taken is included whenever known.

Throughout the war Charleston was in the news. The war had begun there. South Carolina was the first state to secede and the first battle took place at Fort Sumter, where a nearly bloodless Confederate victory galvanized the North to raise an army and navy to put down the rebellion. Charleston held out nearly four years against Federal naval blockade and eighteen months of shelling, the longest siege in military history, before Confederate forces finally evacuated on February 17, 1865. By the next day, Union forces were already arriving to occupy the city.

Since 1861, Northern photographers had covered the war, largely in Virginia. The few Southern artists who took to the field had to give it up within a year when the blockade cut off their Northern suppliers of photographic equipment and chemicals. As Federal armies gradually occupied the South, photographers followed, making images of soldiers, battlefields, campsites, forts, ships, and when possible, battlefield dead. These photographers, shrewd businessmen, wanted images to sell to a Northern public with plenty of money to buy souvenirs to celebrate the progress toward Union victory.

The first arrived in Charleston within two weeks of the evacuation, carrying their own cameras, lenses, chemicals, and glass plates; they also brought portable dark rooms that could be mounted into a rented carriage or wagon. The collodion wet-plate technique of the day required elaborate equipment to prepare a glass plate for the camera. Moments before the photo was made, chemicals had to be poured onto the glass plate in the dark, to sensitize it for the image.

These photographers are all gone now. They are nearly forgotten and their story little told. In the course of study for this volume I have learned a small amount about how they did their job. They left few accounts about themselves or how they worked. Indeed, for many we have no portraits at all. Some were army employees such as George Barnard. Others, such as Isaac Beckett, William James,

Selmer Seibert, Philip Haas, and Washington Peale are known only by their images, and others are still unknown.

Many were hired by galleries such as Mathew Brady's to take pictures for Brady's gallery. Their glass negatives were printed and marketed by the owner of the firm, carrying the gallery's name. Thus, the label "Photo by Brady" merely advertised the plate's owner. The operator, as the man behind the camera was called, was paid very well but received no credit. (This book will give credit to the actual operator, where known.) Brady's operator in Charleston is yet unidentified.

Confederate contributions to the record of Charleston exteriors are, sadly, few. The market was almost entirely for portraits, and little money could be made by taking the camera outside. Seven portrait studios flourished in 1861, all on King Street, clustered near the Bend. This was the fashionable shopping district where one could have his image struck (they advertised, "preserve the image 'ere the substance fade"), continue shopping and perhaps pick up the finished cased image later that afternoon. They were:

> Jesse Bolles – 333 King, corner Liberty,
> George S. Cook – 265 King
> Daniel L. Glen – 221 King
> John J. Mundy – 226 King
> Osborn & Durbec – 245 King
> Charles J. Quinby – 261 King
> Ryan & Gardner – 234 King[1]

These photographers produced ambrotypes and carte-de-visite portraits of the city's gentry, common folk, and free persons of color. The daguerreotype that had introduced photography to the common people since 1839 was considered old-fashioned, though most galleries could produce them on special request.

The newer ambrotype had replaced daguerreotypes. The latter used a silver-coated plate that often reflected like a mirror, making the picture difficult to see at certain angles. The ambrotype was on glass and still required a protective case, but was cheaper, faster, and required fewer poisonous chemicals to produce.

Just before the war, the carte-de-visite (French for "visiting card") became the rage. They measured about 2 1/2" by 4", and unlimited copies from a glass negative could be made for about $2.50 to $3.00 for one dozen. These card photographs, for that is what they were called by the public, were easy to write upon. Names, dates, and places were inscribed—a joy to modern collectors and historians.

Politicians and soldiers posed against the studio's neck-rests, but bodies in action (such as battles) could not be photographed. Indeed, George Cook, who owned Charleston's most successful gallery, saw no business opportunity in images of the Battle of Fort Sumter. His business ledger for April 12, 1861 grouses:

"Shut up, War, War, War $00."

Shortly before the war, the stereopticon viewer was perfected, and one could now buy three-dimensional pictures. Outdoor views became popular and profitable. While portrait negatives could produce a few sales to friends and relatives, prints from a successful outdoor stereoptican view could be sold for years to locals and tourists. Stereoscopic views of exotic foreign places like Egypt were popular but there was little demand for local scenes. Of Charleston's seven portrait galleries operating in 1861, only one is known to have made a few outside images of the city—the partnership of James M. Osborn and F. Eugene Durbec.

Osborn & Durbec introduced the stereo camera to Charleston. Possibly other Charleston artists bought stereo cameras, but none of their prewar marks have been seen on this city's outdoor views. In 1860 or 1861 Osborn & Durbec published a set of at least eight street views of the city. After the 1860 Democratic National Convention, two stereo views of South Carolina Institute Hall were published. That building burned in December 1861, so all views of the intact structure must date before 1862.

During the war, the blockade kept needed chemicals out of the South and one by one, the Charleston artists closed their shops or occasionally worked for Cook, who kept his bustling portrait business well into 1864, serving fully 21 customers on March 8, 1864. By the end of that year, all Charleston galleries had closed. Cook evacuated to Columbia, S. C., where much of his work was lost to Sherman's invading army.

Nearly all his wartime images were cartes-de-visite, with occasional ambrotypes on demand. His work carried no backmarks until he reopened during the Occupation.

At the beginning of March 1865, or possibly a few days earlier, the first Northern photographer arrived to find grass growing in the streets of lower Charleston. Most of the remaining businesses had moved to upper Charleston to escape Federal shells. The tracks of all three railroads running out of the city had been wrecked by Sherman's army, and the North Eastern's depot had been destroyed. Much of Charleston lay desolate or burned. A golden opportunity awaited these artists, for they found a once-elegant city devastated by fire and artillery shells.

In fact, much of Charleston was still elegant and only a part (though a large part) was devastated. Much of Charleston was left unrecorded by these visitors, to the regret of us today who want to learn how people lived in the Confederate South. They did record the dramatic: ruined mansions, shelled buildings, empty streets guarded by Union occupiers. They did it for the dollar, which has shaped so much of the capitalist world, but they left priceless images of a culture that is gone. To-

day these images can be studied for the lifestyle and architecture of that golden age. Charleston today prizes most of the old hovels and mansions of the 1700s and 1800s. These images preserve architecture that is often changed by careless renovation. It is hoped that modern architects and contractors will use these images to preserve old buildings and design new ones to blend with the old.

Street scenes usually appear empty; the camera could not record moving men, horses, and dogs. Only when they stood still for several seconds could their image be fixed on the slow emulsion. But people were there—over 40,000 in 1861—Charleston was then the second largest city in the South.

Charlestonians themselves appear in this book. Emma Holmes described vividly in her diary the horror of the 1861 fire that gutted one mile of her city, destroying a strip two blocks wide, including her home. Augustine T. Smythe was an 18-year old student who attended the signing of the Ordinance of Secession and later wrote letters describing the gradual destruction of his city under unrelenting Union bombardment. But the city, and Emma, and Gus (as he was called by family and friends), persevered. This is their Southern city: its images and their story.

Emma Holmes

Daughter of a prominent Charleston family, she was twenty-two when the war began. Her father, Dr. Henry Holmes, had done well as a physician and plantation owner. He died in the 1850s but left his widow Eliza and eight children secure with a home at 2 Council Street, good friends, and attending house slaves. They could depend on their extended relations for moral, intellectual, and if necessary, financial support.

Her older brothers were soldiers, and one a physician in the Confederate Army. She kept a diary during the whole war that exhibits her intellectual curiosity as well as the excitement of the war. She enjoyed books, church, the company of men, frolics in the country, dinner parties, flagmaking, visiting Confederate Army camps, and the companionship of her friends and extended family.

When her family home burned in the 1861 fire, they moved to her uncle James G. Holmes' mansion on 9 East Bay Street (now 17 & 19 East Battery). They were able to save their clothing, most of their silver and valuables, a little furniture, and the carriage. Her family took refuge in Camden during much of the war. Inflation required her to supplement her family's income by teaching some of the local Camden children.

She took the train to Charleston occasionally to shop and to visit relatives, trying to avoid the Yankee shelling, but fragments from air bursts made these visits hazardous.

Augustine Thomas Smythe

Augustine was the second son of an Irish-born Presbyterian minister, Rev. Thomas Smyth of the Second Presbyterian Church. To avoid confusion with an "Aleck Smyth," formerly "Smith," in Charleston, Augustine added the terminal *e*, which has been used by his descendants ever since.[2] He was eighteen, and in his first year at South Carolina College, when Lincoln was elected president. Gus (as he signed his letters, and was known by his family and friends) attended the signing of the Ordinance of Secession in Charleston. He returned to his studies in Columbia, S. C., but with the excitement over Fort Sumter (and his mother's reluctant permission) he joined Capt. Alex Taylor's militia company, made up largely of his fellow students. After getting their own uniforms and learning drill during their studies, they served only three days active service in Charleston watching the firing on Fort Sumter.

That taste of military service made him transfer, after April 3, 1862, into the Washington Light Infantry, to be near his brother Adger Smyth and an uncle. One of the quality Charleston uniformed companies, it boasted a service dating from 1809 and still serves today. The W.L.I. put 410 soldiers into the Confederate Army, losing 117. One was General Johnston Pettigrew, who commanded the left wing of Pickett's Charge. The W.L.I. fielded three companies; Gus joined Co. A, 25th S.C. Volunteer Regiment. They served around Charleston for much of the war, and he fought in the Battle of Secessionville. His college connections brought him a letter:

Signal Office
August 28th 1862

Dear Smythe,
...It is our desire to collect in the corps as many of our ole fellow students as possible, and Manigault

Augustine T. Smythe, 1863

will detach every one that we recommend for the Corps, he being anxious as any of us to have young men of situation & responsibility. Our duties will be light, except during an actual or expected engagement with the enemy, then we may have a good deal of riding about to do, signaling, &c. By calling down at the Signal Office, in the Bathing House on the Battery, you will know everything connected with the Corps, that can be told an in[itiate.]

...by dropping me a few lines...,signifying your desire..., I can have you detached....

Yrs. Etc,
Wm. R. Atakinson

Gus did reply, and on Oct. 22, 1862, he was "detailed to the Signal Dept., & will report to Capt. Joseph Manigault in the city." He wrote to his Aunt Janey Adger one week later:

...so far I am much pleased with the exchange. I have not yet been assigned to any station, but trust to be kept at the Bathing House. My business hours now are from 9 A. M. To 1 1/2 P.M. & from 4 to 6 P.M. The manual labor is quite hard as the flag & staff are pretty heavy, but then there is not very much of it, & besides there is more interest in it than drilling. As to the accommodations, they are MUCH better than in camp, as we (in town) all stay in houses....

To his sister, Sarah Annie, he wrote on Nov. 10:

...I am now studying the system of the telegraph, as we expect probably to have an instrument here in the Bathing House.... We have a very pleasant set of fellows in the Corps, very many from among my old college friends.

He was promoted to lance sergeant in the Signal Corps on February 5, 1863. This was a temporary promotion, reverting to private if he returned to his permanent unit, Co. A, 25th SCV. Still, the "good bit of riding about" did occur, and Gus was expected to provide his own horse, Don. Accordingly Lance Sgt. Smythe applied since "services of a horse are indispensable, to be allowed the same food & pay for a horse." This request eventually had to be approved by Gen. Beauregard's adjutant. In April 1863 he wrote to the Confederate Secretary of War in Richmond, James S. Seddon, for the position of lieutenant in the Signal Corps. Gus never got a reply.

Though never an officer, he was a confident and well-read lad. At Fort Sumter he messed with the officers. His Signal Corps duties included flag semaphoring among the different Confederate forts in the harbor, telegraphing to the city, and reading the Yankee flag signals among their ironclad ships.

A captured Yankee signal man had divulged their own system, and Gus was able to read the flag signals between their fleet and the USS *New Ironsides*. He was pleased as punch with this unique ability and bragged to his Aunt Janey Adger:

> ...this should not be spoken of, of course, for if it were known by the Yankees they would immediately change & this put us again to sea. So please say nothing of it.

In 1863 the Federal army captured Morris Island, taking nearly two months to secure the three-mile island. Now they were only a mile from Fort Sumter. The Yankees immediately built batteries bearing upon Sumter, intending to destroy what had become a major symbol of secession.

In July the Morris Island batteries started what would become a one and a half year bombardment of Fort Sumter by land and by sea. A small-boat landing was feared. Gus got an additional job while he was temporarily stationed at Fort Sumter. He was placed in charge of twenty men who would throw hand grenades and greek fire down onto any attacking Union sailors and marines. In August he was transferred to CSS *Palmetto State*, one of two Confederate ironclads defending the harbor.

He reported on naval affairs to his family now, expecting much from the underpowered ironclads, and experiments with the plucky torpedo boats. Training on a new submarine named the *Hunley* went awry when a passing steamer swamped the little boat:

> We had quite a sad accident yesterday. A 'machine' we had here & which carried eight or ten men, by some mismanagement filled with water & sank, drowning five men, one belonging to our vessel, & the others to the CHICORA. They were all volunteers for the expedition & fine men too, the best we had. It has cast quite a gloom over us. Strange, isn't it, that while we hear with indifference of men being killed all around us, the drowning of one should affect us so.[3]

In July 1863, Federal heavy artillery opened fire on Charleston. Deliberate destruction of cities was not a usual thing, but Charleston had become an emotional target. This was the "vipers' nest of secession." Northerners felt that South Carolina had led in the treason that had already caused so many American deaths, and Charleston was where the Ordinance of Secession had been signed. It should be destroyed and treated as the ancient Romans had treated Carthage. Army Chief of Staff General Henry Halleck suggested in a letter to Sherman in Savannah in late December 1864 that, "...should you capture Charleston, I hope by some accident that the place be destroyed, and if a little salt should be sown on the site it may prevent the future growth of nullification and secession."

This shelling was random but almost continuous. The resulting terror caused a mass exodus from the city. Gus' parents stuck it out until late August when Dr. and Mrs. Thomas Smyth decided to remove to Summerton, a farming village some 90 miles away. The three railroads were jammed with luggage and passengers trying to get out, but Dr. Smyth managed to get a railroad "car & carried his buggy, horse, cow and some baggage."[4]

This left Augustine in charge of "No. 12" (now 18 Meeting St.) as well as the supervision of the other family properties. He wrote often to his evacuated family. It is these letters, written in a familiar style, that have preserved much of his Confederate Charleston.

The value of first-hand accounts cannot be underestimated. Indeed it is the stuff of history. An antique gun is only metal and wood. Yet it becomes much more than that if we know the man to whom it was issued by a sweaty and overworked ordnance sergeant from out of a wooden Charleston Arsenal box. The soldier cleaned it and carried it in drill, guard duty, and on the march; he was carrying it when an enemy's conical lead bullet tore through his left forearm, shattering his radius and ulna, while he was defending Battery Wagner and aiming at a blue-coated and hatless officer who was trying to clear his own jammed .44 caliber Remington revolver. In his pain, the injured soldier dropped his cocked rifle-musket, as do nearly all wounded men.

Such detail can only be gleaned from writings of men and women who lived through it, and from that, we can start to understand their world and their war. Emma Holmes' diary has been published, but Gus' letters have not. Emma never wrote of firing a gun. Gus fired his musket at the Battle of Secessionville but spent most of his war wielding a telegraph key, telescope, or a signal flag or torch.

This work mines Gus' letters extensively for the first time. It is hoped that Gus and Emma's words will help the modern reader understand more of their war.

Louisa McCord, Gus' fiancée and recipient of his letters.

RESEARCHING THE PHOTOGRAPHS

Many of these artists are little more than names today. Few are well-documented and some remain anonymous.

The established Charleston photographers took few outdoor images of Charleston, and even fewer as a Confederate city. Their money was in portraits and a photographer seldom took his lens outside his gallery. Only one wartime view of the city, that of the Confederate ironclad gunboat CSS *Chicora*, has survived.

Northern Photographers

After the Confederate evacuation on February 17, 1865, Northern photographers flocked down to record the freshly-fallen viper's nest of secession. During March, April, and early May they took their cameras to the docks and lower part of the city to record its defenses, defiance, and destruction. They also visited outlying forts but that is outside the scope of this study. By mid-May they had exposed enough plates to satisfy a Northern audience eager to see the humbled and ruined Rebel city.

The seven Northern artists identified so far, who visited Charleston in 1865, are: George Barnard, Isaac Beckett, James W. Campbell, William E. James, J.T. Reading, Selmer Seibert, and Mathew Brady's operator. An eighth Northern partnership, Haas & Peale, recorded a unique image nearby while the fighting was still going on.

George N. Barnard

A New York state photographer of fifteen years, Barnard moved to New York City and Washington, D.C. in 1859, making stereographic views for Edward Anthony. He is one of the early ones to arrive just after the evacuation, exposing plates in early March 1865. He is also notable for his artistry and for producing the first quality book of Civil War photographs.

When sent to Cuba in 1860 he included in his work a remarkable number of "instantaneous" stereographs.

Typical photography then required exposure time of some ten seconds or more, so stiffly posed images were the norm. Here he was able to reduce this time to about 1/5 second, and was able to record marching Spanish soldiers, a moving sailing ship, and surf!

In 1861 Barnard worked for Mathew Brady in Washington as an "Operator," merely a technician making portraits for Brady's studio. Brady took the credit; it was his studio of course, hence the title "Photo By Brady." Mr. Brady paid well: $11 per day for experienced photographers, in a day where a bricklayer supported his family on $1.50 per day.

Barnard covered the first two years of the war for Brady and Alexander Gardner doing studio portraits and some fine outdoor military scenes. Late in 1863 he was hired by the Topographical Branch of the Department of Engineers of the Army of the Cumberland in Nashville, Tenn. Under the direction of Capt. Orlando Poe, he ran the army's photographic operation. Barnard took images of generals, camps, warehouses, cities, railroads, and copied maps for the Army. He photographed Sherman's occupation of Atlanta, and followed Sherman on his "March To The Sea" to Savannah.

In March 1865 he journeyed to Charleston, taking remarkable images, but apparently not very many of them. Barnard left no written account of his Charleston views of 1865, but I have shadow dated his series of images taken at Battery Ramsay on White Point Garden, featuring the "Whopper," as the second week of March 1865, commencing around 10:30 a.m., by the shadows along the piazza and fence of Mr. DeSaussure's house on the corner of East Bay and South Battery.

In 1866 he published the landmark *Photographic Views of Sherman's Campaign*, retracing his route to shoot some missed or lost scenes.

Barnard returned in 1868 to Charleston for three years, to become a partner in Charles J. Quinby's long-established studio, above 261 King Street. He moved to Chicago in time to be burned out in the disastrous fire of October 8, 1871. Singed but undismayed, he quickly rounded up new apparatus to photograph the still-hot ruins. Back in Charleston in 1873, he bought out the old Quinby rooms. Burned out again in 1875, he rebuilt and stayed until 1880 when he sold out and moved back to New York.[1]

Isaac Beckett

Isaac Beckett of Savannah, Georgia, first advertised on April 15, 1865, his "BECKETT'S PHOTOGRAPHIC GALLERY, on Broughton, between Barnard and Whitaker Streets. Superior pictures at reasonable prices." The next day, the Savannah *Daily Herald* noted:

We have before us some fine photographic views of the ruins of Fort Sumter and the city of Charleston, taken by Mr. Isaac Beckett, of this city. Mr. Beckett is about to open a photographic gallery in Savannah, and he is an accomplished artist.

Born in County Mayo, Ireland, in August 1839, he became a captain in the 56th N.Y. Infantry. He was later in the signal service at Malvern Hill, Lee's Mills, and Seven Pines. After leaving the signal service, he was sent to Beaufort, S. C., as port commissary for the Union army.

Here Isaac became a partner with Samuel A. Cooley, who did extensive photography around the Beaufort area. But on May 12, 1865, Cooley sued "to recover possession of all negatives views taken by Beckett in Charleston, and all instruments."

Beckett's gallery was short-lived. In 1869 he was a clerk, living at 164 Jones Street, Savannah. In 1870, he was a lawyer, beginning a successful career in tracing land titles and making abstracts of property. He died in 1911 and is buried in Bonaventure Cemetery near his wife, Mary.[2]

James W. Campbell

Campbell worked in Charleston in mid-April, 1865, and copyrighted fifteen or more views of the city and Fort Sumter in the District Court of the Southern District of New York on May 23, 1865. This series was reviewed by the *American Journal of Photography* on May 15:

> ...As photographs, war pictures, or an exposition of the punishment of treason, we know of nothing of the kind which is superior...[3]

An experienced photographer, he was a close friend of George Barnard. They often worked together, but on their own enterprises. He worked in Chattanooga in late 1863 with the 20th Army Corps of the Army of the Cumberland. He assisted Barnard in Savannah in December 1864 and possibly in Charleston in 1865 as their work there is similar. After the war he had his business at 575 Broadway, New York.[4]

In 1866, George Barnard took Campbell on his trip to record the Atlanta Campaign for his monumental *Photographic Views of Sherman's Campaign.*[5]

Haas & Peale

Philip Haas and Washington Peale produced images on Morris Island, a sea island just south of Fort Sumter, during the summer of 1863. They recorded the two-month siege of Morris Island. Among their images of the attempt to take Battery Wagner and to shell Fort Sumter is a remarkable action photograph, that will be described fully in Section C.

William E. James and the *Oceanus*

Who was he, and why did he photograph Charleston?

When the public learned of government plans for a big ceremony to celebrate the capture of Charleston, where Brigadier General Robert Anderson would raise his old 1861 flag over Fort Sumter, many New Yorkers wanted to go down to see the show. They could not get free transportation with public officials, but they did not want to miss this adventure. The Sumter Club was organized to charter a ship, a screw propeller, the *Oceanus*, departing New York City on April 8, 1865. It is uncertain whether a Brooklyn photographer named W. E. James was on board to record the expedition, but he was in Charleston on their arrival.

Three days later a sullen ex-Confederate Charleston harbor pilot got the seasick passengers over the bar into the harbor. They steamed past the ruins of Fort Sumter, where a pavilion was being built for Gen. Anderson and his flag-raising celebrants. United States flags flew from all the evacuated Confederate forts in the harbor.

Oceanus tied up to Southern Wharf, on the east side of Charleston. Most wharfs, and the city in general, were in poor condition from eighteen months of shelling and abandonment, but the city was slowly being cleaned up for the celebration and later occupation by the Federal garrison. A book about the expedition, *The Trip Of The Steamer Oceanus To Fort Sumter And Charleston, S. C.,* reported that Mr. James was the agent:

> To Mr. E. Anthony, of the firm "E. & H. T. Anthony," No. 501 Broadway, New York, who had an Artist in the field, and who (James) kindly permitted

William E. James   (Cal Packard)

his copy-righted views to be used for illustration, the committee of publication would tender their hearty thanks, in the name of the "Sumter Club."

This identifies James as one of Anthony's photographers. He traveled to Charleston to produce negatives for Anthony, but he made no demand for credit. Once paid for his negatives, James had no further interest in them. He also agreed to make extra images for *Oceanus* passengers. These were done on his own time, for his own income, and he put his name on these cards. It is doubtful whether James steamed down on *Oceanus*, for he was from their neighborhood, and certainly knew some of the Sumter Club members as clients. But, he was with them at Southern Wharf.

Friday, April 14th.
    Breakfast was ordered promptly at six o'clock. The preliminary business being disposed of, we were requested by our enterprising fellow-citizen, Mr. W. E. James, to bestow us as eligibly as possible on the decks of the steamer, to be instantaneously photographed. Some of our first reflections in Charleston, were made at this moment.[6]

This identifies the backmark imprint of "W. E. James, Photographer, 267 Fulton Street (opposite Clinton), Brooklyn." A friend of mine, Cal Packard, has a collection of James carte-de-visite images that were taken in Charleston, and he has generously allowed me to use them in this volume. Also, Ray Davenport, of Sumter Military Antiques in Charleston, S. C., shared his image collection with me.

In getting to know Mr. James' work, I have seen some fifteen of his Charleston cartes. All of James' work bears his imprint on the front or reverse, but no printed Charleston caption. All those seen, so far, have only a penciled or inked Charleston identification or date.

It may be that Mr. James considered this junket to Charleston to be merely a diversion from his profitable Brooklyn portrait clientele. He made enough prints to satisfy his *Oceanus* patrons, but made little effort to market his Charleston prints to the general public.

In 1987 three stereo views found at the Washington Antique Photo Show turned out to be James work. Among shoe-boxes of stereographic views from all over the U.S., was a good view of the ruins of the Circular Congregational Church and St. Philip's Church. Seven well-dressed ladies and gentlemen had posed for the photographer on the sidewalk by the ruins of the Congregational Church. There was no caption on front or back of the cream card, only a penciled "Ed. C."

In the same shoe-box was a stereo on the same cream-color card stock, showing a ruined building. Again, it had no printed caption of photographer or location. On the reverse, in pencil, is:

Ed. C.
Charleston
April 14th 1865

Third time lucky: also in the shoe-box was another uncaptioned stereo on the same cream-colored card stock, showing a church and two shelled buildings. On the reverse, in the same hand in pencil, is the cryptic:

Ed. C.
Charleston, S. Ca
April 14th 1865

But who took them? When Cal Packard loaned his James collection, it included an identical carte-de-visite version of the dapper ladies and gentlemen in front of the Congregational and St. Philip's churches. This suggests that the cartes and stereos are all views by W. E. James. The clincher is one more stereo, an image of the flag-raising ceremony at Fort Sumter, on the same cream card stock, captioned in pencil on the reverse:

Ed. C
Raising of the flag at
Fort Sumpter
April 14th 1865

Mr. James used a stereo camera to take his pictures. Back home in Brooklyn, he trimmed some of his stereo prints and mounted them as cartes de visite. The cartes all have James' pre-printed name and Brooklyn address on the card stock.

Mr. James Charleston work is scarce, but not rare. *Oceanus* passenger list names 132 well-heeled tourists, and most of them could easily want, and afford, their very own souvenir set of their historic adventure.

James may have printed sets and selected views of his Charleston series for his *Oceanus* clients and marked the names of his clients in pencil for his own convenience. Some sets of his city series may not have the penciled captions, and may be overlooked for what they really are. The four stereo views may be part of an order for *Oceanus* passenger Edward Cary, of the "Sumter Club's" Executive Committee.

J.T. Reading

Mr. Reading sold cartes of Charleston backed with his advertisement:

J. T. Reading & So., Photographers
Cor. John & Whitaker Sts.
Savannah, Geo.

He is difficult to find, both as a photographer and his short-lived studio. The Savannah city directories from 1858 through 1871 do not list him. There is no John Street in Savannah, though St. Julian Street does intersect

Whitaker, in Savannah's commercial area. Reading may have come in with the Union army after Sherman captured Savannah in December 1864 and used cards for his carte de vistes that had been composed by another recently arrived job printer. A local printer would have known the proper Savannah street names.

Reading did make a friend in the Savannah *Daily Herald*, who editorialized on February 13, 1865:

> J. T. Reading and Co., Photographers, at the corner of Whitaker and St. Julian Streets, have sent us a view of the scene of the late [Confederate Naval magazine] conflagration. It is well executed, and gives as accurate an idea of the ruins as can be given in a picture.

Then on April 24, 1865, the *Daily Herald* reported:

> We are informed that Mr. J. T. Reading, corner of St. Julin and Whitaker streets, the well known photographer, took a good negative of the great [Lincoln memorial] gathering, with the stand in Johnson square recently...

Three days later the editor saw proofs of "...the great meeting in Johnson square. It is a fine aspect of the assemblage and an interesting souvenir of this memorable occasion."

Reading did not stay long in Savannah. The 1866 city director lists J. G. Steiger, proprietor of the Sunbeam Photographic Gallery, at the "cor. Whitaker and St. Julian Sts."

Selmer Seibert

In 1865, Seibert produced a series of 63 photographs of "the more important points and defenses of Charleston," for General Richard Delafield, Chief of Engineers. Forty were known to have been taken by Seibert, the balance made either by him or George Barnard. General Delafield spent the war in Washington. He appreciated the value of photographs as a historical record.[7]

Little is available about Seibert, and even his name is uncertain. Another writer identifies him as Samuel Rush Seibert, who was actively experimenting with the daguerreotype when he arrived from Philadelphia to Washington in January 1841.[8]

Most of his work is in the National Archives. Few of their acquisition records were kept, so in 1897 Gen. A. W. Greely attempted to reconstruct just how the Archives assembled their images from the War of the Rebellion. Greely wrote:

> In 1865, under the direction of Gen. Delafield, a series of views were taken by Mr. S. R. Seibert, showing existing conditions of the more important points and defenses of Charleston, S. C. There are

sixty-three of these photographs, of which forty are known to have been taken by Seibert, the balance being attributed to him [although possibly some of them may have been made by Barnard].[9]

In 1897, the War Dept. listed sixty-three negatives in their "Seibert collection", all of the "C" size, larger than 8 x 10 inches. Most are of Fort Sumter, other batteries on Sullivans Island and James Island, and other forts not on the Charleston peninsula; and are outside this study of the city. The three images of the torpedo boats [C-750-752, my images E-2, 3, 4] "were probably made by Mr. Seibert, but the records do not show positively."[10]

His image of Battery Waring, [C-798] is credited as supplied, but not produced by him. I have shadow dated it as part of his own Chisholm's Wharf sequence [my image E-1]. Other views were supplied by him, though he may have actually photographed some of them himself.

Mathew Brady's operators

Mr. Brady's poor eyesight kept him from working behind the lens. He was a businessman, running successful galleries in New York and Washington. He sent operators into the field to produce images for his studio, which he marketed under the title, "Photo by Brady." His as yet unidentified operator worked in Charleston late in April and perhaps early May, recording scenes in Fort Sumter, forts around the city, and several views in the city itself.

Brady sent many of his stereo images to the Anthony Brothers for mass production. In their *Photographic History/ The War For The Union* series, they marketed several Brady-supplied negatives in their catalogue.

Most Charleston views encountered today are stereoscopic scenes mass-produced in 1865 by two aggressive firms, E. & H. T. Anthony of New York, and John P. Soule of Boston. Both marketed them for years after the war. While Soule's stereos are every bit as good as Anthony's, Soule's views are usually trimmed versions of Anthony's stereoviews.

Charleston Photographers

Most galleries in Charleston confined their business to portraits, but we have records of three that did venture outside their studio.

Jesse A. Bolles

In 1856 the Washington Light Infantry hired "our friend Bolles, the artist" to make daguerreotypes of their excursion to the Cowpens Battlefield to build and dedicate a monument to Colonel William Washington. The widow of this Revolutionary War hero had given his battle flag to the W. L. I. which is still treasured by them.

> April 21: On our way we crossed the Bridge at Pacolet,...A beautiful Daguerreotype was taken of this spot by Mr. Bolles as also at Cherokee Springs, and Spartanburg...[11]

In 1857, Bolles produced daguerreotypes and ambrotypes at 281 King (upstairs), at the corner of Liberty Street. On April 26, 1861, Bolles's Temple of Art advertised in the Charleston *Mercury*, pictures taken of Forts Sumter, Moultrie, and the Floating Battery, "Taken immediately after the surrender, previously to any repairs or changes whatever."

He managed to stay in business through 1862, advertising in the *Courier* on December 10 for a "BOY WANTED, TO WORK IN AN AMBROTYPE GALLERY, Inquire at BOLLES GALLERY, corner of King and Liberty-streets."

After the war, Bolles reopened his gallery by 1868. He had relocated to 323 King, at the northeast corner of King and Market Streets, where he sold card photos, cabinet cards, and post war stereos of the city.[12]

His wife, Catharine A. Bolles, ran the business as listed in the 1872-3 directory,[13] but Jesse took it over again through 1878.

Osborn & Durbec

This partnership is the only Charleston firm known to have produced views of their city that have survived. In 1860 or 1861 they exposed a series of eight or more stereo views of White Point Garden. Five of these have been located, and are included in this volume.

James Osborn first appears in a Charleston directory in 1855 as a daguerrean artist, living in his studio over 233 King Street.[14] By 1859 he had taken a partner, F. Eugene Durbec, who lived on Coming Street, near Calhoun.[15] Together the ambitious partners expanded into the more modern ambrotypes, melainotypes (now called tintypes), ivorytypes, and stereoscopic views.

By 1861, they were at 245 King (west side) and recognized by the public by a big camera hung outside their gallery. They exposed ambrotypes and card photographs inside their studio but took their own stereoscopic camera outside for street scenes.

Their early wartime business prospered, recording soldiers and civilians, until the blockade choked off their supplies. Nearly all photographic materials were produced by a few Northern firms such as the Anthony Brothers in New York, and Scoville in Waterbury, Conn. As these sources were stopped by the blockade and their

supplies dried up, the King Street galleries closed their doors. There are no wartime city directories to determine just when these partners folded. They stayed in business for a time by buying supplies from a competitor, George Cook, whose gallery was one block up King Street. Osborn & Durbec bought 1/9th plate ambrotype cases and mats from him as late as October 22, 1861. Durbec dropped out of the partnership. Cook made a last sale of alcohol, iron oxide, and collodion to Mr. Osborn himself on January 28, 1862.[16] Osborn then worked as an operator at George Cook's gallery, at least through September 1863.

James Osborn stayed out of the regular army but did join the S. C. militia. He enlisted in the Lafayette Artillery, 1st Artillery Regiment on September 17, 1861. Its only muster roll in the National Archives, to October 31, 1861, shows him present for duty. He later joined Co. C, 1st Artillery Regiment on July 10, 1863. The National Archives preserves its only roll, which runs to Sept. 26, 1863 and shows him still present.

Osborn saved his negatives, and after the war, opened his own studio at the corner of King and Liberty Streets. He marketed his own prewar images to the Yankee occupiers, under his own name. The first city directory published after the war, in 1867-8, shows J. M. Osborn one last time, as a photographist at 331 King Street.[17] Some images will appear in this volume, under his name alone, as postwar cartes made from stereo views taken in 1860, 1861, and 1865.

The next directory, for 1869-70, showed Mr. Durbec back in business, at 235 King. He had a new photographic partner, Richard Issertel who lived at 21 Vanderhorst Street and had served in Capt. Cordes' Company (German Hussars), 2nd S. C. Cavalry. Their product was the carte-de-visite. All Osborn & Durbec images, as well as Osborn images, are scarce.

Charles J. Quinby

In 1860 this veteran New York "Photographist and Dealer in photographic materials" was living above his shop at 233 King Street.[18] By the next year the Quinby Photograph and Fine Art Gallery had moved above J. R. Read's dry goods store, at 261 King, an excellent address in the heart of Charleston's most fashionable commercial district. He quickly built a thriving business in cased glass ambrotypes and carte-de-visite card photographs.

Mary Boykin Chesnut was mulling over her 38th birthday in her hotel room in Charleston on March 30, 1861, when she heard a loud banging at her door. She threw it wide open:

> Oh, said John Manning, standing there, smiling radiently [sic]. "Pray excuse the noise I made.

I mistook the number. I thought it was Rice's room. That is my excuse. Now that I am here, come go with us to Quinby's. Everybody will be there—who are not on the [Sullivan's] Island. To be photographed is the rage just now.[19]

Mrs. Chesnut did have some card photographs made, but she did not like them: "Got my carte de visite. Mr. Chesnut very good—mine like a washer woman.[20]

Edmund Ruffin, who fired the first Confederate shot that struck Fort Sumter, approved his own card photos, for which Mr. Quinby charged 50 cents.

No exterior images are known by Quinby before or during the war. His card images have various backmarks, some misspelled "Quimby."

In 1865 he quickly accepted the new rulers. He was back in business four days into the occupation, but not as a photographer:

> Mr. C. J. Quinby, well and favorably known to all good citizens, has opened at 233 King street, opposite Hasell, a large and well selected stock of the best brands of segars, smoking and chewing tobacco, and a variety of other articles.[21]

Memories of him in the North were strong and sore-headed. One "N. Parsons" wrote Secretary of War E. M. Stanton on March 18, 1865:

> Charles J. Quimby son of Daniel Quimby of this Town, left here a few years since for the South, where he has been making Thousands of Dolls by a contraband trade—he is now in Charleston S. C., where he is waiting an opportunity for permit to sell some Sea Island Cotton stored in a large Barn there—desires to avail himself of the amnesty proclamation—he is a rebel sympathiser and Mr. Secretary seize the Cotton and put him thro'—a mean dog—and his Father before him—who altho he claims to be loyal has not voted for 3 or 4 Years—Father & Son have been in correspondence since he left—The Father openly boasts that he can have a permit to visit his Son—dont trust him.

Stanton asked Gen. John Hatch, commanding at Charleston to look into the matter, who reported on April 9, 1865:

> Mr. Chas. J. Quinby is considered here as one of the few men who [desired?] to be known as loyal to the Government while the city was held by the rebels. It is not known of the claims acg [sic] cotton, but if so his claims like all others will be made at Washington. No decisions have been made to seizing cotton without reporting to Washington and receiving orders in the case.[22]

Quinby reopened his gallery later in 1865. He produced portraits and large prints, and his later outdoor scenes show skill. He marketed several carte de visite street scenes taken in 1865, but these are usually cropped stereo views taken in 1865 by Northern photographers. Quinby's manager in 1867-68 was another veteran cameraman from the North, Jacob F. Coonley.

George N. Barnard then returned from the North as a partner, and turned Quinby & Co. into one of the finest in the region. Bertha F. Souder bought this studio in 1871. It was operated by her husband or son, Stephen T. Souder.[23] George N. Barnard returned to own the gallery from 1873 until 1880.[24] Frank A. Nowell then owned it after 1880. This genealogy is given so one may trace the ancestry of its product. The firm's stock of negatives went to each new owner, so a wartime image could appear over the imprint of a much later gallery.

Identifying Civil War Images

Today we rarely know exactly when a picture was taken or by whom. Captions are usually lacking, and when present are frequently inaccurate. This lack of captions can be frustrating to anyone wanting to know more about a photograph. It must be understood, however, that these images were not made as historical records or even as journalistic pictures as we know them today. These "views" were made to appeal to the victorious Northern public.

Today we are often left with no information on what otherwise is a splendid view from the 1860s. Fire images from 1861 are mistaken for 1886 earthquake views. Both are often mistaken for damage from Union shells.

Mathew Brady often gets credit for any Civil War photograph, from any place. He never visited Charleston, though he did sell prints from glass negatives he had purchased, or had hired an "operator" to make for him in Charleston.

Only in rare instances do we know actually who stood behind the camera in Charleston. Unless self-employed and marketing their work under their own names, most were only workmen. For example, Northern firms such as the Anthony Brothers hired photographers to produce images that Anthony would then sell under their name. Equipped with cameras and chemicals, these hired artists "went South," captured their images, delivered them to the boss, collected their pay, and moved on. Civil War Charleston views have also been credited to a later photographer, only because he had bought the negative files of the original gallery owner and put his own name on the print. George

Barnard and William James are exceptions. The former insisted on getting credit, and the latter sold his images under his own name.

Shadow Dating

The technique of shadow dating can identify the time and date an image was made, and occasionally identify its cameraman. Accuracy sometimes can be within one or two days for date, and within two minutes for time of day. Many early images of Charleston have survived, but with only a brief caption or none at all. The information may be sketchy and inaccurate.

To understand how this process works, we need to remind ourselves of the relationship between the earth and the sun. It is important to know that the earth revolves around the sun in exactly the same way now as it did in 1865. Since the morning sun rises in the east and sets in the west, it throws a long shadow to the west in the earliest part of the day. That shadow decreases in length as the morning passes, becoming shortest at noon. Then, as the afternoon sun descends to the west, it throws ever-lengthening shadows to the east.

The angle of these shadows changes daily throughout the year. In the winter, when the Sun is low on the southern horizon, the shadows cast to the north are long. As spring arrives, and the Sun climbs higher in the sky, the shadows get shorter. In the summer, the Sun reaches its apex, and thus casts a short shadow. Finally, the Sun falls lower in the sky throughout the fall, and the shadows get longer again. If a building's exterior remains as it was in the 1860s, this progression of the sun can be tracked, allowing us to determine the time of day when that photograph was taken. Once the time is known, then we may be able to date the image. Shadows descend a wall at the same time of day, as spring advances. Seasonal shifts in shadows make shadows climb or descend a wall.

A third problem must be recognized. Which half of the year was the image taken? Was it exposed in the first half of the year or the last half? A spring shadow will be indistinguishable from a fall shadow. For instance, an image taken in February will have a southern angle very close to an image taken in November. An image taken in May will have a southern angle similar to one taken in August.

This book will not have this third problem. All shadow dated images in this volume were made in the spring: Charleston was occupied on February 18, and Boston papers headlined this news on February 22. This was a hot story, and Northern photographers rushed south to capture images they could sell to an eager Northern public. By June this was old news. I have not found any images that could be dated to the second half of 1865.

Once the image's time and date is known, it may be compared with other dated images to identify the artist, for they were here at different times. If just one image has an identified photographer and can be shadow-dated, sometimes even the sequence of his work can be established.

PRE-WAR CHARLESTON

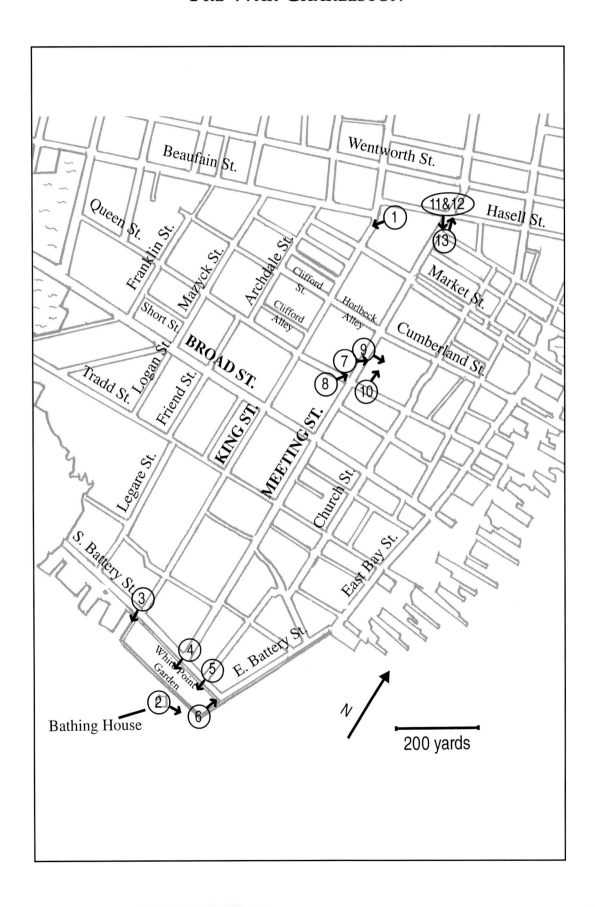

A-1

**Jno. Siegling Music Warehouse, 233 King Street, copy
print from a lost quarter-plate daguerreotype c. 1853.
(Greyscale)**

A-1. John Siegling's Music Warehouse. This is the earliest outdoor photograph taken in Charleston.

This is the oldest surviving Charleston exterior photographic image.

German-born John Siegling started his music store in 1819 on Meeting Street. He relocated to King Street after a fire had cleared this site in 1838. This location was perfect. King Street At The Bend was Charleston's most fashionable shopping area. Four generations of Sieglings made a living on this corner until 1970 when C. Casimer Siegling closed it. He acknowledged that after 150 years his store had become an institution, but he also said that institutions do not make money. Siegling's firm manufactured drums for the Confederate Army. A century later, I purchased fifes here for a bicentennial reenactment unit, the 2nd. S. C. Regiment of Foot.

This image was exposed from a second floor of a shop located on the east side of King Street, just one or two doors south of Hasell Street.

The original thumb-stained daguerreotype is lost. The size of the thumb print, included in later enlargements on paper, indicates that the original image was a "quarter-plate" daguerreotype. It was made on a 3 1/4" x 4" silver-coated copper plate. Its cost was considerable. There is no evidence that George Cook

made this image, but the record books for his Charleston gallery are the only records for a Charleston artist to have survived for this period, so it may be useful to examine his rates. At a time when a bricklayer supported his family in a two-room apartment on $1.50 per day, Cook charged $4.50 for a quarter-plate made at his gallery. The photographer may have charged more to move his apparatus outside his gallery.

Mr. Siegling's neighbor to his south, 231 King (now 241 King) survives in good condition, but Siegling's building (now 243 King) was virtually gutted in the 1980s during renovation into a bookstore.

A-2

White Point Garden, No. 5—view taken from the Bathing House, half of stereo #8, Osborn & Durbec, 1860 or 1861.   (Cal Packard)

This image is copied from a carte-de-visite with a plain back, but the image is identical to an Osborn & Durbec stereo in the South Carolina Historical Society. This carte image is used for its greater clarity and because none of its margins have been trimmed to fit the stereo format.

In 1861, James M. Osborn and F. Eugene Durbec marketed sets of twenty stereographic views of Fort Sumter taken after the Confederate attack. Before then, or possibly at the same time they also published a set of eight or more stereos of Charleston. All bear their label pasted, as does this:

No. 8
from
OSBORN & DURBEC'S
Southern Stereoscopic & Photographic
DEPOT.
223 KING STREET
(Sign of the Big Camera)
CHARLESTON, S. C.

Four of these eight that have survived in libraries and collectors's hands are included here. White Point Garden was Charleston's most popular resort.

Taken from the Bathing House, it shows several people enjoying wooden benches, by immature trees. The harbor light, seen in image A-5, is just out of frame, at left.

In the center is commission merchant Louis DeSaussure's three-story Italian Renaissance Revival

A-1, Modern

A-2. White Point Garden.

A-2, Modern

The Bathing House was a favorite resort for Charlestonians unable to leave the peninsula. It was a comfortable two-story affair built on stilts, reached by an arched bridge into the Ashley. Salt water and fresh water bathing were available, with separate accommodations for ladies and gentlemen. Mrs. Susan Bennett, granddaughter of Gus Smythe, added this comment in the margin of her typescript of Gus' letters: "The Bathing house stood off the battery. One could get ice cream there, and it was quite the thing to go down for a bath and refreshments."

mansion, little more than a year old at the time of secession. His neighbor to the rear, Dr. St. Julien Ravenel of 4 East Bay Street (now 5 East Battery) designed the Confederate steam torpedo boat *David* and built the first one at Stoney Landing, his Cooper River plantation.[1]

In 1994, Dr. Palmer, modern owner of Dr. Ravenel's house and a descendant, said that his ancestor had owned the property down to the White Point, and that he would not have sold it off if he had known how large that corner house would be.

Ships and steamers in the background are tied up to Southern Wharf.

A-3

White Point Garden No. 2—the turnstiles into White Point Garden, left half of stereo #2, Osborn & Durbec, 1860 or 1861.   (SCHS)

While the High Battery along Bay Street was free to anyone, slaves and free persons of color were excluded from the White Point. The turnstiles kept out "cows,

A-3. White Point Garden.

horses, mules, & inebriates," with a penalty of $5. Also prohibited on East Bay or South Bay was the washing of horses and the hanging of fishnets on the railings of the Garden. Additionally, smoking of any pipe or segar, within the enclosure of the Garden at White Point, was not permitted.[2]

Looking to the south, along what later would be an extension of King Street, but was then the western fenced edge of the Garden, is the Ashley River. Here the rice harvest was barged from plantations to Chisolm's Rice Mill and West Point Rice Mill where the grain was husked and cleaned. Then the cleaned rice was put into wood-hooped 350-lb. barrels called tierces for shipping. From the Garden, strollers watched freshly loaded cargoes of Carolina Gold rice sail downriver, from right to left, to begin their journey across the sea. In 1860 alone, South Carolina produced over 119 million pounds of rice, nearly two-thirds of the total grown in the nation.

The first Emancipation Day parade terminated here in late 1865, where recently freed slaves hosted numerous speakers and a huge barbeque.

The modern view shows the paved southern extension of King Street, which once stopped at South Bay Street (now South Battery). Marsh and docks to the

A-3, Modern

right were filled in 1911, when Andrew Buist Murray promoted an Ashley River seawall to create fifty acres of new land for housing. The seven-story Fort Sumter Hotel, opened here at the end of King Street in 1923, is now condominiums.

A-4

White Point Garden, No. 3—from Meeting St. to the Ashley, left half of stereo #3, Osborn & Durbec, 1860 or 1861. (SCHS)

Development of a "public pleasure ground" began in 1848 when the city started filling in what had been a low-water oyster bank. Indians had a village here in the 17th century and threw their discarded oyster shells onto the shoreline, creating a "white point" to early passing ships. The pirate Stede Bonnet and some of his crew were hanged and then buried here below the high-water mark. Palmetto log forts were built here during the Revolution and the War of 1812.

For over ten years cartloads of debris, sand, and oyster shells were dumped for fill, and a granite seawall was

A-4, Modern

A-4. White Point Garden.

built. Shade trees and wood benches were installed. Sheep leveled the grass lawns, which were interspersed with walkways of crushed oyster shells. By the 1850s gas lanterns provided romantic evenings. Charlestonians enjoyed the breeze and view.

Early in the war one could enjoy the park and still be patriotic. On the afternoon of August 7, 1861, "...the German Band voluntarily gave a concert on the Battery for the benefit of the Hospital & Volunteer Aid Societies. Little boys and gentlemen were stationed at different crossings to receive contributions of promenaders and riders. $247.00 was collected."[3]

During the war, a huge flagpole was erected in this circle or the one to its west. From it the Confederate Stars & Bars, and later the Stainless Banner could be seen for miles.

In 1905, the daughters of George Williams built an elegant cast-iron bandstand, in memory of their mother Martha Williams. Their father, George Williams, was a highly successful blockade-runner investor.

A-5

White Point Garden, No. 4—Harbor Light, right half of stereo #4, Osborn & Durbec, 1860 or 1861.   (SCHS)

This harbor light, fueled by whale-oil, guided ships into Charleston's harbor. Its prisms magnified the flame until it could be seen over five miles away, at the harbor's entrance. During the Civil War it was generally kept dark to deny its value to the Union blockading fleet.

It was located in a line with the end of Church Street.

Presently this circle holds a monument built by the Palmetto Guard in 1876. It celebrates the June 1776 defense against a British fleet of four frigates that attacked a South Carolina fort at Sullivans Island. This fort was built of palmetto logs, backed up by sixteen feet of sand. British cannon balls could pass through the logs but were then stopped by the sand.

A-5. White Point Garden.

The monument is topped with a statue of Sargeant William Jasper, of the 2nd South Carolina Regiment of Foot. During the engagement the fort's signal flag, blue with a white crescent, was shot away by a British ball and fell outside the fort. Jasper recovered the flag amid a shower of iron, tied it to a cannon sponge staff and stuck it into the sand on top of the parapet, giving the defenders a shot of adrenaline. Assisted by a fresh supply of gunpowder rushed over by Gen. Charles Lee, the defenders held off the British ships.

Jasper became a hero through the rebellious colonies, particularly in the South. Towns, counties, and babies throughout America have been named after him. To call someone a "tough jasper" meant that he was not to be trifled with. It is singular that the last living Confederate widow receives benefits through her Alabama soldier-husband, William Jasper Martin.

A-5, Modern

A-6

White Point Garden, No. 1—High Battery, from the Garden, stereo half, Osborn & Durbec. (SCHS)

An almost constant summer breeze made this seawall that was High Battery a delightful escape from Charleston's summer humidity. Hurricanes threatened to wash away this lower part of town, so few buildings of any size were built until a stone seawall was completed in 1819. It was capped with a wood-railed flagstone promenade.

The view is to the north, along High Battery, which for years before the War Between The States was the favorite promenade for citizens of quality to stroll and enjoy the breeze, or for lovers who made wonderful plans for their future. Anyone—whites, slaves, and free persons of color—could enjoy and wonder at the dozens of ships in the harbor, who were carrying cotton and rice to the far ports of the globe. Ships came in regularly with cargos of all imagined sorts. Save for New Orleans, this was the busiest port in the American South.

For the next four years, spectators here viewed events that would reshape their entire lives.

On April 12, 1861, around a hundred souls who happened to be on High Battery at 4:30 in the morning witnessed the first shot of the Civil War. It was expected that something was going to happen, but none of them knew just when. In the pre-dawn darkness they saw a flash across the harbor, from the direction of Fort Johnson on James Island. The sputtering fuze of a mortar shell soared almost a mile into the air, paused, and began to descend with increasing speed. It exploded in a flash, directly over Fort Sumter. 16 1/2 seconds later, the sound of this shell's detonation boomed in the ears of these spectators.

Few in the South really wanted this to happen. Gen. P. G. T. Beauregard directed this bombardment from Charles Alston's mansion at 11 East Bay (now 21 East Battery). Fort Sumter's 84-man United States garrison had heavy guns that could block the channel into the port at any time. That they might remain in this second-largest Confederate city put in question the whole idea of secession.

The Federal commander was Major Robert Anderson. Anderson was from Kentucky, and his family owned slaves. Personally he saw no argument in the South's right to secede, but he had a fort to defend. He knew he would have to leave shortly, for he would be out of food in a day or two. Beauregard knew this, but Union sup-

A-6. White Point Garden.

ply ships were already assembling off the bar. Once supplied with food and more soldiers, Anderson could stay indefinitely.

This reinforcement must not happen. Beauregard had cleared it with President Jefferson Davis and his Secretary of War when forty-seven Confederate guns and mortars opened on Sumter.

In the modern view, East Bay Street has been cut through the park, and the seawall has been raised and strengthened.

A-6, Modern

A-7

South Carolina Institute Hall, before it was destroyed in the December 1861 fire, left half of stereo. **(Author's collection)**

Earliest surviving print by Quinby & Co., Charleston, 1865 or later.

To the left is the Circular Congregational Church, and to the right, Nicholas Fehrenbach's Teetotal Restaurant.

This was the largest meeting and exposition hall in five states. It could seat over 2,500 on the floor and in the balconies. Completed in 1854, it was a magnificent brick building, with stuccoed walls scored and painted to resemble cut stone blocks. Two meetings were held in this hall which changed the future of America: the 1860 Democratic Convention and the Secession Convention.

The Democrats met here in April 1860 to nominate their candidate for the November presidential election. The decision to meet in Charleston was made four years earlier, after Northern Democrats nominated James Buchanan for the 1856 election. Buchanan won, for his only opposition was John C. Fremont, candidate of a new third party called the Republicans. Lingering bitterness on the part of the Southern bloc was to be resolved by holding the next convention in the South...Charleston.

This turned out to be a bad idea. Charleston had a fine meeting hall but little else to recommended it. Hotel rooms were insufficient, rail links were a nightmare, and the Democrats were so divided that they eventually ran three men for the November election.

Eight months later another convention met in this hall to take South Carolina out of the Union. It was here the December 20, 1860, Ordinance of Secession for South Carolina was signed. Forever after, it was known as Secession Hall.

The secession convention was planned for Columbia, the state capital, but discovery of smallpox there caused a change to Charleston. A grand reception of dignitaries met the delegates when they steamed into the railroad's passenger station on Line Street. A parade of bands, militia companies, and volunteer fire companies, led them down the peninsula. After meetings in Institute Hall, the delegates convened at St. Andrew's Hall, on Broad Street, where the resolution to secede was approved unanimously.

Actual signing of the secession document would have to be accomplished in a grander location, so another parade led to the magnificent Institute Hall. At 1:15 p.m. on December 20, the first of 170 delegates, Thomas Chiles Perrin of Abbeville District, soberly inked his signature. Two hours later, the audience's adrenaline being barely suppressed, the last signed his, and the deed was done.[4] The audience exploded.

The cheers of the whole assembly continued for some minutes, while every man waved or threw up his hat, & every lady waved her handkerchief. *(Diary of Edmund Ruffin, a witness)*

Five minutes later, the Charleston *Mercury* had the most famous extra ever published, on the streets: "THE UNION IS DISSOLVED!" Delegates and thousands of witnesses flowed into Meeting Street.

One lad of eighteen, Augustine Smythe, who had come from his freshman year at South Carolina College, watched the spectacle from the Institute Hall balcony. After the crowd had thinned, he slid down a column, walked up to the podium, and picked up the ink blotter and one of the pens used in affixing most of the signatures. They still exist today. Years later his widow gave them to Charleston's Confederate Museum.

Who took this image? I have never seen a contemporary print. I have stereos of this image all published after the Federals occupied the city, by Charles Quinby, Stephen T. Souder, and George Barnard.

The phrasing of the long caption on Quinby's stereo indicates that he published it some time after the war:

The Institute Hall, in later years, was known as 'Secession Hall', from the fact that the Ordinance of Secession was ratified within its walls, on the 20th December, 1860.

Quinby & Co. may have been able to take stereo views in 1860. Possibly his neighbor and competitor, George Cook, could have as well, but no prewar or wartime stereos are known to have been published by these galleries. Osborn & Durbec, down the street, did publish stereo views of the city before December 1861. This view was probably taken soon after the signing ceremony, but may possibly have been exposed right after the May 1860 Democratic Convention.

All three were Charleston photographers and successful proprietors of galleries on King Street. Quinby was the first owner of 261 King and was at this address in 1860. In 1871 Bertha F. Souder bought this gallery's equipment, furnishings, and 4,000 negatives. The firm operated under the name of Mrs. Souder's husband or son S[tephen] T. Souder, both of whom had the same name.

Then, on July 1, 1873, George Barnard bought Souder's studio which, by this time, held 7,500 negatives. Barnard had first come to Charleston in 1865, photographing for the Union Army Engineers. While there he established connections with Quinby. Quinby published some of Barnard's negatives under the Quinby & Co. name. In 1880, the Quinby/Souder/Barnard gallery was bought by Frank A. Nowell, who had earlier worked for Souder.[5]

A-7. South Carolina Institute Hall.

So the earliest surviving stereo of this image is by Charles Quinby. Osborn & Durbec produced stereos in 1860-1, which we have seen. No prewar stereos by George Cook have surfaced, and if Osborn & Durbec had included this in their wartime work, it is odd that no print of this famous building has surfaced with their label. To muddy the waters further, I have examples of this stereo published with no makers' mark. Some popular images were pirated and sold anonymously by dealers who wished to leave no evidence of theft.

The 1994 image of an entirely different view was taken on Meeting Street's sidewalk, just north of Queen Street. The 1861 fire destroyed two blocks of Meeting Street as it blazed across the peninsula. An 1892 Circular Church was rebuilt on its old site. Secession Hall was also lost. Its modern replacement, called simply "134 Meeting," was built 40 feet to the south and also covers Mr. Fehrenbach's site.

A-7, Modern

A-8

"Presbyterian Circular Church and 'South Carolina Institute' Meeting Street, Charleston S. C. taken from the Mills House May 10/60," left half of stereo. (SCHS)

This image was taken just after the National Democratic Convention had adjourned. The party had fragmented here in April but was to reassemble at Baltimore. Eventually three men ran for the November presidential election. Northern Democrats chose Stephen Douglas of Illinois, Southern Democrats nominated John C. Breckenridge of Kentucky, and the Constitutional Unionists ran John Bell of Tennessee.

The Republicans nominated Abraham Lincoln of Illinois. He carried no Southern state but won in the electoral college and became president.

Here, in South Carolina Institute Hall, 78 Meeting Street, just six weeks after the November election, South Carolina seceded. This handsome, huge assembly hall took a new name—Secession Hall.

A-8. Circular Congregational Church.

Nicholas Fehrenbach owned his Teetotal Restaurant at 76 Meeting Street and Francis G. Ballot occupied 74. At 72 a handsome curved iron sign proclaimed that here Joseph W. Harrison sells "artists' materials, paints, & oil." Mr. Ballot and W. H. Smith shared 70 at this images' right corner.

The photographer has not been identified. The one example of this stereo found bears no printed caption, only a printed or hand-stamped shield bearing three intertwined initials—one appears to be an "L" and the second a "G." The caption "Presbyterian Circular Church and 'South Carolina Institute' Meeting Street, Charleston S. C." is written on the back in a good legible hand. However the legend incorrectly identifies the church, which is actually the Circular Congregational Church.

A-9

Interior of Secession Hall, stereo half, 1859-1861.   (L. C.)

This southeast corner of Institute Hall shows the purpose for which the edifice was planned—as an exhibition hall for industrial, agricultural and cultural assemblies. Here it is being decorated as an Oriental bazaar, with curtained booths surrounding minarets decorated with flowers. It is a crisp day. Several of the ladies continue to wear their outerwear indoors. Seated boys in the foreground wear close fitting jackets and hacking caps similar to the 1839 military caps. They could pass for Citadel cadets, but they look too young. Their clothing is also typical for civilian boys.[6]

The stage, which will be used in December 1860 to sign the Ordinance of Secession, is decorated with floral Oriental arches. Elaborate floral displays in the hall include kiosks with minaret-shaped turrets extending nearly to the ceiling. There was a fascination with things Oriental.[7]

Photographed from the rear balcony, a corner of the south balcony shows at right. A statue of Minerva fills an alcove in the center. Tables on the right are laden with goods to be sold, but the beribboned table on the left is still empty. Sunlight from the south windows indicate that this was exposed late on a spring or fall morning

This is one of only two Charleston photographic interiors taken before 1870 that have come down to us.

A-10

Interior of Secession Hall, Charleston, where South Carolina passed the Ordinance of Secession, stereo negative, 1859-1861.
(Val. Mus.)

Taken from the south balcony, looking north across the Institute's floor, some of the same boys in A-9 have moved their chairs to be included in this image. Shadows from the left, west side indicate a late afternoon exposure time. The table on the right, also seen in the left of A-9, still has little merchandise.

There is no information on the image to indicate the artist. This is from the Valentine Collection and most of their Charleston images are from George Cook's studio. He moved to Richmond in 1880 and his son Heustis Cook gave most of his father's materials to the Valentine. Whether Cook was the artist, or had bought these two images from some other defunct Charleston gallery's assets is unknown.

This print was taken from a contact print of the entire stereo negative. In preparing a stereo for sale, the overlapping part of the negative is trimmed away to paste two separate and slightly different images onto its cardboard mount.

A-11

Charleston Hotel from Hasell Street, with view south on Meeting Street, carte-de-visite, Summer of 1860 or 1861.

(Gil Barrett)

Presence of two church spires on lower Meeting Street proves this to be a prewar image. The spire next to the telegraph pole is the Circular Congregational's, which burned in 1861.

Outside prewar views are rare; nearly every surviving Charleston photographic exterior dates from the Federal occupation, which began in February 1865. An artist made his money in his studio, producing portraits. Any photographer who took his camera outside, away from his chemicals and equipment, to record a muddy everyday street scene, gathered few sales. While the Charleston Hotel was the most impressive hostelry in town, very few local customers would ever wish to buy a street scene of

A-9. Interior of Secession Hall.

A-10. Interior of Secession Hall.

A-11. Charleston Hotel, image from right lens of stereo camera.

their own city. Charleston as a tourist stop and market for souvenirs was half a century in the future.

So when was it taken, and who made it? Outside photographs became popular in 1859, when Oliver Wendell Holmes developed a hand-held stereopticon viewer, produced by Joseph Bates of Boston. Outside stereo views, appreciated because of the depth produced with two images in the hand-held Holmes-Bates viewer, now became popular.[8] This image then dates almost certainly between late 1859 or December 1861, when the Circular Church burned.

This image is a carte-de-visite, first produced in America in 1860 in New York.[9] The scene is summer. Trees are leafed, and on the left, shirt-sleeved men stand across the street. They stare at the cameraman, who is working from under the Pavilion Hotels balcony. Another shirt-sleeved man wearing suspenders, on the right-hand sidewalk, walks away from the operator. These are likely laborers, for gentlemen were expected to wear a coat or vest when in a public place.[10] Awnings are in use.

Now, why was it taken? Charleston was in the national news when it hosted the Democratic National Convention in late April 1860, and it was a warm April. Delegates would want souvenirs. The city was also in the national news next summer, when Fort Sumter was fired upon.

When was it taken? I favor an April or May 1860 date. An 1861 early summer day should have flags and uniforms, and none are visible. The cloudy day precludes shadow-dating.

Who made it? In 1860 there were seven photographic galleries in Charleston. Two established photographers, Charles Quinby and George Cook, had their neighboring galleries one block away on King Street, near Hasell. Either could set up his camera and have an assistant run downstairs, then one block to hand a fresh collodion and silver nitrate-coated wet-plate to fit onto the back of his camera box. The exposed glass plate could then be rushed back for processing. Stereo views or cartes-de-viste could be available for sale the next day.

Jesse Bolles was two blocks away, at the corner of King and Liberty.[11] He traveled to Cowpens, S.C. in 1856, a round trip distance of over 200 miles by train, and wagon, to photograph the Washington Light Infantry's trip. He made daguerreotypes of their camps, river crossings, soldiers, and of a monument that the W.L.I. constructed on the Cowpens battlefield. That monument survives, and some of the images exist as woodcuts on page 121 of the January 24, 1857, issue of *Frank Leslie's Illustrated Newspaper.* Osborn & Durbec's Photographic Mart at 223 King Street was nearly three blocks away.

A-12. Charleston Hotel, image from left lens of stereo camera.

Cook had the most successful gallery but his surviving account books mention no outside work in this period. He did venture out to photograph the recently deceased. If a person died before having an image made, an artist was often quickly called upon for a last (or only) portrait. When Cook was charging $3.00 for a studio portrait, he was willing to pack up his camera, equipment, and chemicals to make a $15 house call on the corpse.

Osborn & Durbec's photographic tent, with their name painted on it, shows in one of their 1861 Fort Johnston views. Quinby included a photographic tent when he sold his studio after the war. Either Osborn & Durbec or Quinby is favored as the artist for this image.

It shows the humanity of the street. On the left a bearded gentleman in frock coat and wide-brimmed hat chats with two riders in a top buggy.[12] White-washed wooden boxes protect the few shade trees. Poles of the American Telegraph Company run down to their office at 49 Broad Street.[13] A mortar-and-pestle apothecary sign swings above the brick sidewalk. A gas street light, new in 1848, is on the corner.

A spectacular advertisement on the right is the saddle-sign over William Harrell's saddlery shop—an Eagle Head Plantation Saddle. The idea for this saddle

was brought back from the Mexican War. The leather seat was quilted, and planters found it comfortable to sit all day.[14] It was also called a Kentucky Easy Back. General Grant used one during the War.[15] The detail of this advertising saddle of "Harrall, Nichols & Co. Cor Meeting & Hasel" is impressive. It is either a real saddle with a thick lacquer coat of paint, or a tinsmith's masterpiece.

A-12

[Similar to A-11], carte-de-visite, Osborn's Gallery, Summer of 1860 or 1861. (Beaufort)

At first glance, this appears to be simply another print of the above image, though trimmed to the left. The different location of Circular Congregational Church's steeple, behind the telegraph pole, however, shows that this image is a different view. It proves that this was instead photographed as a stereo. This then,

A-11 & 12, Modern

is the left-hand side of a stereo, and the previous image, above, is the right hand side of the same view. Not only is this a rare view, but these are two images, collected from states 600 miles apart, now placed together to recreate a scene that has not been glimpsed in 140 years.

The carriage to the left can be seen in greater detail, and the bearded gentleman speaking to the carriage driver, appears better dressed: note the white collar in a dark frock coat and light trousers. His hat is a light color, befitting a Charleston summer. Part of McCarter & Dawson's Book Store[16] on the corner of Pinckney Street is visible, just north of the Charleston Hotel.

In 1861, Osborn & Durbec published a series of more than forty stereo views of Fort Sumter, surrounding Confederate forts, and some scenes of White Point Garden. Surviving examples are uncommon. Their gallery closed during the war. James M. Osborn worked as an operator for George Cook's studio late in the war. Soon after the Occupation began, he opened a new gallery in his own name, on the corner of King and Liberty streets. He published this single image under his name, and as the survivor of his old firm, very probably used his old negatives to print single cartes. He also made new images in 1865 to market to the public.

In 1997, at the Beaufort (S.C.) County Public Library, I found the carte-de-viste album of William G. Read of 1 Melville Street, Dorchester, Massachusetts. Read had been in Beaufort in 1867. His album contained 60 cartes, all showing images of Beaufort, the Federal operations against Charleston and her defenses, and several Charleston street scenes. Back marks on the Charleston cartes advertised Charleston's Osborn's Gallery, Beckett's Photographic Gallery in Savannah, and J. T. Reading & Co., of Savannah, Ga.

Some time later, Mr. Read sent his album to the Beaufort Township Library by "Am. R. Express Prepaid," along with a script describing each image. This carte, numbered 57 in his private script, contained the description:

> Charleston Hotel, Meeting St. Opened soon after the evacuation of the city by our forces, by Stetson of the Astor House, N.Y. Miserably kept tho' for all that, and is constantly full of Secesh.

The 1998 view, looking south, shows a new office building on the Charleston Hotel site. The Charleston Hotel was demolished in 1960 in favor of a motel, for the motor inn craze was sweeping the nation. Initial plans for a new office building in the 1980s included rebuilding the old Hotel's handsome 1838 Corinthian colonnade, but the owners chose a simpler front with more office space.

Few structures of the 1860s remain on Meeting Street's east side in this area. The block on the west side of Meeting, however, is a Charleston preservation success.

In the 1970s, plans were made to demolish all buildings on the west side of this block, in favor of a parking garage. Instead, the front forty feet of these mostly 19th-century commercial buildings was saved, and the garage built behind. These facades-in-depth house a series of shops and restaurants. The west side of the street is vibrant and the sidewalk full of tourists and shoppers, whereas the east sidewalk of the block is sterile, with no street life.

A-13

Pavilion Hotel. Corner of Meeting and Hazel Sts., carte-de-visite, James E. Osborn, Summer of 1860.   (Beaufort)

When William Read sent his carte album to the Beaufort Township Library, his script described it as:

> ...occupied by various officers of the Army, as quarters & offices. The old Post Office building having been so badly damaged by our shells, a temporary Post Office is situated in the basement of this building.

A-13. Pavillion Hotel.

A-13, Modern

This is a reverse view of Mr. Osborn's views A-11 & A-12 of the Charleston Hotel, exposed when Osborn & Durbec's gallery was flourishing. There is nothing in the view to indicate the date when it was made, except that the shirt-sleeved spectators indicate a warm day.

The presence of a tall sawhorse at the extreme right, also seen in the left edge of A-12, proves that both images were probably made on the same cloudy day. Sawhorses do not stay in one place very long. Osborn already had his camera set up, so he moved his apparatus across the street to the corner of Meeting and Pinckney. Here he exposed another view, perhaps as a souvenir for departing delegates to the 1860 Democratic National Convention. I believe this to be an 1860 image, since the lack of uniforms or flags precludes an 1861 view.

If produced as a stereo, this may be one of the Civil War's lost images. Osborn saved his negatives, as any wise commercial photographer would do. Soon after the Yankees return, he reprinted some of them in carte versions; the view reproduced here, however, has not been found in any other collection.

The Pavilion Hotel survived for years after the war as one of Charleston's better hotels, and was still owned by the H. L. Butterfield family. It was directly on the new horse-trolley line and well served by omnibuses that could meet guests arriving at the three railroad stations. With a good restaurant, it prospered.

The modern view shows that the site still welcomes guests, though with a motel of indifferent architecture. Ezekiel B. Stoddard & Co.'s brick store at "165 and 167 Meeting St., nearly opposite Charleston Hotel... Wholesale Dealers in Boots, Shoes and Trunks..."[17] survives. Mr. Harrell's saddlery warehouse next door survives at the corner of Hasell Street but with a different upper facade. A Sticky Fingers restaurant now occupies the ground floor of both buildings.

AFTERMATH OF THE 1861 FIRE

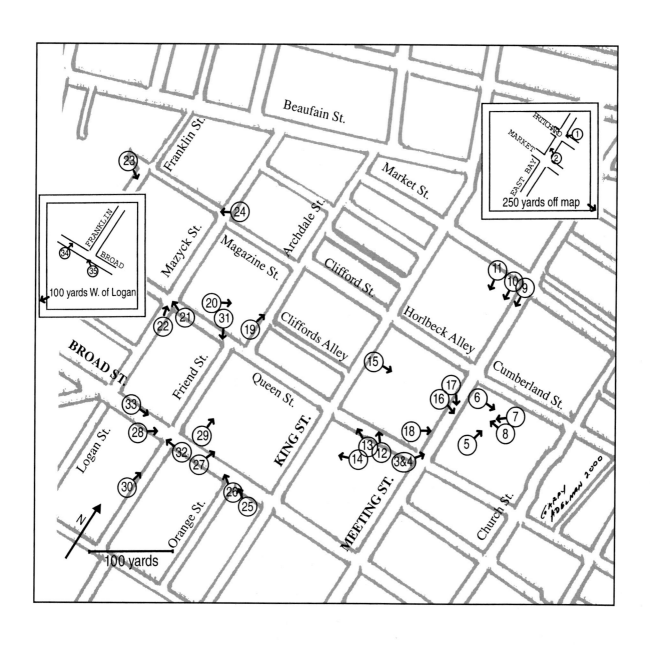

B-1

Ruins of the Pinckney Mansion, Charleston, S. C., glass plate, George Barnard. Plate 59, in his *Photographic Views of Sherman's Campaign*, 1865. (N. A.)

Miss Emma Holmes, in her diary, wrote of the terrible fire of December 11, 1861:

> It swept all the upper part of Hasell & many small streets near, down East Bay where Miss Harriet Pinckney's splendid mansion, once the palace of the Royal Governors & for long successive years the residence of her forefathers, was destroyed. Just one year ago, I went with mother to see her on the 17th, her 85th birthday and my 22nd, but principally to see the interior of the house, which was hung with tapestry, in antique style. Fortunately almost everything was saved through the strenuous exertions of Captain [John] Rutledge and the crew of the *Lady Davis....* The fire later destroyed the old Rutledge house [on Tradd Street] from which poor old Miss Pinckney had to be moved a second time.[1]

The fire began in a shed behind a window sash factory. A Beaufort, S. C., planter had escaped the Federal invasion of Hilton Head with some of his slaves and sought refuge in Charleston, where he found tem-

B-1. Ruins of the Pinckney Mansion.

porary quarters for his slaves in the shed. They were cooking their dinner when their fire spread to a nearby haystack. That stack flared up and the fire spread to nearby buildings. The site of this shed is behind the cameraman's position and to his right. The Charleston *Mercury* reported on December 12:

> About nine o'clock last evening the alarm rang out, calling the citizens to quell the beginnings of a fire, which, in the subsequent extent and rapidity of its ruinous sweep, will compare with the most terrible conflagrations which have ever visited the American continent.... The fire began in Russell & Co's Sash and Blind Factory, at the foot of Hasell-street, and the report—though a vague one—is that it appeared in three places at the same time. Crossing to the other [south] side of Hasell-street, it burned Cameron & Co.'s immense machine Shops....

ment after tenement was first licked by and then enveloped by the fast-spreading flames, the panic became awful. The fierce and roaring march of the fire was indeed a horrid scene; but far more heart-rending was the sight of...thousands—of poor and bewildered families, driven suddenly from their homes, destitute even of their scanty effects. All the available carts, drays, handcarts and wheelbarrows were immediately brought into requisition, but these were altogether inadequate to remove even a tithe of the movables beyond the reach of the devouring element.

Miss Pinckney's mansion was in the block north of North Market, on the west side of East Bay Street. It was not rebuilt. A restaurant currently occupies the site.

B-1, Modern

Emma Holmes gives more detail, writing that the fire, "...evidently the work of an incendiary, broke out in a shed next to [H. P.] Russell's extensive machine shop & soon spread to Cameron's foundry, where an immense amount of Confederate work was destroyed, in rifled cannon, shot & shell."[2] Heavy gusts of wind carried sparks and burning wood over the heads of frantic firemen, and the dead low tide kept a supply of river water from their pumps. The *Mercury* continued:

> Before ten o'clock, the fire had begun raging in several different points in the lower part of the city. The buildings in the stricken neighborhoods were mostly of wood, old, closely built, and surrounded by small out-buildings of an exceedingly flammable character. As tene-

B-2

Pinckney Mansion, glass plate, George Barnard, April or May 1865.   (N.A.)

East Bay Street is recorded from a higher angle. A shell hole hit the roof of Miss Pinckney's brick dependency, seen to the left of her big house. The shell plunged through the shingle roof's ridge pole. This view gives the best street detail of surviving Charleston streets—typically cobblestoned high in the middle with gutters edged with granite curbstones. The brick sidewalks were laid in a herringbone pattern.

Miss Pinckney's chimneys show the white "Charleston Band," an architectural custom almost unique to the city. The stuccoed band over brick, painted white, has no structural value, but was merely a way to make chimneys more attractive. Modern replacement chimneys usually skip this detail. Her burned brick walls held up well through the war.

Everything useful has been salvaged out of Mrs. Pinckney's ruins. The double stairs have been stripped of marble steps and iron hand rails. A sturdy plank fence replaces the old iron property fence. Windows shutters have been stripped from her dependency.

Shadows suggest that B-1 and B-2 were taken on the same morning, probably in April or May of 1865.

B-2. Ruins of the Pinckney Mansion.

B-3

Meeting Street to the north, looking across the Burnt District, glass plate, 1865.   (L. C.)

This photo was taken from the roof of the Mills House Hotel, at its northeast corner. The vantage point and view is nearly identical to A-8's image taken May 8, 1860.

The Burnt District here was two blocks wide, from Queen Street in the foreground across Horlbeck, nearly to Market Street. To the right of center is the Circular Congregational Church. Fire repairs to her capped steeple came to a halt when shelling commenced. Its circular walls survived until the 1886 earthquake.

South of the Circular Congregational ruins are the nearly obliterated Secession Hall and the scant remains of Nicholas Fehrenbach's Teetotal Restaurant. He relocated to Broad until late 1863.

Up the west side, nothing survived the fire or shelling until Jane White's residence and stone yard at 119 Meeting (now 177 Meeting). There is little traffic in this area in 1865, save for blurred images of three pedestrians on the west sidewalk. Two blocks up Meeting Street, beyond Market Street, the street becomes active.

The modern view was taken out of the sixth floor northeast corner room of the rebuilt 1969 Mills House Hotel, room 601. When the new hotel was constructed in 1969, the upper rooms were a bit shorter, but this perspective very nearly matches.

In 1892 an entirely new Circular Congregational Church was begun on its old footprint. The church acquired a forty-foot strip of land along the north edge of the Secession Hall ruins. In the late 1980s a new office building, somewhat copying the lines of the former building, went up. That new structure is much more massive than the former, and also covers the site of Mr. Feherenbach's Teetotal Restaurant.

B-3. Meeting Street, looking across the burnt district.

B-3, Modern

B-4

Circular or "Central" Church, Charleston, S. C., glass plate. (L. C.)

These ruins of the Circular Congregational Church were often miscaptioned by northern photographers as the "Central Church." This exceptionally sharp plate was exposed from the same spot as B-3, but at an earlier hour in the morning. B-4 was probably exposed by a different photographer, as this man's apparatus produced a much sharper image.

The foreground is dominated by the ruins of the church and Secession Hall, but much can be picked out along the right. It shows the progress of the fire from its start along the Cooper River across to the southwest directly toward the Mills House.

B-4. Circular Congregational Church.

The image is clear enough to pick out three shell holes in the stores and warehouses of Hayne Street. These shell holes are seen just to the right of the burnt steeple. This street was one of the fashionable shopping districts of Charleston. One shell was seldom enough to completely destroy a building but the danger a random shell was enough to close down whole areas.

The Circular Congregational Church graveyard to the right of its ruined walls can be seen more clearly in this view. I have not included a modern view as the scene is completely dominated by the 1988 office building at present-day 134 Meeting Street.

B-5

Charleston, S. C., 1865. The bombarded graveyard of the Circular Church, glass plate, also published in stereo by Anthony, and by Soule.   (L. C.)

This tomb blown up by a shell became a popular photographic subject. The photographer set his tripod on top of the tablet stone of Sarah Julia Porcher, who died "1847, in the 53d year of her age." Here he exposed both a large glass plate and a stereo plate from the same spot. This plate was also published as a stereo by John P. Soule of Boston.

A plunging shell exploded on the head of the tall tablet stone, blowing out its decorative ends. By the time this tomb was mended years after the war the identity of the

B-5. Cemetery in rear of Circular Church.

B-5, Modern

original inhabitant was lost. Surviving fragments tell that he was born in 1743. The tomb also contains James Mathews, grandson (?) of the original occupant who died in 1844 at 71, and five more of his family.

A board fence follows the church property line, a wartime economy fence made with very few nails. Iron spikes and nails were expensive in blockaded Charleston, so here posts were dug into the ground. Flexible boards were then woven between every other post, saving nearly half the normal cost of nails. Behind the board fence is a burned mansion on the north side of Cumberland Street.

The modern view of the repaired Mathews family tomb was also taken from the top of Mrs. Porcher's tomb. Her chipped marker is mostly illegible and very fragile. I stood on a sheet of thick plywood to keep from cracking her slab. The Circular Congregational has some of the oldest headstones in Charleston and all stones in this 1865 image have survived to this day.

B-6. Cemetery in rear of Circular Church.

B-6

Cemetery, rear of Circular Church (showing effects of shot and shell), albumin print, April 1865.   (MOLLUS)

Another view of the Mathews family tomb in the Circular Congregational Churchyard, blown up by a Federal shell. The view is to the east, towards St. Philip's Episcopal Church steeple and graveyard. These cemeteries provided a fire break for the 1861 fire, keeping flames from spreading south, until the Circular flamed up. Then the blaze jumped west across Meeting Street.

This view was taken late in the afternoon, with the camera placed at the foot of John Hume's (1762-1811) table top tomb. Looking at the shadow on the left edge of the Mathews' damaged tomb, I was able to place the time at 4:35 p.m. ±5 minutes, on April 13, 1865 ±2 days.

B-6, Modern

B-7

Graveyard of Circular Church and ruins of Secession Hall in distance, Charleston, S. C., stereo half.   (L. C.)

B-7. Cemetery in rear of Circular Church.

Almost a reverse angle of A-8, the view is looking southwest over the first floor remains of Secession Hall. The Circular's ruins are at right. The camera is looking west, positioned near the foot of Eliza Swinton's box tomb (died 1848, at age 64). Mrs. Porcher's low slab, from which B-5 was taken, can be seen in front of the tall flame-topped marker in the right background.

The large brick mausoleum for the Hutson/Perroneau family in the right background of B-8, is at the left edge of this photo. Camera location was under the tree behind the urn-topped stone that is barely visible at the right edge, and in 8 to the left of center.

The Circular Congregational was the oldest cemetery in Charleston. This graveyard, and most of the others in the city were filling up by the 1850s. New cemeteries on Charleston Neck, such as Magnolia Cemetery and others around it, were begun there and have continued to receive Charlestonians and others for over 150 years.

B-7, Modern

B-8

Ruins of Circular Congregational Church, looking west across its graveyard, carte-de-viste, J. T. Reading.   (Beaufort)

Mr. Reading miscaptioned his carte, "Grave of John C. Calhoun, Charleston, S.C." Calhoun was still in St. Philip's care, though moved for a time into their eastern graveyard. This is the only surviving view of the Circular Church graveyard from the back. It does show, on the

left, Mr. and Mrs. John Bee Holmes's 1836 tablet on the end of their children's table-top tomb, and the shelled Mathews family table-top to its right. An urn-topped marble column in the foreground commemorates Eliza Lucilla Simons, who died in 1849 at age 35. To her right is Nathaniel Russell's (1738-1820) short urn-topped square monument. He built the fabulous adamesque mansion at present-day 51 Meeting Street.

Reading visited this city and captured a few Charleston views to add to his Savannah inventory. His gallery closed in 1866.

B-8. Cemetery in rear of Circular Church.

B-8, Modern

Partly screening the Mathews family tomb in the modern photograph is a fluted shaft, capped with a marble wreath, over Major David Ramsay's grave. He fell while his battalion fought off a Union attack led by the 54th Massachusetts Regiment, and his stone reads:

...He fell mortally wounded
Gallantly fighting in the Defence
Of Battery Wagner on Morris Island
On the 18th day of July 1863.
He died on the 4th day of August ensuing.
Aged 32 years 11 months and 10 days

Battery Ramsay, on White Point Garden (D-1 through D-12) was named in his memory.

B-9

Meeting St., Charleston, S. C., looking South, showing the ruins of Circular Church and the Mills House, St. Michael's church in the distance, stereo #3105, Anthony, March 1865. (L. C.)

B-9. Meeting Street, looking South.

Emma Holmes was still at her mother's home on Council Street, anxious for reports of the fire.

...About one, W[illie] Guerard returned & reported the Institute Hall & Circular Church as burning & cousin Henry [DeSaussure]'s in danger. A light rain was then falling & we earnestly prayed for more, but it only lasted a short time & Rosa [his wife] went home. We heard the roaring & crackling of the flames, the crashing of the roofs falling in. & occasionally the report of an explosion as a house was blown up to try and stop the ravages of the fire. But God had decreed that we should be purified through fire as well as blood, & still the

B-9, Modern

flames swept on with inconceivable rapidity & fierceness, not withstanding the almost superhuman efforts of the firemen.[3]

The Charleston *Mercury* reported that by 3 a.m., on Dec. 12, 1861, "In the lower part of the city the fire has done its work in thorough style. Its path is now burned out, and nothing now remains to mark where it has passed, save smoldering piles of cinders and gaunt and smoking walls and chimneys. ...The Theater, Lloyd's Coach Factory opposite, the Express Office, the old Executive Building...have been burned [on Meeting Street]."

Emma Holmes recorded other losses on Meeting Street: the Apprentice's Library, the Southern Express office, "the fine collection of our art gallery was entirely destroyed, but the Savings institution fortunately saved most of its papers."[4]

This image shows ruins of all buildings in the previous descriptions, with the steps of the Charleston Theater in the foreground. This theater was one of the main entertainments of the winter social season, along with St. Cecilia balls and February's horse racing. The theater was never rebuilt. Later in the war shells fell in this area, fortunately doing little additional damage. A shell striking the sidewalk in the foreground caused little more harm than breaking up some flagstone.

The modern view was made on the edge of the sidewalk, just north of the Meeting Street Inn, from what is now 177 Meeting Street. The Meeting Street Inn now occupies the burned Charleston Theater site.

Shadow dating for this view is challanging, as no pre-war buildings survive except St. Michael's steeple, and her clock is not readable in this image. Shadows cast by the pylon with the leaning lamp post, alongside the theater staircase are sharp, and an examination of its shadow onto the sidewalk was useful. In late March, afternoon shadows cast into Meeting Street here are 9/8 as long as the pylon in shadow, at about 2:45 p.m.

B-10

Ruins of Charleston, albumin print, George Barnard, March 1865.

(West Point, Poe collection)

This shows the 1861 fire's desolation better than any other view. Apparently little but St. Michael's Church escaped destruction. The Mills House, to the right of St.

Michael's, survived only through heroic efforts of its staff. Flames swept everything to the east, north, and west of it, and its north side is seen scorched from flames across Queen Street, only thirty-four feet away.

Mr. Barnard set his camera on the second floor piazza of Jane White's home and marble yard on Meeting Street to capture this scene of disaster. He skillfully avoided nearly all wartime reconstruction in the Burnt District.[5]

Shadows cast by lamp posts, the iron fence and gate of desolate lots in the foreground, and the board fence beside the Charleston Theater's steps, show the plate was exposed soon after B-9, around 3 p.m. This image has been used in numerous publications to show wartime destruction to Charleston, though nearly all damage in view was caused by fire, and later salvage clearance in 1862 and 1863. Indeed, Mrs. White's residence apparently was struck only once by Federal artillery, and many buildings behind Barnard's camera location survived the war with little damage.

Mrs. White's piazza was lost in the 1930s but her home and office survives today as a cigar store and upstairs smoking club.[6] A modern view was not attempted, for it would show only the blank north wall of the Meeting Street Inn, once Albert Tiefenthal's 1874 saloon and restaurant. Tiefenthal's residence was upstairs.[7]

B-11

View on Meeting St., Charleston, S. C., looking south, showing St. Michael's church, the Mills House, ruins of Central Church and Theater in ruins in the foreground, glass plate, March 1865. Also published by Anthony as stereo #3072.   **(L. C.)**

Shadows cast by the board fence beside the Charleston Theater's steps, and most specifically St. Michael's clock, show that this picture was exposed at 3:20 p.m., shortly after B-10.

The Mills House Hotel, seen in the right distance, survived the fire with only a scorched north wall. It continued hosting notable wartime visitors such as Generals Beauregard and Wade Hampton until closed down by Federal shells.

Scaffolding around the Circular (miscaptioned "Central") Church shows rebuilding begun soon after the fire, but later postponed by the shelling. This image was prob-

B-10. Meeting Street, looking South, showing fire damage.

ably made by Barnard as the shadows follow very closely Barnard's identified image B-10. The scene is nearly identical. But he changed his lens to produce a paired stereo negative to supply Anthony's demand for their stereopticon market.

A third stereopticon, made on the first floor piazza directly below B-11 was probably taken that same afternoon. This third stereo card was marketed as Anthony's #3104, and it carries the same caption as Anthony's B-11. This view is not reproduced as it reveals much less than B-11.

B-11. Meeting Street, looking South.

B-12

View of ruins, Charleston, S. C., glass plate, March 1865.   (L. C.)

The camera was placed atop the Mills House, facing northwest across King Street toward the Unitarian Church (left) and St. John's Lutheran Church (center.) In the right distance is the Gothic Grace Episcopal Church, consecrated in 1848. Its congregation expanded during the war with refugees from burnt-out churches. Services continued until Grace Episcopal's sanctuary was hit by a shell, and closed January 20, 1864.

The 1861 fire leaped across King Street, from right to left, sparing two brick peaked-roof stores, 163 & 165 King. The former sports a barber pole in 1865. Just behind these, on the right border, is William Enston's three-story brick furniture company. He had the reputation of bringing in the finest furniture from Northern factories.

The fire's northwestern advance was halted by a fire-break formed of graveyards of the Unitarian and Lutheran churches. In the left foreground is O'Mara's Bookstore facing Queen Street, built of salvaged brick in 1862 or 1863. Lacking proof of O'Mara's construction date, I can only assume it was built quickly after the fire.

Confederate patriotism and the conscription of bricklayers, house carpenters, plasterers, shinglers, and slaters into the army slowed reconstruction of the Burnt District. In 1863 the shelling halted it.

To the right of center is a three-story King Street residence, also built of salvage brick, which was plentiful after the fire. Edward Lacassagne had his "china ware & wig maker" business here at 162 King, under his residence before the war. His rebuilt residence survived the shelling with but one hit, in his roof's southeast corner, seen here patched over.

Dating of this image was by examination of the late morning shadows moving across the rear of the Lutheran Church. Shadows cast by the south slope eave match pretty consistently at around 11:20 a.m., and the rising spring sun casts an identical shadow within two days of March 22.

B-12. View of ruins.

B-12, Modern

Matching the 1865 image camera location was not as difficult as expected. The Mills House has been completely rebuilt. It is now seven stories tall compared to the original five, and rooms on the upper floors have lower ceilings. Still, by opening the window at room 601, I was able to get within four feet of matching the scene.

Today, many buildings near the burnt district survive. All three churches have active congregations. In the earthquake of 1886, the Unitarian Church tower crashed through the roof. Its magnificent interior ceiling has been expertly repaired.

During repairs to St. John's Lutheran Church after 1989's Hurricane Hugo, I observed a scabbed roof rafter where a shell had penetrated the south slope, exploding under the roof but over the decorative plaster ceiling and peppering the brick bell tower with shell fragments. In a corner I picked up a four-inch long fragment from that 100-pdr. parrott shell and gave it to the minister.

Mr. O'Mara's brick bookstore in the foreground has since been extended to the rear, stuccoed, lost its chimneys, and has a tin roof. It is now part of the Elliott House Inn, named for Revolutionary war Lieutenant

Colonel Barnard Elliott who was second in command in the 1776 Battle of Fort Sullivan. His descendants owned this site in 1861.

Mr. Lacassagne's brick mansion (renumbered #164 King) was torn down about 1914 to provide the northern lot of the Charleston Library Society. Farther up King Street, the two shops that survived the fire remain today, the second with a new facade, as 179 (now English Patina, Inc.) and 183 (Jack Patla Antiques). Mr. Enston's Furniture Store is now Birlant's Antique Shop. Some quality furniture has been sold there twice: the first time as new, and the second time as an antique.[8]

B-13

Burnt district, west-northwest from the Mills House, copy-print.   (Author's collection)

Taken from atop the northwest corner of the Mills House west extension, this print shows a continuation of ruins from the 1861 fire, along Queen Street in the foreground and King Street in the middle ground.

At two o'clock, a.m., the *Mercury* reporter noted the fire on "all the buildings upon King-street, from Clifford-street up to within a few doors of Broad-street. Crossing King-street, the flames are approaching the rear of the Cathedral, the Unitarian and the English Lutheran Churches.... The Fire Department is making incredible exertions. The men are in the last stages of exhaustion, springing to each occasion with renewed vigor, and such exhibitions of courage and endurance have been rarely witnessed."

But others told Emma Holmes the fire could not be stopped and that her mother's house at 2 Council Street would be lost.

> At two o'clock Willie returned and told mother it was time to pack and move. We had already commenced to put up our jewelry, silver & money &, by three, we had packed our clothing and started for uncle James [Holmes on East Battery], each laden with their own things. The scenes all along the streets were indescribably sad. The pavements loaded with the furniture, clothing, & bedding of refugees who cowered beside them in despair, while others were hurrying with articles for safety to the side from whence we came. When

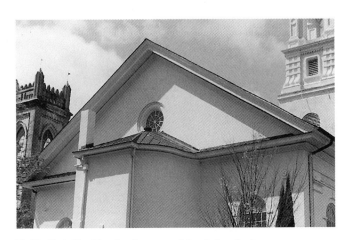

B-12, Detail with shadow used to date photo.

B-13. Burnt District looking from the Mills House.

we reached the Battery the wind was so high we could scarcely breast it. The heavens black as midnight while the waves were white with foam and all illuminated by the intense lurid lights.[9]

Directly across Queen Street in the foreground, is O'Mara's bookstore, built of salvaged brick. It is now hotel rooms for the Elliott House Inn. Clifford Alley leads off King, toward the upper left. It was filled with slaves that were provided lodging away from their masters' property. In 1861 seventy-six slaves and one white man lived here, in ten wood and two brick houses.[10]

Many slaves were given an extraordinary amount of freedom, despite strict laws to the contrary. Charlestonians lived in constant fear of insurrection, for there were far more slaves in South Carolina than whites. The 1822 Denmark Vesey Slave Insurrection, though nipped in the bud, had terrified whites. The successful 1791 Santo Domingo (now Haiti) Slave Revolution reported massacres of white men, women, and children. However, over thirty-five years had now passed with little trouble. With a vigilant police and an organized militia, many slave owners felt secure enough to dismiss their servants at the end of the work day, and give them a pass to go home. The slaves simply showed up for work the next morning.

B-13, Modern

Clifford Alley was gutted in the fire of 1861. Only one brick building, seen in this image, remains today. Diagonally to the southeast of the Unitarian Church is a brick kitchen with a shell-hole to the second floor. This was behind Patrick Darcy's on the corner of Clifford Alley and King.

Reconstruction of the Mills House, though on its original footprint, provided two additional floors to this extension. With the generous cooperation of the Mills House staff allowing me to peer out of several north-side windows on several floors, I was able to get within four feet of matching this view, from room 439.

B-14

Burnt District—from roof of Mills House, Charleston. Scene of the great fire in Dec. 1861, carte-de-visite, Isaac Beckett.

(Beaufort)

This view is taken west, across the Burnt District to the Ashley River. Left of center is St. Finbar's ruins, and in the foreground below St. Finbar's, on King Street, is the graveyard of the Quakers. Their Meeting House was consumed, but that open space served as a firebreak, keeping the fire from spreading south.

Isaac Beckett saw a scene of desolation, as the fire had passed by the Mills House, thanks to heroic work by their staff who kept falling embers from catching fire to the roof. Once past, the fire spread widely from shifting winds and jumped beyond King Street for another third of a mile until finally stopped at the Ashley. St. Finbar's Catholic Cathedral's stark ruins and gutted tower stand on the horizon. To the river, little remains beyond chimneys and ruined brick walls.

Shortly after the occupation, Isaac Beckett photographed several ruined sites in Charleston. He was a partner with or an operator for Samuel A. Cooley, an enterprising photographer in Beaufort, S.C. After their falling-out, Beckett established his own gallery in Savannah, pasting his label on several of his views of Charleston and her forts:

BECKETT'S
Photographic Gallery,
North side of Broughton, between
Barnard and Whitaker Sts,
SAVANNAH, GEORGIA

This is one of sixty cartes of William G. Read, of Dorchester, Mass. Assembled for his own album while he was in Beaufort, S.C., in 1867 or 1868, his images are mostly of Charleston, Fort Sumter, and Fort Moultrie, with views taken in 1860, 1861, and 1865.

B-14. Burnt District, looking West, from the roof of the Mills House.

The back marks are all from Osborn's Charleston Gallery, or from Beckett's or Reading's in Savannah.

The Quaker Cemetery survived until 1969 when the city wanted the property for a parking garage. Its graveyard was searched and the remains, together with the one surviving tombstone, were removed to Mendel Rivers Park on Court House Square. Its iron gates and fence fronting King Street survive in place, in front of the parking garage.

This view is to the west, toward the Ashley River and James Island beyond. It may be matched through Mills House's corner room 439, west window. I have not tried to match with a modern view, for this scene is now blocked by that undistinguished six-story parking garage.

B-15

Ruins in Charleston, S. C. "Photo from nature By G. N. Barnard," glass plate, March 1865. (West Point)

George Barnard photographed this scene of utter desolation from the yard of Christian J. Schwettman's burned home at 166, on the east side of King Street. For scale Barnard placed his usual model, the skinny, mustachioed man in a felt hat, smoking a long-stemmed pipe. He sits in front of a flooded basement. There is simply nothing behind them. This view is to the east, toward the ruined Circular Congregational Church. Bricks have been salvaged and walk paths worn through desolate lots all the way past the burned Circular Church on Meeting Street, to the nearly intact St. Philip's steeple.

Barnard implies that this is destruction from Federal shells, but all damage in this view was in fact caused by the fire of December 1861. The area was called the Burnt

B-15. Burnt District, looking East.

District for years after the war. Reconstruction took years. The *Bird's Eye View of Charleston*, a lithograph map completed in 1872, still clearly illustrated lots emptied by the fire which blazed from the Cooper River to the Ashley.

Harpers Weekly published this view as a woodcut in their July 8, 1865 issue. Their rendering was accurate, but their engraver turned the "man with a smoking pipe" into an old Negro man. Barnard used a very similar glass negative as "plate 60" in his monumental *Photographic Views of SHERMAN'S CAMPAIGN'S* [sic], one of only three Charleston city views published in his book.

Anthony published an almost identical stereo, taken one foot to the north of B-15, titled "Ruins of Central church, St. Philips church in the distance, Ruins of Secession Hall on the right of the picture, on Meeting street, Charleston, S. C." It is No. 3073 in their catalogue. As the camera location was only one foot to the north of #B-15, and shadows are identical, it is a fair assumption that George Barnard produced that third negative, this time in stereo, for sale to the Anthony brothers.

Stretching across the block from King to Meeting, this area is presently owned by South Carolina Electric & Gas. Barnard's camera tripod was set up in what is now its parking lot entrance from King Street.

B-15, Modern

B-16

Circular Congregational Church, St. Philip's Church, and Secession Hall, stereo, William E. James, April 14 or 15, 1865.

(Author's collection)

Circular Congregational Church's burnt-out walls survived the war. Her congregation had met here since 1681 and had prayed within these walls since 1807. Hope of rebuilding on these old walls crumbled with the 1886 earthquake. Emma Holmes mourned her loss:

> The Circular Church is where all my ancestors worshiped and are buried for 175 years. That pulpit has been filled upon the same spot though not in the same church. This was built in 1806, and a few years ago thoroughly done up & refurnished, making it the largest and one of the handsomest churches in the city. Uncle James [Holmes, who lived across the street] saved the Bible & Hymn Book.[11]

There is another large graveyard behind the Circular's—the western graveyard of St. Philip's with its tall 1848 steeple rising, across Church Street, to the rear. On the extreme right is what remains of burnt-out Institute Hall, with its facade completely gone.

Most of these markers in their cemetery survived. Mrs. Eliza Catherine Bryan's in the center has lost its top shaft, but W. Ransom Davis Flud and his wife Martha Jane's 1855 marble stone just to the right, seen sideways, remains intact. Thomas Lehre's tall marble monument, a bit farther to the right also survives.

This captionless stereo of several well-dressed tourists, posing in front of the churchyard's ruined wall, would remain undated and its photographer unidentified if it had not been used as a woodcut in *Trip of the Steamer Oceanus*. All illustrations in *Oceanus* volume are from W. E. James's photographs. (I have seen over a dozen different images, from different operators, of this church.) The same self-assured confident gentleman standing with his legs wide, in light-colored trousers and cane appears opposite page 125 of *Oceanus*. It was bought at the same time as H-6 and I-21, on the same color card, and manuscript "Ed C" as the others.

Cal Packard of Mansfield, Ohio, has a James-captioned carte de visite of this church in his collection with the same people on the sidewalk. Grass in the foreground lines up with the right image of the stereo. This stereo image was trimmed to fit a carte format. James made enough prints and stereopticon views for his *Oceanus* clients, sent other Charleston and Fort Sumter negatives that

B-16. Ruins of the Circular Church.

he had made for Mr. Anthony in New York, and then went back to his more lucrative portrait work. The Charleston work he made for Anthony is not yet identified.

James apparently did not caption his Charleston views when he published them as stereos. This lack of captions makes his work difficult to identify as being from Charleston as opposed to any Brooklyn street scenes he may have made. The three stereos I purchased at Rusty Norton's annual antique photo show in Washington several years ago, have no printed caption or photographer's mark. These stereos are all on the same cream-colored cardboard stock with only penciled notes on the reverse: the customer's initials, date of image, and "Charleston, S. C.," or some of those three.

The modern view is taken from the exit from South Carolina Electric & Gas onto Meeting Street. The church later acquired forty feet of the Institute's northern lot, expanding its graveyard. An additional entrance to their graveyard has been built. While it is assumed that cemeteries do not change very much, and that a marker once placed will not be moved, Mrs. Haynes Miles' 1800 marble and Jeremiah Milner's 1741 slate headstones, to the left of the gate, do not appear in the 1865 images.[12]

B-16, Modern

B-17

The ruins of the Circular Church and Secession Hall, Meeting St., Charleston, S. C., stereo #3102, Anthony, March 1865.   **(L. C.)**

B-17. *Ruins of the Circular Congregational Church.*

B-17, Modern

A handsome wrought-iron gate lies where its building burned almost 3 1/2 years earlier. Some today explain the loss of much of Charleston's early decorative ironwork to the manufacturers of Confederate artillery and projectile factories. It has been established that scrap iron, window sash weights, and Yankee artillery shell fragments were industriously salvaged by patriotic Southerners for the war effort. Gus Smythe recorded that off-duty Confederate soldiers broke into locked homes below Broad to gather copper pumps and drains and brass gas fixtures, getting as much as a dollar per pound from the Ordnance Bureau. That this iron gate had lain in the sand, undisturbed for over three years, shows that much private property was respected, even during wartime shortages. More likely explanations for the loss of Charleston's early

ironwork are scrap iron dealers, Northern collectors, and simple ignorance of the value of this city's historic relics.

James W. Campbell also published this stereo, with its images slightly cropped all round, as number 188 in his "War Views" series. I have seen one of his stereos, with a three cent revenue stamp[13] indicating that stereo card was sold between August 1, 1864 and August 1, 1866, when the revenue act was repealed. This was a war tax of two cents levied on a photograph selling for less than 25 cents, three cents on those selling for 26 to 50 cents, and five cents on those selling from 50 cents to one dollar.

The 1994 view was taken from the north parking lot of South Carolina Electric & Gas.

B-18

Ruins of Circular Congregational Church, and Secession Hall, taken from west side of Meeting St., glass plate.   (N. A.)

By the spring of 1865, when this image was exposed, South Carolina Institute's sandstone or stuccoed brick facade had been salvaged and removed, leaving nothing of its grand entryway. Scaffolding for repairs of the church steeple was up, but the workmen had been conscripted into the Confederate Army. Shelling stopped any further work in this area until after the war. Only days after the Great Fire, enough was still left for Emma to ruminate about the disaster. She wrote of her birthday, on December 17, 1861:

> [several of us] walked among the ruins principally to see the Circular Church & the Cathedral. The walls of the former are perfect & part of the steeple still standing, and, with the moonlight streaming through the windows & the monuments gleaming beyond, the effect was beautiful & reminded us of the Coliseum. While the front view, with the row of Ionic [sic] columns standing as if to guard the sanctuary, brought the ruins of the old Grecian temples vividly before us, as did the broken arches of the Institute Hall.[14]

Unknown to the photographer, for he left no mention in his caption, he had captured in the foreground the scant remains of Governor Francis Pickens' temporary executive headquarters. Only the brick foundation remains of what he used during the 1861 Fort Sumter crisis. General Beauregard also used this building as his headquarters during that time.

B-19

Unitarian and German Lutheran Churches, Charleston, S.C., stereo #3436, Anthony, March 1865.   (L. C.)

St. John's Lutheran Church and the Unitarian Church, on Archdale Street provided a firebreak for the 1861 conflagration. Their graveyards kept the fire from spreading to the north, but did not spare Clifford's Alley (now Jacobs Alley), seen in the right foreground.

Clifford's Alley housed slaves who lodged away from their masters' property. The 1860 city directory listed 76 slaves and one white man living here in wood houses and

B-18. Ruins of the Circular Congregational Church.

B-19. Unitarian and Lutheran churches.

one brick house. Despite constant fears of a slave rebellion, many owners gave remarkable freedom to their slaves. All houses on Clifford's Alley were completely destroyed in the 1861 fire, save the walls of a brick outbuilding, on the north side of that street. A new wall enclosing the cemeteries was built of salvaged bricks, and parts of that brick wall remain today.

St. John's Lutheran Church, to the left, had a remarkable minister, John Bachman. An ornithologist, he befriended John James Audubon while he was working on his famed book on birds. Bachman's daughters married Audubon's sons. During the war he made patriotic speeches, ran some benefits, and on occasion interpreted for some captured German-speaking Federal soldiers.

Church communion service and records for the previous 30 years were lost in the 1865 Columbia fires. Bachman had evacuated to Cheraw where passing Federal soldiers assaulted and robbed him. But he was able to reopen his church in June 1865, claiming that his was

B-19, Modern

the first church to be reopened by its own congregation. Sketchy notes assembled in November 1865 by their vestry and wardens record that:

> ...our Church was Struck with One Shell, which went thru' the roof into the Gallery, Slightly injuring our Organ and Organ Gallery. The Injury to the roof Mr. [F. C.] Blum has repaired also the damage to the Ceiling. The Organ is Still to be repaired. Several Shells fell in the Yard doing Considerable Injury to Some of the Monuments.
>
> ...[We have little money from collections and pew rents].... There is a few hundred Dollars on deposit in the Savings Institution belonging to the Colored Members of the church, being the next proceeds of the Sale of a portion of their Grave Yard. They have recently made Some application to be for Some Aid to enable them to erect a fence around their Lot, but I can See no prospect of helping them. I think all the Pensioners on our Alms fund have gone to their final rest.[15]

The Unitarian Church has been abused through two wars. Unfinished and unconsecrated before the Revolution, the building was used as a barracks for South Carolina militia. When the British returned in 1780, they used the weary structure as a stable. Later finished with a beautiful Gothic interior and exterior, in 1865 it was taken over by the Federals. They assigned it to the 127th New York Volunteers, and advertised on March 3, 1865, in the Charleston *Courier* that services would be scheduled at 10:30 a.m. and 4 p.m. on Sundays.

In the 1886 earthquake, much of the Unitarian's tower fell. Of all possible directions, unfortunately, it toppled to the east, crashing through its ornate ceiling.

Shadowdating suggests that this photo was taken in March 1865, at 2:20 p.m. ±5 minutes.

B-20

The Ruins of Charleston, S. C., showing the Sister Churches, stereo, Anthony.   (L. C.)

The view is across 1861 rubble from destroyed wood and brick residences on the north side of Queen Street, west of Archdale. These were blown up with gunpowder to try to arrest the fire and keep it from burning the convent at the corner, crossing Mazyck Street (out of the picture to the left), and spreading to burn a block of public buildings.

Sacrifice of these structures saved the Medical University, Roper Hospital, Marine Hospital (for sailors—it also served occasionally as a teaching hospital to study exotic diseases brought from foreign ports), City Jail, and the Workhouse.

The Ruins of Charleston, S. C., showing the Sister Churches.

Entered according to Act of Congress in the year 1865, by E. & H. T. Anthony & Co. in the Clerk's Office of the District Court of the U.S. for the So. District of New-York.

B-20. Ruins in front of the "Sister Churches."

B-21

Roper Hospital, Charleston, S. C., glass plate, also published by Anthony as stereo #3119. (L. C.)

Roper Hospital was finished in 1852 with a handsome central section containing a library, lecture amphitheater, and apartments for physicians. Well-ventilated arcaded wings held patients. Colonel Thomas Roper's son died without an heir, and his $30,000 legacy was used to build Charleston's first community hospital.

Special efforts were made during the 1861 fire to save Roper Hospital and other public structures around it. This hospital, the Medical College, Marine Hospital, Jail, and Workhouse filled a whole block. General Ripley had fourteen houses north of Queen blown up to try to stop the fire at Mazyck Street (now Logan). This effort succeeded and also saved the Roman Catholic Orphanage on the northeast corner of Queen and Mazyck streets. A corner wall of that orphanage can be seen at the right. Sister M. Charles (Curtin), of the Sisters of Charity of Our Lady of Mercy remembered:

> [After 11 o'c,] at last the men came from the camp, and their most earnest efforts seemed to be directed towards saving the Convent. Never was more devotion shown than that which actuated the men of Charleston that night. The...Protestants and Catholics alike, if anything the Protestants predominated in their earnest unselfish sympathy. They moved all our furniture [away];...took down shutters, blinds and everything that might catch the sparks.... They took the law into their own hands and blew up the surrounding buildings. The beautiful Cathedral went without an effort to save it.... Some men were heard to say, "Let us try to save the Church." Others replied, "We cannot save both, and the Sisters have first claim."[16]
>
> ...All the outbuildings, however, had perished, and the firefighters had found it necessary to blow up the Sisters' kitchen and the orphans' refectory in a last ditch effort to save the whole.[17]

Roper Hospital became an unofficial Confederate Hospital. Its steward was instructed not to charge volunteers from South Carolina, and over 1,100 military patients were treated over a three month period. When a shell burst within 50 feet of the hospital, the patients were moved to the Normal School at Morris and Jasper Court.[18]

This is a late April view. Mr. Anthony's operator exposed his glass plate from the second-floor piazza of Thomas and John Hancock's brick house at 101 Queen (now

B-21. Roper Hospital.

B-21, Modern

Dena Panos' 129 Queen). This was the only house west of the Mills House on the south side to survive the fire until the saving of Henry Ross' at 113 Queen, three doors west of Mazyck Street. The Hancock's house did not escape the war entirely—a shell hole in the attic can be traced today. The streets here are dirt, with stone crosswalks at the corners.

B-22

Charleston, S. C. Roper's Hospital, glass plate, March 1865. (L. C.)

This looks northwest across Mazyck and Queen streets. It is early March, before weeds in the burned lots on both sides of Mazyck had leafed out. After missing the Hancock house on Queen, the fire burned both southern corners of Mazyck, and raced southwest toward the Ashley River. The following year Yankee prisoners arrived. Eventually the prisoners of war were placed in one of four locations—here at Roper Hospital, the Jail Yard (B-25), the Work House (B-26), and later at the Race Course (K-1). F. R. Jackson, Co. F, 7th Conn. was sent to Roper Hospital:

I lost my left arm in battle on James Island, S. C.... Here were confined all of the prisoners taken on June 16th [1862], who were seriously wounded.

Sister Xavier came to the hospital daily, accompanied by another Sister and...gave fruit, cornbread, cake, meat, gruel, arrowroot, and sometimes chicken broth. She brought me daily either a bottle of wine or of brandy, generally a bottle of old Malaga wine. There were eight wounded men confined in our cell, only one of whom, Capt. Lawler, was a Roman Catholic. All received the same attention....

Sister Xavier brought...lint, medicines and money...and made our two months of prison life in Charleston a perfect Heaven on earth, compared to what we experienced after leaving that place.[19]

After the shelling began, the patients were moved out of range, and it became a prison for Union officers. About 300 captured Union officers were confined here. At least one officer almost enjoyed his stay.

We were permitted to burn gas [lights] until nine o'clock p.m., which luxury we fully enjoyed.... I should not omit to speak of the long

B-22. Roper Hospital.

piazza at the front, on which I have spent so many hours with my pipe for my companion....

One day a fire broke out close by the hospital, which was no sooner perceived by General Foster than he opened all his guns. The prisoners crowded to the windows, and as shell after shell came crashing down in close proximity, frightening the darkey firemen so that it was almost impossible to get any work out of them, we raised cheer upon cheer, which were not abated when one shell burst directly over us, and a piece came whizzing into the room, wounding slightly one of our number....

In early October [1864] yellow fever appeared and the prisoners were moved out.[20]

Years later, in 1869, Capt. John O'Rourke, Battery "l", 1st Illinois Light Artillery thanked Sister M. Xavier of the Sisters of Charity of Our Lady of Mercy:

I...remember...every morning...your ambulance at our prison gates, your kind words..."How are you today, Sir" "Be of good cheer." "Are you feeling better?" "You will be exchanged soon" "Have you any messages to send to your men on the fair grounds?"

...I cannot forget the morning [we] were ordered away...I met you and Sister Teresa...at the gate and showed you to a room where a few of my comrades were lying sick of the yellow fever. You encouraged them with kind words and promised me you would take care of them, yourself.... Even doctors fled from the plague...I received letters from them after they recovered; they...blessed you, because they said they owed their lives to you.[21]

In 1865 Federal authorities took over the property for several months. Roper reopened with difficulty and remained open until the earthquake of 1886. Its central tower survived, but the wings were demolished around 1911. Roper moved to Lucas and Calhoun Streets in 1904. The old central tower survived as the Marlborough Apartments into the 1980s when its northeast corner collapsed. The tower continued to deteriorate until Hurricane Hugo blew off much of the roof in 1989. A quick demolition followed. Today 140 Queen's large house and garden fills the site. All that remains of this handsome public building is the sandstone fence base bordering the property along Queen and Logan. Mazyck Street has been renamed the north end of Logan Street.

B-23

City Jail, right half of stereo, March 1865.
(West Point)

The Charleston District Jail, constructed in 1802, with later 1820s additions by Robert Mills and 1850s additions by Barbot and Seyle. South Carolina-born Mr. Mills was also the architect of the Washington Monument in the District of Columbia. Mills describes it as:

...a large three-story brick building with very roomy and comfortable accommodations. There has been lately added to it a four-story wing building, devoted exclusively to the confinement of criminals. It is divided into solitary cells, one for each criminal, and the whole made general fire proof. A spacious court is attached...[22]

During the war captured Union enlisted men were confined here, but not under the lock-up regime described by Mr. Mills for common criminals. Mills' wing, with the innovative solitary cells, had been replaced in the 1850s by Barbot & Seyle's octagonal wing, with the octagonal tower.

What to do with captured soldiers from Negro regiments was something of a dilemma. Brigadier General Johnson Hagood, C.S.A., reported from Secessionville, James Island, on July 16, 1863, "Thirteen prisoners Fifty-fourth Massachusetts, black. What shall I do with them?" General Beauregard told him to send them to town "under a strong guard, without their uniform." Soon almost one hundred more were captured in the failed Union assault on Battery Wagner.

For 200 years the South lived in fear of slave insurrection. Capture of armed Negroes in Union blue indicated to many that the war would turn into a massacre of white men, women, and children. Confederate authorities argued that Union officers of Negro regiments should be treated as "inciting to Negro insurrection," and slaves returned to slavery. But these were all, or nearly all, free Northern blacks. They had never been slaves. This issue was never really settled during the war, and captured Negro soldiers were usually confined with the white prisoners of war.[23]

The 54th Massachusetts' wounded men were sent to the Negro Hospital at Rikersville, near Magnolia Cemetery, for treatment. This was a hospital for slaves recruited from the plantations to build Confederate fortifications and the government had to feed, clothe, and care for their health. When recovered, the 54th prisoners joined their comrades at the jail.

B-23. City Jail.

The irony of their confinement in the District Jail was they lived better than their white comrades. The jail in summer was stifling. Blacks were kept separate from the other captured Yankees, outside in tents in the prison yard, and they were worked harder than the whites. The black "Quarters" outside were cleaner and airier, the 54th's men stuck together to help each other, and they got more exercise when put on work details "outside." Also, they had opportunities to get food and other help from the town Negroes.

In 1864 Federal prisoners from Andersonville Prison were transferred here:

> They were crowded into the yard of the City Jail where the ground soon became filthy with the overflowing sinks and vermin which had shared the exodus from Andersonville. The rations, however, were superior to any they had received for months...and after their release the prisoners looked back on Charleston as the "oasis" of their prison experiences. Aiding this sentiment were the visits of the Sisters of Charity of Charleston who came among them distributing gifts to the well and bestowing care and medicines upon the sick.[24]

The top floor and tower were lost in the 1886 earthquake, but the jail was not closed until the 1930s. In the 1980s it was a private museum, and is now used for city storage. Shadow dating suggests that this image was taken in late March 1865, at approximately 5:15 p.m.

B-23, Modern

B-24

Workhouse and Jail, Charleston, S. C. place of confinement of Union prisoners in 1864, carte-de-visite, Beckett's Photographic Gallery, Savannah, Georgia. (Beaufort)

William Read described the use of this public building in 1865, when he later gave his images to the Beaufort Library as, "Workhouse and Jail, Magazine St. The first building, on the left, is occupied as quarters of the detachment of the 54th N.Y. V[eteran] V[olunteers] and detachment of the 47th Pen. Vols.—who garrison the town." The Workhouse was part of a complex of public buildings filling the whole block, in all of which Union prisoners were housed. Robert Mills described it in 1826:

B-24, Modern

B-24. Workhouse and Jail.

The work house, adjoining the jail is appropriated entirely to the confinement and punishment of slaves. These were formerly compelled only occasionally to work; no means then existing of employing them regularly and effectually. The last year the City Council ordered the erection of a tread-mill; this has proved a valuable appendage to the prison, and will supersede every other species of punishment there.[25]

Emma Holmes described how the whole square narrowly escaped the 1861 fire:

The square on which the Mills House is built was saved, but the whole other side of Queen was burnt down to the Roper Hospital, fourteen houses being blown up to save the latter & the Medical College, Marine Hospital, Jail, Workhouse, & other public houses which otherwise must inevitably have been destroyed. For the wind circled in eddies, driving the flames in every direction & carrying showers of flakes to an immense distance.[26]

After the shelling began, most public buildings and hospitals were moved uptown, out of range. Federal prisoners captured at Morris Island and other nearby islands were sent to these buildings to have their wounds treated and to be imprisoned. Lieutenant Henry H. Belfield, 8th Iowa Cavalry, was captured at Lovejoy Station, Georgia, on July 29, 1864, when Stoneman's Raid failed. He described the building:

...[the] City Workhouse then used as a prison for Union officers. It was a stone building built on three sides of a quadrangle, the fourth side being a brick wall. The windows had iron gratings...The number of officers in the prison numbered six hundred...We had been turned loose in the prison. I obtained a cell on the second floor and slept on a pine board. I soon found my way to the roof from which I hoped to study the topography of the city. But a few bullets from the guards below soon warned me that I was on forbidden ground.

Our rations were principally meal, flour, mouldy rice, beans (largely worms), with occasional issue of sweet potatoes, salt pork, or fresh beef. The amount of food issued was never sufficient...at about eight o'clock every morning roll was called. By slipping a few men from one rank to another it was very easy to increase or decrease the normal six hundred, to the great annoyance of the prison officials.

The most common game was cards. Some carved into ornaments or toys the bone issued with the beef. One showed great skill...reminding one

of Chinese or japanese work in ivory. The demand for books was great—the supply extremely small.

[I] held classes in Latin and Algebra, the slate roof furnishing slates and pencils. Of course there was some musical talent and singing was not uncommon.[27]

B-25

Catholic Cathedral, Charleston, S. C. 1865, glass plate, March 30, 1865.   (N. A)

These were the last buildings on Broad Street to escape the great fire as it roared west. St. Finbar's Cathedral and St. Andrews Hall flamed up, but Dr. Thomas Gadsden's mansion (center) and James Rose's porticoed residence (right) escaped the conflagration.[28]

Rose's brick house at the right, with four columns, was Gen. P. G. T. Beauregard's headquarters from early September to November 1863, when intense shelling caused him to move further out of range uptown to what is now known as the Aiken-Rhett Mansion, on Elizabeth Street (Image J-11.) It was here that the *Courier* reported that on November 3, 1863:

PRESIDENT DAVIS IN CHARLESTON.

About ten o'clock, it being rumored that the President was at the General Commanding's Headquarters, in Broad Street, a large crowd gathered to catch a glimpse of him as he passed out to the carriage.

The next day the *Courier* continued, "The President... visited James's Island...accompanied by Generals Beauregard, Gilmer, etc.... The party started from Headquarters in Broad-Street, and proceeded to the headquarters of Colonel Rhett on Commercial Wharf...."

This handsome porticoed brick townhouse with four columns was finished in 1829 by rice planter Col. Thomas Pinckney as his winter residence for Charleston's social season. Charleston in January and February boasted the theater, racing, and the St. Cecilia Ball. Planters must supervise the spring planting and fall harvest in person, but the threat of malaria kept whites away from their rice plantations in the summer. He spent those months in Pendleton District. Later, his widow rented her place to James Rose during the war. Rose made it available to the general for his headquarters.

B-25. Catholic Cathedral.

A shell had burst in Broad Street, showering Beauregard's headquarters' stuccoed fence with fragments of iron. This image was taken from the sidewalk in front of what is now 109 Broad. It shows the handsome decorative brick wall separating Dr. Gadsden's mansion from neighboring St. Andrew's Hall. That wall had occasionally supported planking, allowing revelers in Dr. Gadsden's parlor to join other celebrators across the wall at St. Andrew's. The decorative pigeonhole top of this wall was largely blown down during Hurricane Hugo in 1989, but the Diocese has chosen not to replace it.

Shadow dating this image suggests it was taken around 12:15 p.m. on March 30, 1865 ±3 days.

When the modern view was taken, I was fortunate to catch retired Lt. Gen. William Westmoreland on his way to the post office.

B-25 & 26, Modern

B-26

Roman Catholic Cathedral burnt by the great fire in 1861, and Dr. Gadsden's House destroyed by the bombardment, Charleston, S. C., left half of stereo, by one of Mathew Brady's operators, April 1865, also published by Anthony as stereo #3438.   (MOLLUS)

Dr. Thomas Gadsden's handsome brick mansion was struck at least once by a Federal shell, exploding in the top corner. Another shell burst below in the street, peppering the neighbor's street wall. His house was built c. 1763 by John Rutledge, member of the Continental Congress and first president of the Republic of South Carolina. Rutledge later was governor of S. C., Chief Justice of the U. S. Supreme Court, and an author of the Constitution.

Fashionable houses were built of stone in the 18th century and later, but with no building stone within 100 miles of Charleston, here the best were built of brick. The brick was often stuccoed and scored to make the surface look like stone blocks. The effect is finished by painting each of the "blocks" slightly differently to complete the desired look.

Dr. Gadsden, a successful land owner and slave trader, renovated his home in 1853, adding terra cotta window lintels and pressed metal corner quoins. He also ordered cast ironwork by Charleston's Christopher Werner, incorporating Federal eagles and South Carolina palmetto trees into the corner columns.

Brady's operator used a very wide angle lens when he exposed this stereo at about 12:30 p.m., standard time, the first week of April 1865. There was little traffic, so he was able to work with his tripod set up some nine feet into the street. The modern view may be matched perpendicular to parking meter B-81, in front of 113 Broad.

B-26. Dr. Gadsden's House.

B-27

Saint Andrew's Society Hall, glass plate.

(N. A.)

Built in 1815 for a Scottish benevolent society, it honored Lafayette in 1825 and Daniel Webster in 1847. For years the balls of the Jockey Club and the St. Cecilia were held here. Here too the South Carolina secession convention met on December 19 and 20, 1860. Planned for the capital in Columbia, rumors of smallpox there moved it to Charleston. The 169 delegates steamed into the South Carolina Railroad's Camden Depot on Ann Street, on the afternoon train.[30] After a fifteen-gun salute representing the number of slave states, a parade of militia and volunteer firemen escorted the delegates down Meeting Street to the Mills House. Mrs. St. Julien Ravenel, in her 1906 book, *Charleston, The Place And The People*, remembered the St. Andrews Society Hall:

B-27, Modern

B-27. Saint Andrew's Society Hall.

[the] ...scene of so many joyous entertainments, was the place of meeting. The delegates occupied the gilt, velvet-covered chairs sacred to the chaperons of the St. Cecilia; and the president, Mr. Jamison of Barnwell, stood on the dais below the beautiful picture of the young Victoria, in her coronation robes, painted from life by Sully for the faithful Scotchmen.

The time was too grave for thought of these accessories.

St. Andrews Hall was lost in the great fire of 1861. There was hope the blaze might pass to the north, but when neighboring St. Finbar's Church caught, the Hall was doomed. Burning shingles from the massive church set alight her roof and she was gone in a short time, burned to the walls. Emma Holmes penned on December 16, 1861, that, "From St. Andrew's Hall, many of the portraits were saved, and the walls now stand in their strength, swept bare within."[31]

The Society never rebuilt. Its ruins stood until the 1886 earthquake, after which only the iron fence and handsome brick east property wall remained to remind passers-by of a lost elegance. Even the east brick property wall has been neglected in recent years. Hurricane Hugo blew down most of the handsome decorative pierced brick wall top in 1989, and the bricks were trucked off a few months later. The 1819 iron fence and gate survive today.

Dr. Thomas Gadsden's neighboring mansion survived the fire in good order. This is a 1988 view, taken before Hurricane Hugo damaged the brick wall and before Dr. Gadsden's house was renovated into a handsome bed-and-breakfast named for its 1763 builder, John Rutledge.

B-28

Cathedral of St. John and St. Finbar, glass plate, April 1865, also published by Anthony as stereo #3075.   (L. C.)

Visible behind the burned residence of Judge James L. Petigru at Broad and Friend, and his neighbor William Schneirle's flooded basement, are the remains of a Catholic church consecrated seven years before the great fire. The Gothic cathedral's tower rose 200 feet, and could be seen from the harbor's mouth. Emma Holmes spent her 23rd birthday, December 17, six days after the conflagration:

...very quietly writing & seeing friends & after tea...[several of us] walked among the ruins.... The Cathedral is also very beautiful, the walls all standing and the spires [sic] all along the side reminded me of the statues on the Vatican while the general offices was that of some old Gothic minister—indeed everything is so transformed by the work of a single night that it seems as if we were carried centuries back and stood among the ruins of some ancient city. How desolate seemed the few solitary houses still standing....[32]

Judge Petigru's nephew was Maj. Gen. Johnston Pettigrew, who commanded the Confederate left flank in Pickett's Charge at Gettysburg and was killed shortly after at Falling Waters. Judge Petigru, a noted Unionist, gave us the famous grumpy quote when his state seceded from the Union: "South Carolina is too small for a republic and too large for an insane asylum." The judge, who was against secession, owned seventeen slaves.[33]

The modern view was taken in the front yard of present-day 131 Broad Street. Joseph Mattheson, Jr., has this identical view published in stereo by Anthony as "Ruins of the Catholic Cathedral, Charleston, S. C."

B-29

Interior of St. Finbar's ruins, glass plate.
(N. A.)

Charlestonians thought the Cathedral of St. John the Baptist and St. Finbar was fireproof. Many who had already been burned out, but had been able to save something, desperately stored their goods here.

But this new Gothic cathedral, popularly called St. Finbar's, and completed only in 1854, was not. Its gutted remains lie exposed to the weather in 1865. It had been magnificent; with a nave of 54 feet high, side aisles of 25 feet, and a tower and spire of 200 feet.

In 1865, on a late morning hour around April when this view was taken, looking north, there was hope of eventually rebuilding what had been the largest religious structure in South Carolina. Salvaged brick lay stacked for reuse. But Charleston's economy was wrecked in the war and a new Cathedral of St. John's would not be completed until 1907. That handsome new church was built along roughly the same lines as before, and slightly larger. A planned 100-foot tall tower still has not been built.

B-28. (left) Cathedral of St. John and St. Finbar.

B-29. (below) Interior of St. Finbar.

B-28, Modern

B-30

St. Finbar's from Friend Street, glass plate, George Barnard. (N. A.)

Mr. Barnard skillfully placed his camera to dramatically capture the Burnt District. The fire-gutted Cathedral stands out against the horizon, and his trademark "skinny-man-with-a-pipe," this time reading a paper, sits among rubble of houses along Friend Street. Brick walls of J. F. Baker's home at 12 Friend, in the foreground, have fallen into the sandy street. A chimney remains of neighboring free person of color Henrietta White's frame house at 16 Friend. Of Mrs. Lindsay's large wood house on the corner, 105 Broad, only the base of a chimney remains.[34]

Fine wood and brick houses have survived behind Barnard's camera but his lens catches the full width of the fire. Nothing is left of the upper block of Friend, across Queen, and up Archdale in the extreme rear. Auctioneer Thomas Ryan's white frame dwelling survived, at 17 Archdale Street, corner of Magazine. This (now 19 Archdale) had been built for rice planter Philip Porcher in the 1770s and remained in the Porcher family for nearly a century.

To preserve the feeling of utter desolation, Barnard cleverly placed his camera so St. Finbar's walls screen the intact Unitarian and Lutheran Churches on Archdale. Today, Friend Street, some eight feet wider, has been renamed as the upper extension of Legare Street. A modern view is almost useless, as the Cathedral is screened by a wall and a huge cedar tree.

B-30. Ruins of St. Finbar from Friend Street.

B-31

Panoramic View, the ruins of Charleston, S. C., Roman Catholic Cathedral in the distance, glass plate, also published by Anthony in stereo. (L. C.)

B-31. View of ruins and Roman Catholic Cathedral.

Anthony's operator had an eye for composition and scale, seating his assistant on the stripped ruins of a double staircase to nowhere. Even the marble steps have been removed. Before the fire, this was a wood house on a raised brick basement, then numbered 91 Queen. It was owned by Mrs. St. John Ball, and occupied by a Miss A. Clissey. The house filled all of the front of a small property, 40' x 60', and second from the corner. The staircase indicates that it had been an elegant house.[35]

Behind Mrs. Ball's lot are the ruins of one of Charleston's new prides. Emma Holmes lamented, "The whole of Friend St, from Queen, was burnt, including the very large new Public School, nearly to Tradd."[36] A replacement school was completed twenty years later, named the Crafts School, and closely resembling the lost free public school's 1859 architecture. A north wing was added in 1915. Mrs. Ball's property is now part of the Crafts House Condominium parking lot.[37]

B-31, Modern

B-32

View of the Ruins, carte-de-visite, James, April 14 or 15, 1865.   (Cal Packard)

This view is to the west down Broad Street, from Friend Street (now Legare). Every house on the north side of Broad for four blocks was lost, save Mr. O'Connor's (see B-35) which is seen at the extreme left.

The *Mercury* reported, "the whole of Broad-street is on fire from Mr. Gadsden's to Mazyck-street. The residences of Messrs. Geo. M. Coffin, Jas. L. Pettigru, and others nearby are consumed. The flames have now crossed Broad-street, and as the wind has not lulled, it is impossible to say where they will stop, short of the river." Speaking of this area the next day, the paper mused that the flames "seemed to devote their whole fury against the elegant private residences which have so long been the pride of the southwestern portion of our city. As these beautiful homesteads succumbed, one after another, to the resistless march of the destroying element, the scene was awful."[38] Emma Holmes considered these, on the north side of Broad, to be "some of the finest private residences in the city...Mr. Coffin's, Mr. Isaac Porcher's, Mr. James Heyward's, Mr. Alfred Huger's, the latter quite an antique & for many years occupied by the same family..."[39]

B-33

Broad St., Charleston, S. C., looking east, with the ruins of the Roman Catholic Cathedral and St. Michael's Church in the distance, glass plate, also published by Anthony as stereo #3102, April 1865.   (L. C.)

Broad Street was devastated from the Cathedral nearly to the Ashley River. It took nearly 25 years to fill the void with new homes:

Throughout that awful night, we watched the weary hours at the windows and still the flames leaped madly on the demoniac fury, & now the spire of our beautiful Cathedral is wrapped in flames. There it towered above everything the grandest sight I've ever beheld; arch after arch fell in & still the cross glittered & burned high over all. Then the roof caught & we saw that too fall in.[40]

The Cathedral, which was filled to overflowing with the silver, clothing, furniture and valuables of scores of people, believing it to be fireproof, [was lost]. Bishop [Patrick N.] Lynch's library was also lost there. The residence of the Sisters of Charity was partially burnt.[41]

B-32. View of ruins, looking West down Broad Street.

B-33. View of ruins.

Burning shingles carried by the updraft carried past frustrated firefighters, over Friend Street (now Legare Street), and the fire continued toward the photographer's location. Successively, the roofs of the four houses in the foreground caught fire.

At left are the ruins of Postmaster Alfred Huger's brick mansion. As houses blazed around him he sat in the street in shock, in a chair from his house. For the rest of his life he claimed he was just being stoic. Huger (pronounced "U-gee") had been Charleston's postmaster since 1835. When South Carolina seceded in 1860, Governor Pickens appointed him postmaster of the entire state, but the U.S. government kept the Federal postal system going in Charleston until May 31, 1861. Washington wanted to maintain a vestige of Federal service, and power, in the seceding states as long as possible. Confederate authorities were content with this as it gave them more time to start up their own postal system. The Confederate Post Office took over June 1, 1861. Postmaster General John Reagan of Texas merely swore in the veteran U.S. postmasters to be Confederate postmasters and Huger's job went on. Mr. Huger never worked for the

U.S. Post Office again, but was able to rebuild his home on the same lot.

Shadow dating this image is hazardous, as everything this side of John Rutledge's house has completely changed. I have made an attempt, using shadows from the lamp-post in the right foreground. The shadows suggest a date in late April, and a time of about 12:50, DST.

B-33, Modern

B-34

House where the Union Officers were confined under fire, Broad St., Charleston, S. C., stereo #3101, Anthony, April 1865. (L. C.)

In June 1864, the Confederate provost-marshal refitted Mr. M. P. O'Connor's house at 142 Broad Street (now 180), as a prison for high ranking Federal officers, including General Truman Seymour who had been captured in Virginia on May 6, 1864, in the Battle of the Wilderness. Seymour was not a stranger to Charleston. He had been a captain under Anderson at Fort Sumter in 1861 and in 1863 led the attack against Battery Wagner. The hope was that the Yankees would stop shelling the city for fear of hitting their own generals. This hope failed. The Federals simply brought down 600 captured Rebel officers and put them in a stockade on Morris Island where they were in danger from Confederate artillery fire. It was a standoff, and both sides continued to shell each other.

Gus Smythe grumbled that the Federal officers were living too well. The Confederates had built a bath house for them and ran a gas line so they would have light. Further, they were put in a part of the city that came under fire scarcely once in two months.

By-the-way, we are to have a guard to keep shells from the Steeple & City now in the shape of a number of Yankee officers & men, including Gen. Seymour, who are to be put in the Guard House & Court House, & notification went to the Yankees of the fact. Wonder how it will act. They will hardly fire on their own men.[42]

...The Yankee prisoners are in Mr. Conner's house at the corner of Broad & Rutledge Sts. It is

B-34. House where Union officers were confined under fire.

a splendid house & a delightful situation. They have a large yard & empty lot to walk in, & the other day the Govt. sent round & had gas fixtures put up that they might have light, all at the expense of the Confederacy. They are on their parole not to leave the premises, but there is also a guard stationed round them, & a great many people go round to see them. They are quite a good looking set, & very well dressed. Have plenty of money which they spend for coffee & sugar, &c. It seems a shame to treat them so well.

As we have now got the credit of putting them in shell range, we ought to do so & not leave them out there where a shell does not drop once in two months. They seem perfectly contented with their situation, & well they may be for they are much better off than in camp.[43]

...The Yankee officers flourish finely in their cool house at the foot of Broad St. The Govt. Supplies them with gas, sending the other day to have fixtures set up in the house for them, & is now building them a Bathing House. Surely are kind to them. Wonder if our officers on Morris Isl. will be treated as well.[44]

The History of the Ninety-Seventh Regiment New York Volunteers admitted that treatment was generous. Their Lt. Col. John Spofford was captured at Gettysburg. He escaped from Libby Prison Feb. 9, 1864, and got 27 miles away from Richmond before recapture on the third night. He was in civilian clothes, but was identified by a bone match safe in his pocket, marked "Libby." On June 10 he was sent to Charleston:

After lodging in jail a week they were placed in dwelling houses on the water front, and here until the 3d of August, they were daily witnesses of our artillery practice, but fortunately received no harm. In other respects their condition was better here than in any of the prisons where they had been confined.[45]

Spofford, and General Seymour with the others, was exchanged to Hilton Head, S. C., and rejoined his regiment which was besieging Petersburg, Va.

Mr. O'Connor's 1850s Greek Revival house, with its Temple-Of-The-Winds columns, was warped to the east by the 1886 earthquake. It survives in good condition, as does the house behind (1 Trapman). This view is presently blocked by a magnificent magnolia tree next to O'Connor's and a later brick property wall along the sidewalk. The modern view was recorded to the east, on the sidewalk in front of a marvelous house built soon after the war by the Gibbs family.

Using the shadows from the roof overhang, I believe that this photo was taken before 4:00 p.m. in mid-April.

B-35

O'Connor House, where the Union Officers were imprisoned, under fire, on Broad St. near the Ashley Road, Charleston, S. C., stereo, George Barnard, marketed by Anthony, April 1865. (L.C.)

I identified this image as Barnard's by his trademark skinny bearded man with a felt hat and pipe, in the foreground. This assistant and two others pose among the ruins of a burned house on the south side of Broad Street. Barnard's composition shows the desolate state of the area. O'Connor's house is the only unburnt house along the north side of Broad for four blocks. He records empty lots on both sides and carefully excludes other surviving houses in the background that were north of the Burnt District.

Shadows along the south side clapboards indicate the image was taken within six days of April 2, in the late morning hours. The location of Barnard's camera is the driveway of present-day 171 Broad. The foreground ruins were in present-day 173 Broad. No present-day photograph is possible because a brick house from the 1870s blocks the view.

B-34, Modern

B-35. O'Connor's house on Broad Street.

NAVAL ATTACKS—1863

Few images document the naval attack and defense of Charleston harbor. The saga of the Federal naval blockade and Confederate attempts to break it were hard to capture on collodion, for their fights were full of movement and often at night. Haas & Peale and an as yet unidentified artist in Charleston recorded two important views.

"Haas & Peale" appears scratched into the corner of 25 glass negatives produced by them during July, August, and September, 1863, on Morris Island and Folly Island. Their work is detailed, well-focused, and well posed. Some ninety images from their expedition have survived. They had an extraordinary amount of cooperation from the Army in making the photographs. Artillery batteries have men posed in firing position, a guard parading an army thief stops to pose, and surgeons perform an operation in a wall tent. They took the only known images of the Swamp Angel Battery, with its burst 200-pdr. Parrott laying atop its sand-bag parapet. Sailors pose by their guns in the Whitworth Naval battery. They posed an entire mounted battery; men, horses, guns, and all. The imprint on their mounted images reads: "Photo<u>d</u> by Haas & Peale, Morris island and Hilton Head, S. C."

But who are "Haas & Peale?" They scratched their name on twenty five of their 4 3/4" by 7 1/2" glass negatives, but left little about themselves. Milton Kaplan of the Library of Congress has made the major study of this pair.[1] Kaplan discovered First Lieutenant Philip Haas, Co. A, 1st New York Engineers. He enlisted in September 1861 and their Regimental Order Book has a letter mentioning him on May 13, 1862 from Tybee Island, asking for "a leave of absence for thirty days to go north—my supply of photographic material being entirely exhausted which require to be selected with great care." On February 6, 1863, he requested a carpenter to do some work in the "Photograph Bureau." The National Archives has a March 31, 1863 letter asking that his photographic assistant not be returned to active service. He resigned May 25, 1863, and two days later requested the Quartermaster take charge of some photographic equipment he was using, "they being gov't property."

Unlike a soldier, who could be thrown into battle with little or no training in 1861, a photographer needed considerable experience inside and outside of the gallery to be useful in the field. There was no military school for Civil War photographers. All learned their trade in prewar galleries, so there should have been some record of Haas before he joined the army.

William and Estelle Marder with Sally Pierce in *The Daguerrean Annual* for 1995, found him in the 1850 U.S. Census.[2] Mr. Haas was born in Germany around 1808. At the time of the census he lived in New York with his five children, along with Hannah Ezekiel (age 62), and Margaret Hearney (18), born in Ireland. Mrs. Haas was dead or absent, and the family was cared for by an elderly woman, possibly a grandmother, and an Irish servant.

By 1835 he was a lithographer and print publisher in what was then called Washington City. In 1834 he published a lithographic portrait of Amos Kendall, a founder of Gallaudet College for the deaf. Shortly after the invention of the daguerreotype in 1839, he mastered that art. This image was one-of-a-kind and could not be reproduced, but its accuracy was so superior to the pencil or paint brush that Haas soon used this method in his successful lithograph printing business. He published a lithograph made directly from his own 1843 daguerreotype of John Quincy Adams. The former president, aged but still active, penned in his diary for March 16:

> According to promise I walked up to Mr. Haas' shop about 9, my hands in woolen lined gloves bitterly pinched with cold. Found Horace Everett there for the same purpose of being fascimileed. Haas took him once, and then with his consent took me three times, the second of which he said was very good—for the operation is delicate: subject to many imperceptible accidents, and fails at least twice out of three times.[3]

Haas moved to New York, where he ran successful daguerreotype studios up and down Broadway from 1845 to 1860. Marder, Marder, and Pierce have found him enlisting in the Union army on September 23, 1861, at the age of 53. He apparently took ten years off his age in order to be accepted.[4]

Despite all this evidence, 55 is old for a lieutenant working in the field along the Georgia and South Carolina coast during the summer, so until records can be found with Lt. Haas' age, the New York identity must remain somewhat suspect. Of Peale, the *British Journal of Photography* reported in their December 1, 1863, issue:

> The photographer attached to General Gillmore's army, at Charleston, Mr. Washington Peale, writes home that he has had many narrow escapes. One day he was working within a mile of the enemy's guns, and as he had to climb a pole which had been erected for his accommodation, with a platform on the top, and a ladder to facilitate the ascent, several solid shot were thrown at him, all well aimed, but faulty in range. At last a shell exploded near him, part of which struck the ladder while he was in the act of descending, and inflicted some severe bruises on his person, but did not interrupt his work. He complained of the monotony of the endless sand reaches, and descants at length on a ramble he had taken inland among the trees, describing the birds and the flowers as if he enjoyed them exceedingly. His intention originally was to have gone north with an arctic expedition, and his outfit was procured with that intention; but the affair fell through, and he is now in a much warmer climate than he had expected to have been in.

Washington Peale (1825-1868) the son of James Peale, Jr., of Philadelphia, was a painter in New York City before the war. Philip Haas (if he is the same artist) and Washington Peale are thus identified as working for General Gillmore in 1863. *Harper's Weekly's* August 15, 1863, issue published a woodcut of Gen. Gillmore, based upon Lt. Haas' photograph. After the war, their images appeared as lithographs or woodcut illustrations in several books, but without credit to whoever produced the images.[5]

Haas and his partner Peale, returned as civilians to cover the Federal operations against Morris Island and Fort Sumter in the summer of 1863. The Library of Congress holds many of their original glass negatives. This work is full of life and detail. They worked among the front siege lines, and also made images of Confederate-held Fort Sumter being pulverized by Union artillery. They used a long lens to catch details of its Second National Flag above the ramparts.

C-1

The ironclad fleet and the frigate USS *New Ironsides* off Charleston, glass plate, Haas & Peale, September 8, 1863.   (L. C.)

Among their negatives is a bland shoreline scene, with Union soldiers' tents pitched almost up to the high tide mark. The Library of Congress recorded it as simply an "Unidentified Camp Scene." It shows a wide beach at low tide; tracks in the sand show where many soldiers and wagons have marched onto the beach and away from the camera. Soldiers stand along the shoreline, looking into the distance away from the camera.

That last point is odd. Most soldiers insist on gazing directly toward a camera. Years ago I saw an enlargement of this image. It appeared to have something on the horizon, possibly a ship. My curiosity was renewed recently and a close friend, Jim Nicholson, enhanced my print. More detail showed a warship with a puff alongside. Was this a battle scene? Is this a cannon firing from a warship? No sails were visible. High freeboard precluded a monitor. Is it USS *New Ironsides* firing a broadside at some unseen Confederate target?

Logic said no. Exposures in the 1860s were usually measured in five to twenty seconds or so. Motion of battle was impossible to capture on a glass plate. A regiment marching, horses galloping, guns rolling backward in recoil, flashing musketry, were all impossible to catch. The hazard to the operator and his assistant trying to sensitize a wet plate in the field, place it against their camera, expose with a steady hand, and develop the plate before it dried, all precluded even a try. Static soldiers and guns could be recorded, but not the action of a battle.

Some tried. Confederate George Cook, atop Fort Sumter, exposed a plate to some Federal ironclads. He was rewarded with some blurs from his two tries, and a shell knocked some of his plates into a cistern. He also recorded the flash of a Federal shell burst inside Fort Sumter's parade ground, but had to heavily retouch his negative to get anything recognizable. The equipment was not equal to the enterprise.

Others had more success in peacetime. In 1859 Anthony sold New York stereos of Broadway which froze pedestrians, horses, and an omnibus in motion. In 1860 George N. Barnard made "instantaneous" views in Cuba. Barnard captured ships in motion, spray from waves crashing on the shoreline, and a column of Spanish soldiers marching from Catholic Mass. He used the brilliant summer sun, an emulsion more

C-1. USS New Ironsides firing on Forts Sumter and Moultrie.

C-1, detail—center right   ↑ *One monitor*

C-1, detail—left   *Two monitors side-by-side (2 stacks)* ↑

C-1, detail—right   ↑ *USS New Ironsides*

C-1, detail—center left   *Two monitors* ↑

sensitive than usual, redeveloped the underexposed negative, and a good darkroom printer. These professionals' fastest exposure could be one-sixth of a second.[6]

I looked at the other Haas & Peale images. One, showing nine Federal ships on the horizon, was sharp enough to pick out a supply schooner, two brigs, and a steamer. Waves lapped toward the shore, making an "instantaneous photograph." I requested the Library of Congress to print enlargements along the horizon of this seaside scene with soldiers gazing away from the camera, and to print from their own copy negative. Jim's enhancement of my third-generation print produced wonderful results, but the first-generation prints were marvelous. This is the first photographic record of naval ships in battle, and probably the only clear battle image produced in the Civil War.

This ship is indeed USS *New Ironsides*, with her stern facing the camera. A longboat trails from her stern. Her stubby single stack and signal rigging are clear. *New Ironsides* was built with masts for a full set of sails, but her engines proved so reliable that these masts were soon removed. Smoke belches from one or more of her port guns. She has been firing for some time; gun smoke billows away to the left for over half a mile inland. Other Federal ships are visible. Four or more monitors are off her port side. These are single-turreted ships with pilot-house atop the turret. Each monitor has a single smoke stack aft of the turret. The extreme left monitor appears to have two stacks, indicating an additional fifth monitor either in front of it or behind. The Confederate shoreline is on the horizon.

The image was produced less than 25 years after photography's invention, yet this large glass negative contains tremendous detail. When was it made? Haas & Peale left no caption for their image, so we must examine it for clues.

1. Sullivan's Island is in the extreme background. One or more Confederate forts are visible.

2. The image was produced on Morris Island. In 1863, Sullivan's Island could not be seen from Folly Island.

3. USS *New Ironsides* blockaded Charleston from February 1863 to June 1864. She was damaged but serviceable after CSS *David* rammed a torpedo into her side on October 5, 1863. Ordered to the Philadelphia Navy Yard on May 23, 1864 for a refit, she never returned to Charleston.[7]

4. It is morning. *New Ironsides'* right side is in the sun. Men and wagons throw shadows to the left. A soldier's shouldered musket barrel and bayonet glint on its right.

5. Five or more monitors are in this fight.

6. It is just after low tide. The beach is wide in the foreground. The anchored *New Ironsides'* longboat has swung to the left on the new incoming tide.

7. The fight has lasted for some time. Smoke from the frigate's guns have drifted to the left (west) for over half a mile.

In February 1863, the ironclad frigate USS *New Ironsides* took station in the blockade off Charleston, just days after the CSS *Chicora* and *Palmetto State* had scattered the Union fleet. She was the largest ship to go on blockade duty, and her arrival gave the Federal squadron much heart.

General Gillmore's Federal troops captured much of Morris Island in July but were blocked by Battery Wagner, which led to a two-month siege of that important Rebel fort. Union camps crowded onto the lower end of Morris Island, allowing a view of Sullivan's Island from Morris Island's beach. *New Ironsides* was used in the July and August bombardments that pounded Battery Wagner.

Federal infantry charged into Wagner the morning of September 7, to discover that the Confederates had evacuated it only hours earlier. That same day the monitor *Weehawken* ran aground at high tide, trying to lay harbor markers for a small-boat attack on Fort Sumter. Admiral Dahlgren used his other monitors and *New Ironsides* to make a diversionary attack on Fort Moultrie. *Weehawken* got into the fight, sending one of her own shells into a Fort Moultrie gun pit. That explosion set off the gun's ready ammunition, killing several Rebel artillerymen. The Confederates did not notice *Weehawken's* stranding until evening. Tugs worked all night trying to pull her off as the Union fleet stood by. This set the stage for the only situation that filled the seven requirements.

Dawn of September 8 found *Weehawken* still stranded. Dahlgren ordered his five monitors and the frigate to fire on Forts Sumter and Moultrie. In the early morning hours the monitors *Passaic*, *Montauk*, *Patapsco*, *Lehigh*, and *Nahant* steamed in to attack the Rebel defenses on Sullivan's Island and Fort Sumter.[8]

Once on station to fire at the Rebel batteries, they kept moving slowly to provide a poor target. *Ironsides* anchored, fore and aft across the channel. Springs were rigged to her anchor lines so she could fire without straining those lines. *Ironsides* could fire all her broadside guns, one by one, to the northwest at Fort Moultrie on Sullivan's Island, or her crew could pull on her anchor lines to warp the whole ship to fire west at Fort Sumter. She was the biggest ship to serve in the entire blockade, mounting sixteen eleven-inch

Dahlgren smoothbore guns and a 150-pdr. Parrott rifle on each side. Her longboat swung to the west with the incoming tide.

With the dawn, soldiers off duty wandered to the wide beach—it was low tide—to see the show. Companies filed down to the beach to the upper end of Morris Island to prepare for this night's planned small boat attack on Fort Sumter. Marching was easier on a hard sand beach. Haas & Peale woke to find a splendid opportunity to photograph a battle. They could hear naval guns. Dressing rapidly, they made their way to the beach where they saw the Union fleet in action. Normally ships move too fast for a plate to catch a sharp image, since an exposure usually required several seconds. The monitors were steaming about slowly, but *New Ironsides* was motionless, firing at anchor. The ships were two to three miles away but the morning was clear. There was no haze. A bright September sun might provide enough light to try an "instantaneous" image. Hastily assembling camera, lens, chemicals, tripod, developing tent and all, they rushed through the crowded Federal camps. Gaining a vantage point on the beach they needed over half an hour to put up their developing tent, erect camera and lens upon their tripod, focus on the distant naval battle, sensitize a glass plate, and put it into the back of their camera.

His exposure was quick; it had to be, to freeze the action. *New Ironsides* has just fired a gun. She had warped to bear her port broadside on Fort Sumter and was slowly firing gun after gun, one aimed shot after another. Clouds of smoke drift west. Anchored against the incoming tide to provide a stable platform, her longboat, trailing from the stern, has swung to the port. Her signal masts and massive stack are well-defined.

The tide, in the foreground, is at maximum low. It has just changed, for *New Ironsides'* longboat has swung to her port side with the incoming tide. It is around 10 a.m. My friend Jim Nicholson ran the computer program "Tide 226": the morning low tide at Charleston, on September 8 is 10:05 a.m., standard time. The local Coast Guard base says low tide would be about five minutes earlier at Morris Island.

West of *New Ironsides* are the monitors *Passaic*, *Montauk*, *Patapsco*, *Lehigh*, and *Nahant*. They all point generally to the east, steaming slowly against the tide so that their single turret remains relatively stationary. Their crew can turn their turret to aim on any Rebel fort. Each monitor's pilot house is atop their turret, and has a single stack astern. What appears to be a monitor with two stacks is really two ships, with turrets superimposed.

Behind the ships is Confederate-held Sullivan's Island. With Wagner and Morris Island gone, it was essential to hold this island. With Fort Sumter, this was now the outer defense of Charleston. Since Confederate control of the island offered them protection, blockade runners still hugged this shore to slip past the Union navy.

By this stage of the war, few houses remained on Sullivan's Island, which, before the war, had been Charleston's summer seaside resort. The earliest letter from Gus in 1853, has him inviting his 31-year old Aunt Janey Adger to bring her bathing dress to Rev. Smyth's summer house on the island. By 1863 he wrote his parents that he feared their house was down too. The large earthwork to the far left may be Fort Beauregard, which eventually mounted thirteen heavy guns. Confederate batteries Rutledge and Fort Moultrie appear to be out of view to the west.

The partners had succeeded only because of their ambition, and the extraordinarily clear morning. The summer haze was lacking. Assuming their camera was on lower Morris Island, about one mile south of Battery Wagner (which had just been evacuated September 6), the Federal ships were from 1 1/2 to 2 1/2 miles away, and Sullivan's Island with its sandy beach was visible at low tide, over three miles. It is difficult to determine what is in the extreme distance. It may be the tree line of Mount Pleasant, nearly five miles away, or more probably drifting gun smoke.

They captured their view just in time. *New Ironsides* and the monitors were almost out of ammunition when this image was made and they soon withdrew to the east. *Weehawken* floated herself at high tide, quickly steaming out to sea. There was no time for a second image of this battle.

Philip Haas & Washington Peale were pleased with themselves. With less than half an hour left of low tide, they proudly posed themselves for their own portrait, with an assistant working the lens.

But this battle scene was not marketable. USS *New Ironsides*, from the stern, was not recognizable, and the technology of 1863 would not allow an enlargement where the ships could be identified. These artists' notes have not survived. This image is their monument, and we are fortunate that the technology of the late 20th century has finally allowed us to give Haas & Peale their due.

C-2

CSS *Chicora*, carte-de-visite, postwar copy, published by S. T. Souder, 1871-73.
(Charles Peery Collection)

This is the only known image of a Charleston iron-clad. It is also the only known image of a Confederate warship flying the Stars and Bars.

Launched in August 1862, *Chicora* was one of two Charleston ironclads intended to drive away the Union blockading fleet. If the Federal blockading fleet could be scattered for just a day or two, and the deed witnessed by British, French, and Spanish consuls, international law provided that thirty days must pass before a blockade could be reinstated. During that time Confederates could ship out thousands of bales of cotton and import tons of arms and equipment.

Her commander was John R. Tucker of Virginia, an energetic veteran with 35 years' experience in the U.S. Navy. His crew had a large proportion of trained seamen, including three free Negroes enlisted aboard. She also acquired battle-trained veterans transferred from CSS *Arkansas*, which had fought her way through the entire U.S. fleet during the Vicksburg campaign.[9]

Chicora had four inches of armor plate. She was armed with two rifled 6.4" Brooke guns and two 8" smoothbore Dahlgrens. Her fore and aft Brooke guns could be swiveled to a right or left gunport. Adding the Dahlgrens, which were mounted amidships, this ironclad had a formidable three-gun broadside.

By January, *Chicora*'s guns, armor, and crew were ready for action. She and her larger consort, CSS *Palmetto State,* had only one major weakness, their engines. Both had to borrow engines from smaller steamers, which produced a top speed of only five knots in still waters. Fighting a tide, they could barely make headway. Still, their morale was tremendous. Commanded by veteran officers who had resigned from the U.S. Navy when their states seceded, and manned by well-trained sailors, they were ready.

In the pre-dawn hours of January 31, 1863, Commodore Duncan N. Ingraham steamed his small fleet past the bar, into the Union navy. The CSS *Palmetto State* surprised the USS *Mercedita* and rammed her, sending a 68-lb. shell crashing through a boiler and blowing a hole over four feet square through her port side. Her captain struck his colors.

The *Chicora* caught up with the fight. She had hoped to ram one of the enemy, but her engines were so weak that she might not later be able to pull clear of a sinking victim.

P. C. Coker, in his *Charleston's Maritime Heritage*, has studied this fight:

Captain Tucker had taken *Chicora* past her consort to starboard and engaged in a gunnery duel with two other blockaders, *U.S.S. Quaker City* and the paddle steamer *U.S.S. Keystone State*. *Quaker City* took a shell in her engine room. Having heard *Palmetto State's* shot at *Mercedita*, Captain LeRoy of *Keystone State* ordered his crew to action stations. When *Chicora* loomed up out of the mist, LeRoy opened fire...he got off three telling shots from his port broadside. *Keystone State* turned seaward, quickly came up to twelve knots, and left her antagonist behind. As the distance opened and the gathering light improved visibility, *Keystone State* turned to attack. Turning the tables, she tried to ram *Chicora*. The range rapidly closed as both sides exchanged fire. A shot from *Chicora* passed through both steam drums in *Keystone State's* engine rooms, scalding and killing several men. Additional shells crashed into her hull and exploded on her deck, and steam escaping from below added to her crew's confusion. Water poured into her bilges from two holes below the waterline and caused her to heel to starboard.[10]

Chicora was only 500 yards away and maneuvering to rake the unfortunate *Keystone State*. Aboard her, water was pouring in through two holes below the waterline, and she was heeling over to starboard. Captain LeRoy decided to surrender. He was on deck, tearing up some papers.

The flag had just been hauled down and Lt. [Thomas H.] Eastman [the Executive officer] had asked "Who hauled down the flag?" The Captain replied "I ordered it down. We are disabled and at the mercy of the Ram who can rake and sink us. It is a useless sacrifice of life to resist further." Lt. Eastman threw his sword upon the deck saying "God D—n it. I will have nothing to do with it." The Captain said "What would you do? Will you take the responsibility?" Eastman instantly replied, "yes sir, I'll take the responsibility," and picking up his sword sang out to the officer on the poop deck cooly and calmly, "Hoist up the flag. Resume firing."[11]

Aboard the *Chicora*, Tucker ceased firing when *Keystone State's* flag had been lowered. Aboard the stricken ship, however,

...his chief engineer reported that the engines would work for a few more minutes on their vacuum, and, before Lieutenant Bier from *Chicora* could lower a boat to take possession, the blockader got up steam and slowly moved away. *Chicora* hesitated before resuming fire on a ship that supposedly had surrendered. As the gap widened, Captain LeRoy rehoisted his colors, resumed fire with his rifled gun, and escaped. The steamer *U.S.S. Memphis* towed him to Port Royal.[12]

The blockading fleet scattered and the British, French, and Spanish consuls came out, agreeing no blockader was in sight. CSS *Chicora* and *Palmetto State* steamed home to cheers and celebrations. Federal killed and wounded totaled 47. Ingraham's Confederate fleet lost no men.

Washington refused to acknowledge that the blockade had been broken. Days later, the USS *New Ironsides* joined the Charleston station. With sixteen 11-inch smoothbore guns and two 150-pdr. Parrott rifles she was the strongest ship in the Union navy. Shortly more ironclads joined her. The CSS *Chicora*, *Palmetto State*, and later on, the *Charleston,* proved too weak for the job expected of them, but the Federal fleet did not know this and demanded more ironclads to defend themselves.[13]

Chicora served until the evacuation, though by early 1864 her engines had nearly failed and she became a floating battery.

This is the only Confederate image of wartime Charleston. It shows the stern and starboard of the CSS *Chicora*, moored at one of many palmetto log wharfs that lined the Cooper River. Her gun shutters are open and a Brooke rifle protrudes from the stern gunport. A Dahlgren smoothbore has been run out of its own starboard gun port. Her hand-operated bilge pump is on her stern. The image contrast has been improved by computer, but no other enhancement has been performed.

She appears to be new and in good order. She was painted pale blue-grey to make her nearly invisible on a sea. This was the only paint job she received, and she eventually rusted to a brown. She flies the Stars and Bars, the Confederate National Flag. This flag was replaced in the summer of 1863 by the new Second National Flag, the Stainless Banner.

C-2. CSS Chicora.

Charles Peery of Charleston, owner of this image, recognizes sailors in British uniform in the longboat. Others support his interpretation. The combination of a new paint job, the early Confederate flag, a longboat bearing what appears to be the British naval jack, three British officers atop the casemate (one on the extreme left, and two to the left of the mast in the center) indicate that this image was exposed shortly after CSS *Chicora*'s victory, probably in January or February 1863.

David Norris, in *Military Images* magazine,[14] has researched that these British were from HMS *Peterel*, which arrived January 1, 1863, and remained six weeks. The pro-Southern British consul in Charleston, Robert Bunch, was worried about a Union attack on Charleston, and that the Emancipation Proclamation could incite a slave revolt. Commander George W. Watson brought *Peterel* into the harbor to protect the city's British citizens. Watson could do this as the Federal blockade did not extend to warships of foreign powers.

Consul Bunch and Commander Watson watched *Chicora*'s and *Palmetto State*'s naval fight from Fort Sumter as guests of General Ripley, and agreed that the blockade had been lifted. During *Peterel*'s visit time her rudder was repaired and Watson's officers and crew enjoyed the city. Emma Holmes recorded on January 20, 1863:

> ...Beauregard's staff last week gave a Soiree— they called it—for they did not pretend to have a handsome supper—but otherwise it was a ball. A [railroad passenger] carload of ladies went down from Columbia—the fashionables there, as well as those who had taken refuge from Charleston...Rosa Bull says it was a ball of strangers, for the city is full of them, foreigners too, &, though she enjoyed it, it was not thoroughly— One partner was a

Frenchman, whose English was indescribable— only three square dances all evening, and she staid till near three o'clock. There are both an English & French vessel in the harbor & the officers have been dining at Mr. Bulls. The Frenchmen were there last Summer & belong to the *Milan*.[15]

Of the English consul Robert Bunch, on February 14, 1863, Miss Emma wrote that he "has just been recalled after a residence of ten years in Charleston, to the mutual regret of both parties. A handsome public dinner with farewell addresses was given him. Mr. H. Pinckney Walker has taken his place."[16]

Several images survive of the *Chicora*, all in the carte size. The oval implies that a carte negative copy was made from a large print that had been trimmed into an oval and pasted onto a cardboard mount. I have examined five of these *Chicora* cartes, most with blank backs. This is the best of the lot and is the only one back-marked. The name is S. T. Souder.

Stephen T. Souder, however, was not a wartime photographer. He worked in Charleston from 1871 to 1873. As related earlier, Souder had bought out George N. Barnard's gallery, who had in turn bought out Charles Quinby, the wartime proprietor of the gallery. It is possible that Quinby produced this image, and its negative was one of the 4,000 included in Quinby's file at the time of sale. Souder's file had increased by another 3,500 negatives when Bertha Souder sold the gallery back to Barnard in 1873. It is unlikely that Souder could produce so many additional negatives in such a short time by himself. He may have bought negatives as other Charleston galleries folded.[17] Another solution is that it was made by an officer of HMS *Peterel*, the British warship visiting Charleston early in 1863. Some ship's officers were skilled in photography.

CHARLESTON DEFENSES

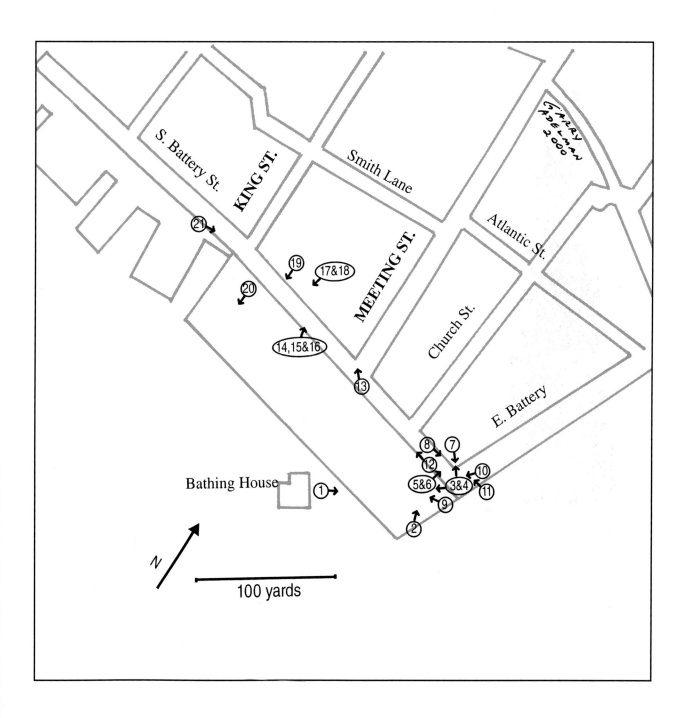

D-1

South Battery, stereo half, published in large format by George Cook, Charleston, S. C.
(Valentine Museum)

From atop the Bathing House, the photographer pointed his camera to the north, to record the largest of seventeen fortifications defending Charleston's inner harbor. His camera location is the same as Osborn & Durbec's 1860-61 photo of the Bathing House (A-6). The reader can see how a peaceful park was turned into one of Charleston's major harbor defenses.

South Carolina was concerned that the Federal navy might penetrate their outer works on Sullivans Island, Fort Sumter, and Morris Island, into the main harbor. The British had done that in 1780 during the American Revolution, when they took their licks passing Sullivan's Island, and sailed into the lightly defended harbor. After a two-month siege, Charleston fell to the British.

Not wanting a repeat, Confederates started an inner harbor defense in 1862. Along the east end of White Point Garden, they built a work holding five gun pits, named Battery Ramsay. It was named after Major David Ramsay, who fell defending Battery Wagner on July 18, 1863. Dirt was excavated from nearby vacant lots. Much fill was taken from inside the Garden itself, taking care to leave a pedestal of dirt supporting those trees within the garden.

This photo shows the Battery Ramsay's white flagpole that would never again fly the Confederate Stainless Banner. Federal ships now fill the harbor. The ship in center background has been identified as the Charleston-built USS *John Adams* by Priestly Coker in his *Charleston's Maritime Heritage*.[1]

A modern view is impossible, as the Bathing House disappeared early in this century.

George Cook marketed this print after the war, but it is doubtful he made this image.

D-2

Battery Ramsay, glass plate, George Barnard,
March 14, 1865.   (N. A.)

This is the first of a series of at least eight images produced here by Barnard on the same day, within three days of March 11, 1865. Nearest of four guns that eventually armed this work is a captured 11-inch Dahlgren. Two of these smoothbores were salvaged from USS *Keokuk*. She was sunk after nine Federal ironclads tried to pound and capture Fort Sumter by themselves, without aid of the Federal army.

D-1. South Battery.

D-2. Battery Ramsay.

Their assault of April 7, 1863, failed. Confederate artillery was prepared, and the pounders became the poundees. *Keokuk* came closer to Fort Sumter than any other ship and was hit over 90 times. She limped off, sinking that evening in shallow water. At low tide, her two turrets and perforated smoke stack could still be seen. The U.S. Navy wrote her off; she was badly torn up and a winter storm would scatter her wreckage.

The Confederates were short of many things and routinely visited the wreck for souvenirs and anything useful. Her two eleven-inch guns were discovered to be in good shape. This was a windfall. Southern foundries could produce ten-inch guns, but an eleven-inch was beyond their capability. In a masterful effort, Confederate salvors recovered both guns, working at night and in cold water, barely 1,000 yards away from the Federal shoreline.

Keokuk's Dahlgren is identified by the shaved-off side of her muzzle. Embrasures in the turrets of this experimental ship were cut too small to allow her guns to stick out. These were muzzleloaders, and the #1 artillery crewman rammed charge and ball from inside her protective turret. The loaded gun then normally was run out through the embrasure and fired. A cannon fired from inside the turret produces a dreadful concussion to cannoneers, so rather than enlarge the openings, the outside diameter of her two guns was shaved to allow the muzzle to be run out through the opening.

All guns in White Point Garden were scrapped after the War. This Dahlgren's mate was recovered from her Sullivan's Island battery site about 1900, under the super-

D-2, Modern

vision of Mayor Adger Smyth, Gus' older brother. It was mounted at the site of Battery Ramsay on an 1860s U.S. Arsenal iron carriage and chassis.

Image D-2 was timed around 10 a.m. ±10 minutes using the shadows in the piazza of Louis deSaussure's three story mansion on the corner, and by shadows under the eaves of a pre-Revolutionary War house at the left rear. This was an establishing shot for his series. Barnard knew if his later views were failures, this image would stand on its own.

Confederate engineers filled the foreground of this sodded earthwork to two feet above present level. I raised my camera seven feet from the seawall's present level to match this scene, about 75 feet from the corner of East Bay and Murray Boulevard.

D-3

Ruins of 650 lb. Blakely, in Battery Ramsay, next to Louis deSaussure's house, corner East Bay and South Battery, glass plate, George Barnard, March 14, 1865. **(N. A.)**

This gun was blown up at the Evacuation, Feb. 17, 1865. Its breech, visible in front of the gate, tumbled sixteen yards to the rear. Another 500-lb. chunk of the gun sailed north past deSaussure's roof, over the next roof, and into Alfred F. Ravenel's attic at 5 East Bay.

It was originally one of a pair. These two were the largest guns ever used by the Confederacy. Both were run through the blockade on August 18, 1863, by

Fraser & Trenholms' ship *Gibraltar*, into Wilmington, N.C., in a daring daylight run. Gus wrote on August 25 that, "one of the two large guns lately arrived in Wilmington by the *Sumter*, these are English guns-Blakely pattern guns, 15 inches in diameter of bore, & shoot a bolt weighing 760 or 780 lbs. They are rifled, and their range is six miles."[2]

His rumor was close. They were 12.75-inch Blakely rifled guns, shipped from Liverpool, with their carriages and 150 solid shot weighing 650 lbs. each, and 50 shells of 450 lbs. Each gun tube alone weighed some 50,000 pounds. Only the carriage of the first gun had arrived in Charleston by that day, and its parts alone filled seven railroad cars. The first gun arrived four days later.

D-3. Ruins of the Blakely Gun.

The "Whopper" lay this afternoon at the corner of King & Hazel Sts, on its way to the Battery.... This is a great gun & is expected to do wonders.[3]

Three days later, Gus added:

The big gun is down on the battery, & will be mounted to-morrow or next day as they are laying the foundation & fixing the carriage for it to-day. The other is coming on, & will be mounted on Fort Johnson "they say."[4]

Confederate artillerymen were eager to test the Whopper, but had not received its instruction manual. They also could not puzzle out the purpose of a bronze cavity cast into the rear of the breech. This cavity was supposed to be empty and serve as an air cushion to help absorb the recoil when the gun was fired. The gunner incorrectly filled that cavity with gunpowder, causing a major disaster. Though the gun crew chose a light charge for this first shot, they still attached an extra-long lanyard and pulled it from the protection of a dugout.

That shell flew some 800 yards, and then skipped an additional 200 yards down the Cooper River. This was respectable, having used only two degrees of elevation and only forty pounds of gunpowder when the service charge called for fifty pounds. But when the white gun smoke cleared, its cast-iron breech was discovered to be cracked in eleven places:

I saw it myself & felt the cracks with my fingers.[5]

The big gun has been taken down & now stands down in the green, neglected & despised.... They talk of repairing the whopper, but I am afraid they can't. The cause of its bursting turns out to be that they put the cartridge of powder into what was intended for an air chamber & not for powder, thro' ignorance of the structure of the gun. The instructions from the maker which accompanied it, were only received here yesterday instead of coming with it. This I heard from an Artillery Officer to-day.[6]

Five months later, on Feb. 12, Gus wrote, "They are preparing I think, to mount a new gun by deSaussure's house.... They have take the cracked big gun to Eason's shop and are going to make it good as new, they say."[7]

Eason did his work well. The repaired gun was fitted with a new breech and returned to Battery Ramsay. It was mounted in its own gun chamber in front of Mr. deSaussure's house and did good service until purposely burst during the evacuation in February 1865. Some of the gun still does good service in 2000. The breech (with Eason's work intact) was taken to the Charleston Arsenal by April, and is today a trophy at the U.S. Military Academy at West Point, along with the muzzle end of the other Blakely that had been burst at Frazier's Wharf.

In 1976, I noticed ditch diggers having a problem, working at the corner of East Bay & South Battery. Buried 12" x 12" beams obstructed their labor. A chain saw quickly cleared through the obstruction, that turned out to be the wooden foundation that had supported the Whopper. I picked up a neatly sawn three-inch 12" x 12" segment, the white pine still fragrant in the damp soil.

When estimating the time of day this image was taken, around 11:00-11:30 a.m., I relied upon the stuccoed brick property line wall and posts. The right gate post and the two further to the right have leaned outward over the years, but shadows on the left gate post are still valid markers.

D-3, Modern

D-4

Three gun battery on "The Battery," Charleston, S. C. The gun in the distance was taken from the wreck of the U.S. Ironclad "Keokuk," glass plate, George Barnard, March 14, 1865, also published by Anthony as stereo #3068.   **(L. C.)**

I had just taken this modern view of D-3, and was seeking the original location of the photographer to match D-4 when I discovered that the camera locations were the same. From the identical camera site, I judge this is also a Barnard image. That veteran cameraman simply pivoted his apparatus and exposed a fresh plate to his new view. The business sense of Barnard and Anthony told them that by making two different images of the same battery, they could sell more stereos.

Both guns in the foreground are 10-inch Columbiad smooth-bore cannon, cast in Richmond. These and the *Keokuk* gun described in image D-2, all appear set at maximum elevation, because retreating Confederates removed the elevating equipment. Unable or unwilling to burst these other guns, the gun crews knew that a lack of that gear would still render these weapons useless. Two unused Confederate wicker gabions lay in the foreground. They were probably found abandoned nearby and put there by Barnard to break up an otherwise uninteresting foreground.

At the right rear is the Bathing House. Recognizing the splendid view of most of Charleston Harbor, Confederates made it their Signal Corps headquarters. A tower was built on top. From here Gus Smythe signaled to forts and ships with flags by day and torches by night. Here he learned how to use the telegraph key to communicate directly with James Island and Fort Sumter. Gus could walk to work, and with the harbor breeze, this part of his war was rather comfortable. Occupying Federals made use of it. The Charleston *Courier* started an ad on April 27, 1865:

D-4. "The Battery."

D-4, Modern

SALT WATER BATHS
THE WHITE POINT SALT WATER BATH-
ING Establishment having been thoroughly repaired, will be RE-OPENED ON THE FIRST OF
MAY. No expense has been spared to render this
former favorite resort as attractive as in the past.
The Ladies' Department has been fitted up with
every convenience. The Gentlemen's Department
has also been very neatly arranged. ICE CREAMS
and other REFRESHMENTS will be kept on hand.
The proprietor will give his own personal attention
to visitors. Besides having engaged polite and
experienced waiters and assistants.

M. McMANMON

D-5

**View on the Battery, Charleston, S.C. Re-
mains of the large Blakely gun, burst by the
rebels before the evacuation, glass plate,
George Barnard, March 14, 1865, also published by Anthony as stereo #3080.   (L. C.)**

Barnard advanced his camera onto the sodded
bombproofs' first level to record the rear wheels and chassis of the ruins of this largest of Confederate guns.

The blast blew fragments hundreds of feet away. The
absent Mr. deSaussure's windows were shattered, walls
cracked, boards knocked off his piazza, and his roof was

torn. One 500-lb. piece of this barrel flew over Mr.
deSaussure's house, over planter St. Julien Ravenel's
neighboring mansion, and then crashed through the roof
of Alfred Ravenel's mansion. It remains there today, resting on the rafters over the master bedroom—a symbol of
pride to the current owner.

The photographer posed soldiers by wicker gabions
to show the gun's massiveness. These are probably the
same gabions seen in, and moved from, D-4. Gabions
are wicker baskets that could be quickly carried into
place, and filled with dirt to create a strong breastwork
on short notice.

The original negative survives at the Library of
Congress. Though deteriorated, it is used because it is
clearer than any period prints. The apparent damage
to the first floor piazza is loss of albumen from the
glass negative.

Barnard had previously exposed a nearly identical
view, at about 11:10 a.m. but I have chosen not to use
it because this image shows more detail in the shadows. Using those shadows I estimate that this photo
was taken around 11:45-noon on March 14, 1865.

D-6

**View on the "Battery" with wreck of the 12-
inch Blakely gun, Charleston, glass plate,
George Barnard,[8] March 14, 1865.**
(West Point)

Barnard kept his 11" x 15" camera on the same tripod as D-5, but with a wider lens. He captured a splendid panorama showing the devastation of war to a city.
At first glance the buildings seem little damaged, but
all had been empty for over one year.

The promenade of High Battery, on the right, was
deserted. In 1861, strollers enjoyed the finest view and
loveliest breeze that could be had in Charleston. Here
the waterfront was, and still is, pleasant in the day and
romantic at night. Any visitor could enjoy the same
ambience that had caused these wealthiest of planters
to locate their town houses here on High Battery.

More of Mr. deSaussure's mansion is seen. He was
an extremely successful auctioneer, selling everything
from ships to slaves. From his three piazzas he enjoyed the breeze and view of White Point Garden and
this confluence of the Ashley and Cooper rivers. On

D-5. View of the "Battery" and ruins of the Blakely gun.

Sketch of the Blakely on arrival in August 1863

D-5 & 6, Modern

D-6. View of the "Battery" and ruins of the Blakely gun.

the warmest August afternoon, opening French doors onto the piazza and raising window sashes on the north side lets the breeze through.

Time of day was established to be 12:20 ±10 minutes by the unchanged second piazza deck's east edge, casting an identical shadow down the south wall. Today his mansion is divided into three condominiums. Occupants of the top floor nearly always catch a breeze, and did not think it necessary to install central air conditioning until 1997.

Barnard-captioned prints of this view at West Point and the National Archives established this shadow dated March 1865 series as all by Barnard.

D-7

Charleston, S.C. 1865. Remains of Blakely gun destroyed by Confederates before evacuation, glass plate, George Barnard, March 1865, Brady Coll. Photo.   **(L. C.)**

Barnard returned in the afternoon for the good eastern light to continue his series. He took this view from behind the fifth column of Mr. deSaussure's second floor piazza to record more of the Blakely's ruin and the Cooper River. On the horizon is James Island, and to the left behind the moving ship in the distance can be seen the northern tip of Morris Island.

Here was its target area. Any Federal ships having passed the outer defenses of Sullivan's Island and Fort Sumter then became a target to twelve forts of the inner defenses. The Blakely gun was "designed for direct shots at short range...the turret of a monitor would be caved in

D-7. Ruins of Blakely gun.

by one plumb shot as completely as a tall silk hat would be crushed by a blow of the fist of a strong man."[9]

I have assumed this to be a continuation of Barnard's series, as the brush and unused gabion baskets still remain in the background, and shadows cast from the left wheel still indicate a mid-March sun. Again, Barnard's negatives have been scattered, but shadow dating has allowed his work and story to be assembled again, in the order he exposed his negatives.[10]

Two different stereo views were made here, in quick succession. This image was published by Anthony as the "Wreck of the large Blakely Gun, on the Battery, Charleston, S.C." published by Anthony (copy in L. C.). Another differing only in changes of ships in the harbor was published by Soule, #358. "Looking down the Harbor. Ruins of Blakely Gun in Foreground" (copy in West Point, and also in the collection of Jeffrey Krause).

The modern view, from the same second floor piazza, was taken in 1992.

D-7, Modern

D-8

Ruins of the Blakely, with the burst breech in the foreground, glass plate, George Barnard, March 1865.   **(N. A.)**

D-8. Ruins of Blakely gun.

D-8, Modern

Later in the afternoon, Barnard returned to record the burst Blakely's breech. When departing Confederates wrecked it with several charges and a plugged muzzle, the blast blew the breech sixteen yards away. Barnard dressed up his scene by moving a Blakely shell seen in lower right in D-7 onto a wood block at the left.

This breech has survived. It was taken to the Arsenal, on Ashley Avenue, and years later transported to the U.S. Military Academy at West Point, N.Y., where it is on display next to her sister gun's muzzle.

D-9

View on the Point Battery, Charleston, S.C., showing the gun in the Cheevrs battery, looking S. W., Anthony, April or May, 1865.
(L. C.)

I have been unable to learn why this was captioned as "Cheevrs battery." The nearest to this name was Battery Cheves, on James Island. That 2-gun battery on the harbor side was named for Capt. Langdon Cheves who was killed when the Federals captured the south end of Morris Island on July 10, 1863.[11]

This is the same 10-inch Columbiad smoothbore seen to the right of D-2. While otherwise undated, a tall flagpole to the right of the prewar harbor lantern tower[12] has its flag at half mast. The flag's position dates this image as taken after word of Lincoln's assassination reached Charleston. This flagpole is also seen in image A-5.

An educated guess may be made of the identity of civilians in this image. Les Jensen, an authority on Confederate uniforms, notes the right-hand man in an ill-fitting Confederate jacket, and third from the left in

D-9. View of the Columbiad at "Point Battery."

D-9, Modern

Confederate trousers. All are laborers, for at least two are in shirt-sleeves, and a gentleman would not go outside coatless. When "Sumter Club" passengers of *Ocèanus* explored the big guns on the Battery on April 14 or 15, Irishmen were engaged in removing them. The only instance of animosity taking palpable form toward any passengers of the *Oceanus* occurred at this point. One gentleman, standing a few yards from the spot, with his back to the workmen, was struck on the leg by a stone, intentionally thrown by one of the Irishmen.[13]

D-10

**Wrecked carriage of Blakely gun on Battery,
glass plate, April 1865.**   **(L. C.)**

D-10. Ruins of Blakely gun.

Taken later in the year than the Barnard images, the sun is high enough to take the bombproof's north side out of the shade, for a good morning view. Removal of earth has continued from the right, out and behind the camera's view, nearly up to the gun. A short Union soldier poses, sitting on a Blakely shell. Most gun and carriage fragments have been carted away.

Shadow dating of the next image, D-11, of shadows in the bombproof's doorway indicates that view was taken about one week after this view, or within a few days of April 15.

Anthony sold this image as stereo #3090, "The ruins of the 600 lb Blakely Gun, Frazier's Wharf, Charleston, S.C., exploded by the Rebels at the time of the evacuation." This caption is in error. Fraser's Wharf battery, seen in H-15, 16, 17, & 18, is surrounded by buildings. Presence of nearby trees proves that this is clearly Battery Ramsay's Blakely.

D-11

Charleston, S. C. South Battery; dismantled Blakely gun in foreground, April 21, 1865.
(L. C.)

Concussion from the bursting Blakely blew slate shingles off the roof of Mr. deSaussure's brick dependency, some 100 feet away. The view is west, up South Bay. The breech is gone, removed to the Arsenal. Edward Ball, on the *Oceanus*, took "the band back with him from the breech of the Blakely gun."[14]

D-11. Ruins of Blakely gun.

One must be careful in shadow-dating this, and previous photos, by this house. The fence's two closest columns now lean outward, and no longer throw the same shadow as in 1865. The gate's column just to the west is still upright, and throws a valid shadow placing the date and time at April 21 ± two days, at about 11:30 a.m.

I have seen an Anthony stereo, #3089, "South Battery, Charleston, S. C., looking N. E. Ruins of Blakely Gun in the foreground." Also, the South Carolina Historical Society has a large print, on an original mount, from a different negative taken with the camera moved a couple of feet to the right:

SOUTH BATTERY, Charleston, S.C.
View looking West, showing the ruins of the
600-lb. Blakely Gun, exploded by the rebels on
evacuating the city

D-11, Modern

Charles Quinby, a Charleston photographer, also published this second view as a carte-de-visite. There is no evidence that he was back in business by mid April, producing views for his own use. He may have pirated this view, as he sold this and many other 1865 Northern photographers' views under his own name about 1868. Though George Barnard worked for Quinby after the war, and eventually bought his gallery, this image is not from Barnard's March series on Battery Ramsay. It is still questionable just who took this photograph.

D-12

Bay Street, Charleston, S. C., carte-de-visite, William E. James, April 14 or 15, 1865.
(Beaufort)

Mr. James climbed atop the Blakely's "bombproof" with his camera, to record this view west, up South Bay Street, now named South Battery. This was an ammunition storage magazine framed with heavy beams and mounded over with dirt. Its entrance was on a side not threatened by plunging enemy shells. Gun crews could take shelter inside. Federal work crews have just cleaned out the gutters, shoveling dirt into the center of South Battery.

On the right is the widow M. E. Brown's wood mansion. The oldest building in the area, Thomas Savage built it in the late 1760s. Its next owner was Col. William Washington, distant cousin of George, and a Continental cavalry hero of the Revolutionary War battles of Cowpens and Eutaw Springs. He married into the prosperous Elliott family and became a planter on his wife's inheritance. This was his town house.

Just to the right of center is Williams Middleton's mansion, seen in James' image D-13.

D-13

Williams Middleton's townhouse, carte-de-visite, William E. James, April 14 or 15, 1865.
(Cal Packard)

An image of 1 Meeting Street, the fine 1845 brick mansion of Williams Middleton, was preserved only because the Brooklyn photographer thought it to be Federal Commandant "Gen. Hatch's Headquarters-Charleston." James was mistaken, but he gave us a rare surviving view of this mansion as built. Its piazza was changed after the 1886 earthquake.

Mr. Middleton was one of the most successful rice and cotton planters of the Low Country and signed the Ordinance of Secession in 1860. His grandfather, Arthur Middleton, had signed the Declaration of Independence.

After the shelling of Charleston began, Middleton spent less and less time in the city. With so many people evacuating the shelled area, lower Meeting

D-12. View of Bay Street.

D-13. Williams Middleton's townhouse.

D-12, Modern

D-13, Modern

Street became nearly empty of civilians. Gus reported to his mother on January 11, 1865, that there was "very little law in the city." Eventually only soldiers stationed at different batteries and at the Bathing House remained. Some of those soldiers broke into unguarded mansions to steal copper pumps, lead guttering, and brass light fixtures to sell to the government for scrap. A solitary guard in a house was seldom enough to keep the gangs out. Williams Middleton's nephew, Benti, was in the Signal Corps with Gus and they moved in together to 17 Meeting Street, for mutual support:

> I have not been very well, but...[at least] I am not alone now. Benti Middleton, a friend of mine is here also. He is now stationed in town & will mess with me. This will be pleasant company for me. He furnishes his share of provisions of course, so we shall get along finely. This will be better than going by myself.[15]

Gus and Benti had some help around the house. He wrote his mother three days later that, "Phillip & I get along splendidly. He is a first rate servant. After the war I should like to own him, he is so cleanly & so reliable."

Number 1 Meeting Street began furnishing shelter to a different sort. Gus continued in his letter to his mother on January 11, 1865, that, "A company of marines have been quartered in Mr. Middleton's house on the corner. He has a great deal of furniture there & came down trying to oust them of it, but with no success. They were too well fixed & declined leaving."

Williams Middleton lost nearly everything at the end of the war. He lost #1 Meeting Street because he could not pay the Federal taxes. His country house was lost when Major Eliphas Smith and four companies of the 56th New York Regiment marched up Ashley River Road specifically to burn it. The major and his officers enjoyed a lunch in the magnificent paneled dining room. He then set a fire under the staircase, and closed the door behind him.

D-14

Charleston, S. C., 1865. Headquarters of Gen. John P. Hatch, South Battery, glass plate, May 1, 1865.   **(L. C.)**

D-15

Gen. Hatch's Headquarters, (26 South Bay / Battery), albumin print, May 1, 1865.

(MOLLUS)

D-16

Gen. Hatch's Headquarters, copy print, May 1, 1865.   **(N. A)**

Brevet Maj. Gen. Hatch commanded the Federal garrison of Charleston, and for his headquarters took over Col. John A. S. Ashe's 1853 Italianate mansion on 26 South Battery. He furnished his residence with borrowings from nearby homes and public buildings, notably the City Hall.

When news of President Abraham Lincoln's assassination arrived in Charleston about April 19 [first published in the *Courier* April 20] Hatch thought that occupied Charleston should mourn too. He had black mourning cloth wrapped around neighboring houses. The columns of photographer George S. Cook's home at 28 South Battery, and silversmith James Spear's home at 30 were wrapped, probably without their knowledge.

George Cook, Charleston's most successful photographer, the only one able to afford a mansion, had evacuated his family to Columbia, S. C., late in 1864. His and Spear's closed batten shutters indicate they had not yet returned to Charleston. The two were close friends, with Cook's King Street gallery located above Spear's silversmith ground floor shop. Together they had bought a large house lot on South Battery, divided it up, and each built their own handsome residences. Their new homes were finished just before the war.

Had Cook and Spear already returned, those shutters should have been open for breezes off the bay to cool the house from warm late April days. Since this had not been done, it is plain that the rooms are unoccupied.

D-14. General Hatch's Headquarters.

D-15. General Hatch's Headquarters.

D-14, 15, 16, Modern

D-16. General Hatch's Headquarters.

I found the three images of General Hatch's headquarters from different collections: Library of Congress, MOLLUS, and the National Archives. Shadow dating indicates that all three images were made the same day, or nearly so. On the morning of May 1 (± 2 days), a photographer visited Hatch's residence. He took image D-14, with the general's headquarters flag hanging limp from the second floor piazza rail. Possibly Hatch was not satisfied, for a tree in D-14's right corner blocked much of the general's house, and that offending tree quickly disappeared.

Around 2 p.m., probably on the same day, General Hatch posed again. He took a chair on the piazza, for image D-15. This second was clearly superior in composition, but a safety shot is prudent, and at about 2:20 p.m., the photographer exposed image D-16

These images were dated and timed by comparing how shadows crept up and along walls. In D-14, shadows under the eastern eaves of Mr. Cook's mansion determine that it was exposed late in a spring morning, at the end of April or early May. The time of day for D-15 and D-16 were determined by shadows cast from the right edge of Cook's fourth floor balcony. A tighter date was found by shadows from the cornice cast down along the

wall. Scored and highlighted "joints" in these stucco walls allowed a precise date. Later paint has obscured these "joints," but the owner Mrs. Amalie Walker allowed me to run thin black masking tape to emphasize those overpainted "joints." Comparison of shadows along Cook's balcony and Col. Ashe's southern wall shows those images were made the same day, May 1 (± 2 days).

D-17

General John P. Hatch, Charleston, S. C., collodion print. (MOLLUS)

The general also wanted his individual portrait taken and posed behind 26 South Battery, wearing a Lincoln mourning ribbon pinned to his uniform coat. The vase to the left holds a single pure white magnolia blossom festooned with mourning ribbons.

D-17. General John P. Hatch.

D-18

Brevet Major General John Porter Hatch and Staff. Charleston, S. C. 1865, collodion print.   (MOLLUS)

D-18. General John P. Hatch and Staff.

D-17 & 18, Modern

To escape harsh shadows and street dust, the photographer took General Hatch and his staff behind his headquarters and carefully posed them on the back steps. The only identified officer is Captain J. Grace, ordnance officer of the 54th Massachusetts, standing in the center, above the seated Federal navy officer.

26 South Battery has been remarkably well-preserved. The owner, Mrs. Amalie Walker, graciously gave permission to examine her home in 1992, to shadow-date it. When the house was being built, an effort was made to make the brick house (as most are in Charleston) appear to be built of stone. A fool-the-eye technique of scoring stucco walls was done to give the look of stone blocks. Often each "block" was painted a different shade to increase the effect, with "joints" highlighted in white. Here the exterior original stucco remains mostly intact, including the lines etched when the stucco was still wet.

The rear of Col. Ashe's mansion has also survived well, with only the back steps and balustrade moved. Mrs. Walker posed with her daughter Legare, at the same spot General Hatch occupied 119 years earlier. I learned, at the same time, that the 1865 photographer had to use a very wide angle lens to capture his scene.

D-19

King Street Battery, glass plate. (N. A.)

This battery, with Battery Ramsey, was in White Point Garden, once an exclusive park for citizens.

Its two heavy smoothbore guns covered the Ashley River, should any Federal ships pass Battery Ramsay, to the left and out of camera range.

I believe the photographer, caught in a rainstorm, took refuge under James Spear's portico, at what is now 30 South Battery, and discovered it to be an excellent vantage point to photograph the King Street battery with what would now be a 50mm lens. The shower over, he set up boxes or planks to raise his tripod two feet off the portico floor and get a clear view over Spear's iron fence.

W. Bonner Thomason allowed me to match up this 1865 view from under his portico. Spear's 1861 iron fence survives, though screened by an ancient yew bush. I closed Mr. Spear's gate; it was open in the 1865 view and I thought it attractive enough to be filmed in 1995.

D-19. King Street Battery.

D-19, Modern

D-20

King Street Battery, collodion print.   (N. A.)

The weather cleared and the photographer, probably the same that produced D-19, crossed South Battery toward White Point Gardens for a closer view of the King Street Battery. The well-sodded earthworks look to be in good order. The left gun is at maximum elevation. It is dangerous to fire a gun at maximum elevation, for the pressure may burst the tube. Departing Confederates often disabled their guns by removing the elevating gear.

This battery was well-situated. A Federal fleet ascending the Ashley first had to pass Battery Ramsay, out of view to the left. Then the fleet had to either stop to slug it out with King Street or shoot on the move, for Confederate gunners had placed aiming stakes out in the shallow river, with their ranges well marked. Its guns were protected by a large earthen mound to the left, and each gun had traverses to protect from any Federal shot except a well-aimed direct, head-on shot. Bombproofs and a magazine protected the ammunition and cannoneers.

White Point was pretty used up by war's end. Earth and grass had been dug out to build and sod the earthworks. Sensitive Confederate engineers saved many trees by leaving a pedestal of earth around them. It is tempting to believe these trees survive today, but a 1938 tornado nearly cleared the park.

Slaves and free persons of color were not allowed into the Garden before the 1865 Federal occupation. Then, and for many years after, the freed people held a grand Emancipation Day parade that ended at White Point with a huge picnic and patriotic speeches.

D-20. King Street Battery.

D-20, Modern

D-21

King Street at South Bay, glass plate, April 11, 1865.   **(N. A.)**

Looking east on what is now South Battery, the Blakely gun pit is barely visible at the far end of the sandy street. Strangely quiet is the area around General Hatch's headquarters, at center in the photo. His headquarters flag is there, but except for a blur on the right in the park opposite his headquarters, scarcely a guard is present. In the foreground, on the corner at 18 South Bay (now 34 South Battery,) is James W. Wilkinson's handsome three-story 18th century house. Gus witnessed:

...on Saturday a narrow miss. I was on the Battery when I heard a shell coming. It passed over &

struck the pavement just by a crowd of women & soldiers who were collected there, not six feet from them. It struck the pavement of the house east of Wilkinson's. It is wonderful the little loss of life by the shelling.[16]

By the cornice's shadow on James Spear's white house with triple-hooded chimney (D-14), two doors down from Mr. Wilkinson's, I estimate this was photographed around 1:30 p.m. within one day of April 11, 1865. It could not have been made much later, for Federals had not yet wrapped the columns of Spear's house with mourning for Lincoln's assassination.

The modern picture shows that Mr. Wilkinson's residence has lost its top floor and portico over the years, but retains its iron fence and the iron spikes that once secured the wooden street sign "KING ST."

D-21. King Street at South Bay.

D-21, Modern

ASHLEY RIVER

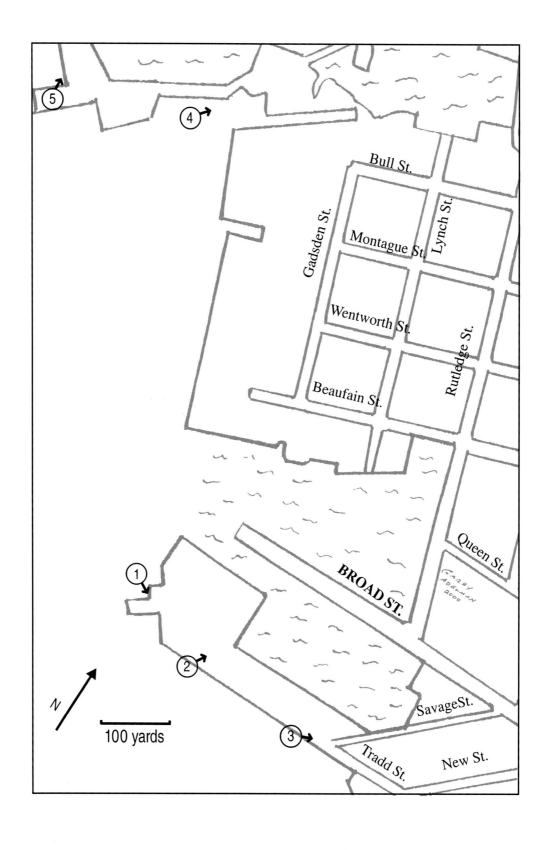

Bull St.

Gadsden St.

Lynch St.

Montague St.

Wentworth St.

Rutledge St.

Beaufain St.

Queen St.

BROAD ST.

Savage St.

Tradd St.

New St.

N

100 yards

E-1

"Battery Waring" on the wharf of Chisolm's Rice Mill, glass plate, Selmer Seibert, March 20, 1865. (N. A)

This two-gun battery was built facing the Ashley River, on the dock area of Chisolm's Rice Mill. Both guns are eleven-inch smoothbores.[1] This battery was at least partly in service by October 7, 1863, as Gus wrote to his sister from his signal station on CSS *Palmetto State*:

photograph within two days of March 20, at about 4:30 p.m. Selmer Seibert positioned his wet-plate camera at the end of Chisolm's wharf, looking to the east. At the right end of the battery is the listing smokestack of a derelict *David*.

Mr. Seibert has an eye for good lighting in his photography. This series of three views needed good shadows for detail, and those details could best be recorded in the late afternoon of a sunny day. It is not unreasonable to assume he waited for an afternoon that offered good late shadows, and he intentionally set up his cam-

E-1. Battery Waring.

My dear Sarah Annie;
...This A.M. they have [sic] firing the gun at Chisolm's Mill, practicing, & with good effect too, as far as we can judge.

When this photograph was made in 1865, evacuating Confederates had disabled the near gun, to the right, by chopping up the wood carriage and removing its elevating screw or wedge. The gun just behind is level, still capable of firing. The National Archives 1897 "Subject Catalogue No. 5, List of the Photographs and Photographic Negatives Relating to the War For The Union, Now In the War Department Library," identified the artist, on page 18, as "probably made by Mr. Seibert, but the records do not show positively." This is the first in a series of three views taken at the end of the same day. Shadows, on the roof of the left extension of the superintendent's house in the center of the photo, date the

E-1, Modern

era with a prepared wet-plate for this subject. Then he could rapidly move to the next two subjects, E-2 and E-3.

Surviving today is the frame house in the center, with two chimneys. It was the superintendent's house for Chisolm's Mill, now numbered 190 Tradd Street. The view is to the east—St. Michael's steeple is left of center. The marsh to the right was filled in around 1911. Most buildings seen behind that marsh survive along Limehouse and Greenhill streets. Today Chisolm's Mill and the site of Battery Waring are occupied by the Coast Guard Station and Tradd Street's westward extension.

E-2

David Torpedo Boat, by Chisholm's Mill Miller's and Engineer's House, glass plate, Selmer Seibert, March 20, 1865.   (N. A.)

After Mr. Seibert had finished processing his Battery Waring glass plate (E-1) and found it good, he quickly loaded his camera back into a two-horse huckster's wagon

he had fitted up into a portable darkroom.[2] He drove east on Chisolm's Causeway (present-day Tradd Street.) Seibert parked in front of Mr. Chisolm's superintendent's house shown in E-1 and unloaded his apparatus from the wagon in the background. He climbed down and set up his camera and tripod on the beach. An assistant sensitized a glass plate, then handed it to Seibert down on the beach, who slid it into the back of his view camera. At 5:05 p.m. he recorded a most remarkable artifact.

This was the original CSS *David*, that had attacked and damaged USS *New Ironsides* on October 5, 1863. It was a wooden steam ram built at Stoney Landing plantation up the Cooper River. Its armament was one 30-foot pole mounting an 80-lb. torpedo, and one shotgun for the captain. The Confederates had spunk taking on the most powerful ship of the blockading fleet. Its four man crew steamed through the Federal fleet, taking advantage of their only two assets: three feet of freeboard and the fact that it could pass for a floating log.

The Confederates' audacious attack did enough damage to send *New Ironsides* north for a refit. Figuring that they could do a lot with a little, they began work on eight more Davids, but could get engines for only three. The original *David*, and possibly more, were plated on the top with strips of quarter-inch plow steel. James M. Eason's Iron Works charged the Navy $655.97 plus hauling, to plate the "torpedo Boat 'David.'"[3]

E-2. The Torpedo Boat David.

E-2, Modern

Still, the Federals never knew how few became operational. They knew the Davids were small enough to steam down any river to attack, and that they could be carried on a railroad flatcar and launched alongside any bridge. Their very existence, and the knowledge that the Rebels would use them, caused anchored Federal ships to rig log fenders to keep Rebel torpedoes away.

A stack and some remaining armor plate prove this had been one of the operational torpedo boats. I believe this to be the original CSS *David*, though derelict and rotted through aft of the stack, and with a broken propeller. She is otherwise complete, with the full length of her torpedo boom, or nearly so.

Mr. Chisolm's miller, David McDougal, lived here, with James McDougal, engineer for Chisolm's rice mill. It has survived with an added second floor piazza, and additions to the north and west. This photo was dated by shadows along the eave of the house, and timed by the shadow under the piazza to about 5:05 p.m. and within two days of March 20. Sparse leaves indicate a spring date. These shadows tie in with those of image E-1, so I am placing Battery Waring's image as first and this second in a series exposed by Seibert the same afternoon.

Around 1911 the beach in front of Chisolm's causeway was filled in as part of a seawall project to create about fifty acres of residential construction along the Ashley River. If anything remains of the torpedo boat's hull which was already derelict and rotten in 1865, it would be under the pavement and near the south curb.

The foreground has been filled, and modern plantings preclude an effective ground level view, so I shot the modern view from Tom Taylor's back balcony at 108 Murray Boulevard, March 19, 1998.[4]

E-3

"Torpedo Boat" in front of John Ashe Alston's mansion, on Chisolm's Causeway, glass plate, Selmer Seibert, March 23, 1865. (N. A.)

This David looks incomplete and more neglected than the one in image E-2. It is barnacle-encrusted following a permanent list and rotted through. No armor, engine, or stack have been installed, and only the lifting device has been fitted to receive its ramming spar & charge of 80 pounds of gunpowder.[5]

Behind the torpedo boat is a splendid mansion in the estate of John Ashe Alston. His widow lived here in 1860, enjoying a splendid waterfront view across the Ashley River to James Island, until shelling caused her to evacuate. In 1865, her yard is overgrown. Mrs. Alston did return, to live here many more years.[6]

This mansion was built in the 1830s for Col. Alexander Hext Chisolm with expected profits from his rice mill. Tradd Street stopped here at the corner of Savage Street, and Chisolm's Causeway continued west to the Ashley. To the right, across the Burnt District, can be glimpsed St. Philip's spire. "At 7:45 A.M. the fire still rages and has reached the water's edge at Tradd St. & Chisholms Mill Causeway. This is certainly a disasterus [sic] fire."[7]

Shadows date this image to March 24 or a couple of days earlier, at 5:30 p.m. ± 5 minutes. An 1880s house presently throws an afternoon shadow over the mansion's west side, but enough light along Mr. Alston's portico times it at about 5:30 p.m. It took about half an hour for Seibert to reload his apparatus into his wagon, drive two blocks further to the east, set up back on the beach, load a fresh plate into his camera box, and take off his lens cap for the exposure. At this time the afternoon light fades fast. This was his last shot of the day.

The irony of these two views should strike the reader with dramatic intensity. Although taken from the same position, at the same time of year, the emotional contrast is overwhelming. In the war view CSS *David* is a symbol of the violence of war and the heroism of its crew. The modern view showing the basketball hoop and backboard represents a kinder, gentler transposition of the violent past.[8]

E-3. Torpedo boat in front on John A. Alston's mansion.

E-3, Modern

E-4

Cigar-shaped steamer, at Bennett's Steam Mill, glass plate, Selmer Seibert.   (N. A.)

Confederate records shed little light on the purpose of this unfinished steamer, left at the end of the war on a mud flat in a lumber pond near Bennett's sawmill. She does not appear to have been iron-plated. Some have suggested it was to be a blockade runner with a low free-board to escape detection by the Yankee blockaders. Rear Admiral John A. Dahlgren of the U.S. Navy was exploring Charleston to evaluate just what the Rebel navy had done to thwart Federal attempts to capture this major Confederate blockade-running port. He wrote in his diary of March 24, 1865, that he, "Went around into the Ashley and saw three torpedo boats; wanted repair; also one big fellow, 150 feet long, to hold 250 bales of cotton; machinery complete, and only wanting being put together."[9] This is exactly what the Federal navy did. After installing her machinery to make her operational, they took her to the Washington Navy Yard as a war prize.

The next day he saw on the Cooper River, "three torpedo boats; one new and nearly completed. Divers at

E-4. *"Steamer" at Bennett's Steam Mill.*

E-4, Modern

work trying to raise the sunken torpedo boats that were in service." He noticed the sunken and blown-up remains of CSS *Chicora*, CSS *Charleston*, and CSS *Palmetto State*. Two more incomplete ironclads were burned at the ways. He was impressed with

> ...the new rebel ironclad *Columbia*. She had caught on a bank, as reported, coming out of dock, lodged and broke her back. She is a remarkably fine, powerful vessel, mounting six guns, 6-inch plating on casemate, with a new double engine, a really formidable customer, and very strongly built, with great capacity as a ram. She would have stood a good fight with one of our ironclads. She was injured about two weeks before the evacu-

ation; had her guns in at the time.... The rebels fired on Saturday, at 4 in the morning....

April 1...At 7 took an early breakfast and started to look at the ironclad ram *Columbia*. Fox thought it worth while to try and float her.[10]

Two of the torpedo boats were raised and one put in good order so as to steam around the harbor at about five knots. One was taken to the U.S. Naval Academy at Annapolis, Maryland. *Columbia* was also raised and found to have little damage from her grounding. Her steam-power was in good order, only needing a new stack-pipe, smoke-box, and some interior piping.[11] Dahlgren was impressed with the refitted ironclad:

> May 22. About 10 the new acquisition, the rebel ram *Columbia*, cast off from the wharf and with steam up and anchored. About 5 up anchor with the first of the ebb and steamed down the harbor. I got on board and went as far as Sumter. She passed on and anchored in the roads near the bar. She seemed to make about 4 knots with 32 turns, and can make 40....
> May 23. The ram crossed the bar about 8 a.m. The *Vanderbilt* took her in tow [to a northern port].[12]

At the center of the eastern horizon is the cupola of the Orphan House. To its right is the steeple of Citadel Square Baptist Church, and to its left is the short steeple of Second Presbyterian Church.

E-5

West Point Rice Mill, stereo, April 1865.
(West Point)

Largest of several rice mills in Charleston, the West Point Rice Mill prepared rice for the foreign market. The 1840s mill operated on tidal power. After a disastrous fire on November 13, 1860, it was rebuilt with two modern steam engines.[13]

According to Bernard E. Powers, Jr., in his *Black Charlestonians—A Social History, 1822-85,* the West Point mill was "considered the most efficient rice mill in antebellum South Carolina. In 1860 it owned 160 slaves, and among them were included many engineers, carpenters, blacksmiths, and coopers."[14]

The rice industry required large numbers of slaves. Whites could not work the rice fields, for they usually died of malaria. Many Africans and their descendants, on the other hand, developed a general natural immunity to

E-5. West Point Rice Mill.

that chronic disease, absent in America before European colonization. Along with rice they brought in malaria too.[15]

Fabulous fortunes were made in the rice trade. Only Calcutta exported more rice annually than did South Carolina. Its most popular variety, "Carolina Gold," was sold all over the world. A popular saying among these planters relaxing in their town houses or country seats was "cotton is king, and rice is gold." The Low Country rice industry died around 1911, but rice is still akin to potatoes in coastal Georgia and South Carolina. Local supermarkets regularly stock rice in 30-lb. sacks for their household customers.

Though foreign trade was stopped by the blockade, West Point was out of range of Federal shells and continued pounding rice for citizens and Confederate soldiers until late December 1864.[16] Since hard money was scarce

during the war, Confederate taxes could be paid "in kind" and many planters settled up with part of their crop. After the evacuation, enough rice was left in Confederate warehouses in Charleston for the Federal government to feed the poor for over four months.

Operations resumed in early March 1865 under a new government. They hired the same workers that had previously been slaves owned by the mill.[17] Smoke from the north stack indicates that one of the two steam engines were operating.

Shadows on the gable end date this image to early April 1865 and at some time before 11 a.m.

The 1996 view shows that most of the West Point Mill's exterior survives today as part of the City Marina on Lockwood Drive. It houses offices, with an upscale restaurant on the ground floor.

E-5, Modern

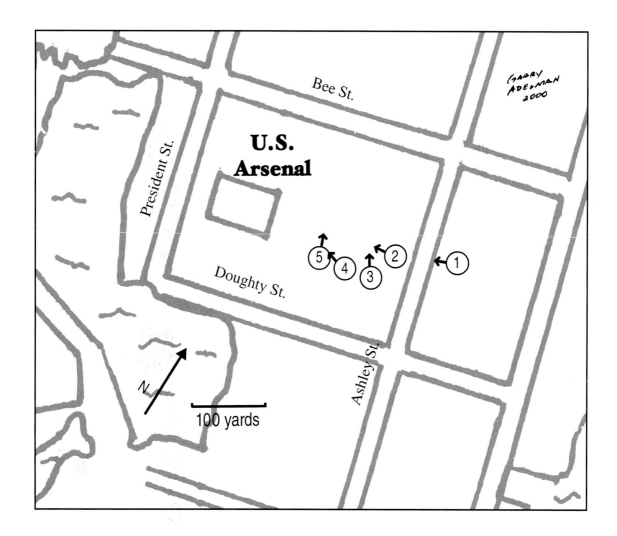

F-1

Charleston Arsenal entrance gate, stereo half, Jesse A. Bolles, late 1860s.

(Author's collection)

Anticipating secession, Gov. W. R. Gist posted a state militia guard outside the U.S. Arsenal on November 9, 1860, to prevent Major Anderson from sending arms to Fort Moultrie. The Washington Light Infantry was the first unit, posting one officer and 22 men, and starting a Confederate service that would put 410 men into the Confederate Army, including Sgt. Augustine Smythe and Brig. Gen. Johnston Pettigrew. One hundred seventeen of them would not come back. Charleston families provided handsome suppers for the men on watch. They were relieved on December 23 by the German Riflemen.

The arsenal became a major source of small arms and artillery ammunition for the city, and crates marked "Charleston Arsenal" appeared in the Army of Tennessee

F-1. Entrance gate to Charleston Arsenal.

F-1, Modern

and the Army of Northern Virginia. Pistols, muskets and artillery pieces were repaired here. Equipment for banding old artillery tubes was built and installed.

President Jefferson Davis steamed into Charleston on the Savannah Railroad on November 2, 1863. The *Mercury* reported, "His special train arrived about one p.m., to a salute of fifteen guns...The President was in the lead carriage of the procession with General Beauregard and Mayor Magrath." The procession, escorted by the Charleston Light Dragoons in front, and Capt. Skinner's Company of Dunnovant's cavalry regiment, crossed the "New Bridge" over the Ashley River, on Spring Street:

> The sidewalks and windows along the route were crowded with faces anxious to get a glimpse of the Chief Magistrate of the Confederacy. ...When the cortege had reached the corner of Rutledge Avenue, it was greeted by three

hearty cheers from the stalwart operatives of the Charleston arsenal under Maj. Trezevant. They had erected at this point a neat pyramid of shot and shell, flanked by small cannon, the whole surmounted by the star-crossed battle flag. At other points of the line of march the Confederate ensign was tastefully displayed and bouquets of fresh flowers were handed to the President as he passed.[1]

During the evacuation demolitions were laid, but did not go off. Residents in the area carefully returned to their homes. Federal troops reoccupied the Arsenal on Feb. 18, 1865.

Bolles' undated stereo is probably a view from the late 1860s or later, indicated by closer-fitting Federal uniforms of the occupiers. In 1880 the Charleston Arsenal was turned over by the Federal government to Rev. Toomer Porter for a boy's school. Porter Military Academy moved from here in 1965 and it is now the coed Porter-Gaud private school.

All buildings but the artillery shed (now St. Luke's Chapel) and Colcock Hall, a two-story brick building built by the Confederates in 1863, were demolished in the 1960s for expansion of the Medical College of South Carolina.

F-2

Charleston Arsenal, to west, glass plate.
(N. A.)

The 12.75-inch Blakely rifle's burst breech has been moved from Battery Ramsay in White Point Garden, with other war trophies. This arsenal became the sole source of heavy projectiles for the guns defending Charleston. Safety was generally good but Gus reported one accident, writing that, "There was an explosion at the Arsenal yesterday in the rocket room, which killed two & wounded three. No serious damage done to the building, only an outer room destroyed.[2]

On the evacuation of Charleston in 1865, machinery tools, ammunition, and arms were evacuated on the Northeastern Railroad, but this train, with many more engines and over a hundred boxcars and other rolling stock were burned in Potter's Raid north of Charleston in May. Enough was left in these buildings to impress Admiral Dahlgren when he was surveying captured rebel property:

March 17 In the afternoon I went to see the arsenal, a very complete place of arms, exhibiting the means and manner of the best work.[3]

F-2. Charleston Arsenal.

F-3

Charleston Arsenal, South Carolina, albumin print. **(MOLLUS)**

War trophies were gathered to the Arsenal yard, as the government wished to examine the Confederate war machine for ideas they could adopt.

The Blakely's breech, seen in F-2, is to the left. Along the curb are Confederate heavy artillery projectiles and other gear. From left to right are the "Blakely Gun Band" from Battery Ramsay, two "600 lb. Blakely shell, made Charleston, S. C." and two "600 lb. Blakely Shot, Charleston, S. C." Other painted projectiles along the curb are several Harding shot, two Whitworth shell, two Eason shot, and a Preston shell. A roll of blockade-run rubber-insulated telegraph wire, and two fragments from the burst Blakely rifle are on the right end.

In the foreground are two stands of heavy artillery grape, several wood keg torpedoes, and on the right, a floating torpedo. Many of these were taken north, but apparently much was scrapped in a few years and most of the remainder melted in the scrap metal drives of World

F-3, Modern

War I and World War II. The Battery Ramsay Blakely's breech is presently at the U.S. Military Academy at West Point.

The building at extreme right is the corner of Colcock Hall, one of the few permanent brick structures constructed by the Confederacy. It survives today as offices.

F-3. Confederate shells and torpedoes at Charleston Arsenal.

F-4

Union artillery at the Charleston Arsenal, albumin print. (L. C.)

Six 100-pdr. Parrott rifled cannon line the south curb of Charleston Arsenal's street. It is this type of gun, the 100 and 200-pounder Parrotts that sent most of the projectiles into Charleston for the 545-day Siege of Charleston.

Two large United States flags are arrayed over the street, and another is just visible at right, next to the building with awnings used for Federal offices.

Brevet Major Francis H. Parker (West Point, 1861) was placed in charge of the arsenal.[4] He wrote of his work:

I have been very busy since I came here, there being a good deal of [repair] work going on at the arsenal and quite a large force of Mechanics and Laborers employed. Immense quantities of stores and material coming in all the time. All the Ordnance Depots, forts, batteries, regiments in the Dept. [of North and South Carolina] pouring their contents into this arsenal...I have started a mess with two of my clerks, one an ex-U. S. Officer and the other an ex-Rebel soldier. We live very comfortably in the office building, it being large with six rooms. We use three of them for office purposes and three for sleeping and eating. ...Sea food of all kinds is remarkably cheap and plentiful. Very good fish, oysters, shrimps, &c. are sold in the streets by hundreds of negroes from morning till night. I hardly [need] ever go outside of the arsenal grounds except occasionally to take a ride.[5]

Parker's obituary in the *Pittsburgh Dispatch*, Feb. 23, 1897 recorded:

In 1865, when the hatred of the South for the North still existed to a very large extent, for the wound that had been made had not yet healed...he was frequently attacked by Southerners who could not so soon forget the past. One day while walking, in company with a lady, an ex-Confederate soldier addressed an insulting remark to Colonel Parker. Placing the lady in charge of a friend as soon as possible, he returned, found the man who had insulted him and who had been joined by several friends, and successfully fought the entire crowd. After this experience he passed the remainder of his time in that city unmolested.

By next spring, Parker had received his permanent commission as Captain in the Regular Army, and its rate of pay. His work was winding down:

I have reduced my force of hired men, mechanics & laborers a great deal; suspended all repairing work and closed shop and will soon reduce more still, things being pretty much put to rights and in shape. Before long the officers here will have little else to do but look after the enlisted men and see that the property is kept safe.[6]

The season is later than F-2 or F-3, for the trees are in full leaf. This camera is directed to the west like the previous exposures, but this scene is closer to the Arsenal's main building.

F-4. Parrott guns at the Arsenal.

F-5

**View in the Arsenal Yard, Charleston, S. C.
Captured Blakely Guns in the foreground, stereo, Anthony, April or May 1865.** **(L. C.)**

Numerous British-made Blakely's patent rifled cannon made it through the blockade and they did good service to the Confederacy. Anthony's caption identifying the four guns laying on the ground is puzzling, for at least two do not seem to match surviving guns designed by the former Royal Artillery Capt. Alexander Theophilis Blakely. He was a pioneer in the banding of cannon and he continually experimented to improve his guns. Warren Ripley, in his landmark *Artillery and Ammunition of the Civil War*, identifies at least nine of his models of field guns that made it to America, and several different siege & garrison models.

Mr. Ripley feels the two rifles on the right look to be Federal-made Wiard rifled guns. The entire breech area is cast in bulbous shape, but does not have the trunnion band that Blakely often used. Neither have cascabels.[7] The third resembles a 3.6-inch Type-4 Blakely with trunnion band missing. It also lacks a cascabel.[8] The fourth looks like a 2.9-inch Confederate-cast Parrott.[9]

Mounted field pieces along the road include a 12-lb. bronze mountain howitzer on the right foreground. It is probably Confederate, since it has been brought to the arsenal with no implements, only a vent cover strapped over the breech. Mottled shadows thrown by leafed-out trees make it difficult to examine these mounted guns in detail. The others appear to be standard Union 3-inch ordnance rifles.

F-5. Ordnance in the yard at Charleston Arsenal.

F-5, Modern

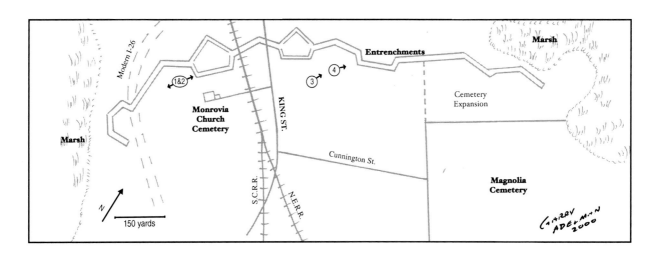

G-1

Charleston Neck, atop South Magazine, to Ashley River, glass plate.   **(N. A.)**

Concerned that the Federals might somehow attack Charleston down the peninsula, Confederate engineers laid out this strong line at the peninsula's narrowest point. Here the Cooper River and Ashley River are separated by less than three hundred yards of level ground, with wide impassable marshes on each flank.

In the left foreground, just behind the clothesline filled with soldier's laundry, is a diverted creek that could be plugged or unplugged to help fill the moat. The Ashley River runs from left to right, 150 yards across pluff mud, impossible to cross. The works are well built, with approaches cleared of trees and brush, sodded to prevent erosion, and planked on the inside, with firing steps for defending infantry. Apparently no artillery was ever in place here, but ammunition magazines and gun positions had all been prepared for any emergency. Colonel Arthur Manigault's mobile siege train could move quickly up the peninsula and go into action.

Nothing remains of these works on Charleston Neck. The South Magazine's site is covered by Davis' Warehouse, just north of Monrovia Church's graveyard.

G-1. Charleston Neck looking toward the Ashley River.

G-1, Modern

these works variously with infantry, artillery, and at an early date, the 54th Massachusetts Regiment. A cannon, with its filled limber, is in position on the ramp.

Construction of Charleston earthworks was done by slave labor. Planters sent a percentage of their field hands to Charleston, where the slaves would be fed, housed, clothed, and worked by Confederate authorities. This hospital for slaves was well-staffed, for if a slave died, his owner must be indemnified by the government.

G-2

Charleston Neck, atop South Magazine, to north, glass plate.　　　(N. A.)

The photographer swiveled his camera around to expose this northerly view. The South Carolina Railroad runs from right to left in the middle distance, over a trestle crossing the moat. Beyond and parallel to the rails is Meeting Street. Woods beyond the Neck were cleared for 200 yards. The white frame house is part of Rikersville, a small community just outside of the city. Here was the slave hospital. Its chief surgeon, Dr. Todd of Kentucky, was a brother-in-law of Abraham Lincoln.

When these views were made, Confederate forces were still active in South Carolina. Federals garrisoned

...who should I see but your man edward, with a knapsack on his back & a canteen on, come down from Pendleton with some more from Uncle R.'s place, to work on the fortifications. He looks hail & fat... I saw Dan at No. 36. He is also down with 900 others from Pendleton, volunteers, labor sent for 30 days. He comes from Uncle Joe, of course. ...Uncle R. Has sent down 5 or 6 hands.[1]

No Negro, slave or free person of color, was officially allowed to join the Confederate Army until 1865, but they did serve as teamsters, servants, musicians, and in almost any other supporting role throughout the war. Three free blacks were regularly enrolled in the Confederate Navy on the *Chicora*. Surprised Federals recorded hundreds of instances of blacks, in Rebel uniform, shooting at them.

Today, Frank Ford's Redi-Mix Concrete Company fills the area to the railroad.

G-2. Charleston Neck looking North.

G-3

Charleston Neck. North magazine and photographer's wagon, glass plate.   (N. A.)

The photographer rode beyond the railroad, through Rikersville and beyond Meeting Street Road, to make a third plate. North Magazine had apparently been poorly built, as it appears badly eroded. The top is barely covered, and the corner beams exposed. A new sodded and vented magazine is at the right. Though never attacked, the Neck always had a small garrison. Two abandoned brick fireplaces in the foreground had warmed two Confederate tents only two months before.

The modern view shows Magnolia Cemetery in the right background. In 1849, with Charleston's church-yards filling up, a group of investors established the Magnolia Cemetery Company one mile outside the city limits. Its reputation is reviving as a well-maintained, attractive place to bring the family on a Sunday afternoon to have a picnic lunch among one's ancestors. Over eight hundred defenders of Charleston are interred here, including the first and second crews of the Confederate submarine *Hunley*. Here also are some 84 identified South Carolina dead from Gettysburg.

Several independent graveyards are nearby. Appearance of this area has completely changed, and Magnolia Cemetery has expanded over part of these defenses. The modern view was made with the assistance of Magnolia's director, Beverly Donald.

G-3. Charleston Neck looking at the North Magazine.

G-3, Modern

G-4

Charleston Neck, atop North Mazagine, to Belvedere and northern Line, glass plate.

(N. A.)

Taken from atop the new, sodded magazine, the damaged steps on the lower left, are also seen to the extreme right of G-3. Inside the center wall are prepared pintles for three more Confederate gun positions. Above these are tents of the Federal garrison.

Along the tree line is Belvedere Plantation and the Cooper River. In the 1850s that plantation boasted the first golf course in the South, since loyalist Scots golfers departed Charleston after the Revolution. Belvedere has been replaced by a tank farm. Woodwork from the plantation house was salvaged by Dr. William H. Frampton. He installed it in houses he owned at 40 Rutledge Avenue and 98 King Street, and in his office at 98 Broad Street. The old Country Club of Charleston has moved to James Island.

Today, Monrovia Street and Algonquin Road follow behind where the Neck works were located.

G-4. View of the works along Charleston Neck.

COOPER RIVER WATERFRONT

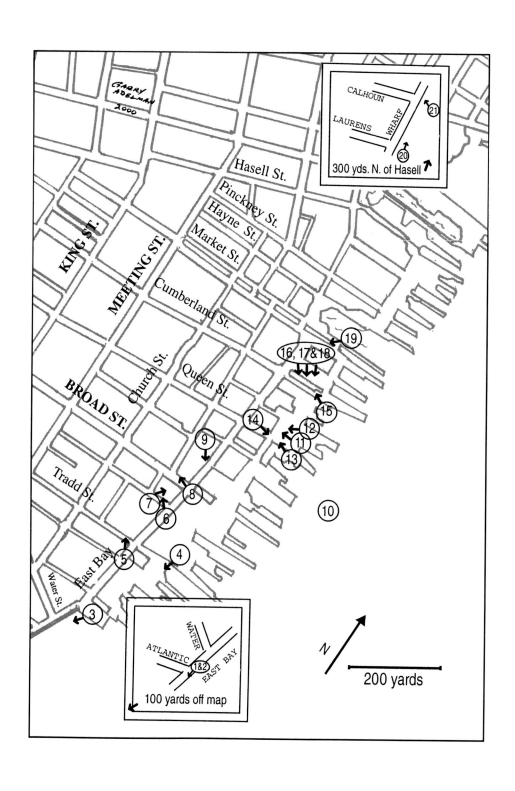

H-1. Mansions along East Bay looking South.

H-1

View on the Battery, Charleston, S. C., looking south, showing the grand promenade, stereo half, Anthony #3079, mid-March, 1865.
(West Point)

Almost all of the mansions on East Bay Street were hit, but the shell that struck Daniel Heyward's on the corner of Atlantic, caused a fire that gutted it. More useful to the occupying Yankees was the neighboring mansion of Charles Alston, a prominent Georgetown rice planter. It boasted a handsome cast-iron verandah. Union Gen. Rufus Saxton took it over for his residence. He had formed the first Negro Regiment in 1862, the 1st S. C. Regiment (colored) near Beaufort, S.C. Now he led the Freedman's Bureau to help the newly-freed slaves with

H-1, Modern

food, clothing, education, an orphan's home, and a home for aged and infirm blacks.[1]

The granite-faced seawall, built to protect this low-lying tip of Charleston from hurricanes, became a favorite promenade. A breeze could be enjoyed almost any time, even muggy July and August evenings. Federal occupiers have already cleared the road of nearly two years' accumulation of debris and bushes.

The modern view shows Charles Drayton's home on Mr. Heyward's corner lot. About twenty years after the war he built his new home here in the modern Eastlake style, using profits from phosphate deposits discovered around his Drayton Hall property on the Ashley River.

Shadows cast by the seawall fence fall nearly perpendicular to the seawall suggesting this image was taken in mid-March. Shadows on the verandah put the time at around 9:15 a.m.

H-2

Ruins of Daniel Heyward's mansion, on East Bay at Atlantic, albumin print. (MOLLUS)

Mr. Heyward's fire-gutted house has collapsed into its front yard and fence. General Saxton has not moved into Charles Alston's town house yet. Its windows are shuttered in this late morning image, and his yard is still overgrown.

H-2. Ruins of Daniel Heyward's mansion.

H-3

East Bay Street, from John Milnor's house, glass plate, March, 1865.   (N. A.)

Taken from the second-floor balcony of John Milnor's residence.[2] It shows East Bay even more spruced up. Gutters have just been dug out on both sides down the street to Mr. Alston's property. The Federals used soldiers and hired workers to clean out flooded cellars, cisterns, drains and neglected outhouses. They cleared bushes and small trees out of the middle of streets little used during the bombardment. This was not done out of respect for property owners, but for the health of the newly-freed slaves in town. Health of the Union garrison was also considered. They occupied the city for eleven years.

Cotton broker and signer of the Ordinance of Secession Francis J. Porcher's pedimented mansion at 15 East Bay (now 29 East Battery, with a square portico and semicircular front piazza added in the 1890s), and Daniel Ravenel's frame home with a bay window (17 East Bay, now 31 East Battery) fill the block to Water Street. To the

H-3, Modern

right of center is Rev. T. R. C. Peck's brick home at 19 East Bay (now 33 East Battery, with a mansard roof). Mrs. Mary A. Wragg's at 21 is gone.[3] Shadows suggest this image was taken at the end of March around 10:20 a.m.

H-3. East Bay Street from John Milnor's house.

H-4

Three gun battery on Vanderhoff's Wharf, Charleston, S. C., right half of stereo, Anthony # 3069.   **(L. C.)**

The stereo's caption says it is a three gun battery, which is properly named Vanderhorst's Wharf, but only two guns are visible. These were identified by Warren Ripley as a 10-inch Columbiad on the left, and a banded rifle on the right, with no muzzle flare. The 1865 "U. S.

Coast Survey, of Defences Of Charleston" shows a two-gun work, with a "7 inch Rifled" in the near gun chamber, and a "10 inch Columbiad" in the far chamber. On Dec. 23, 1864, Gus wrote his Mother:

Oh it is very cold this morning (in St. Michael's steeple). I am here all in a heap by my stove, while the wind whistles around. ...Porter's fleet is off Wilmington. So that is where they will attack. We expected it here, but are ready for them. Among other batteries they have built one on the wharf south of Grandfather's

H-4. Three-gun battery on Vanderhoff's Wharf.

with two guns, and to clear the view up Cooper River they have pulled down the sheds on both wharves, and are also going to take away the last building of the row of counting houses, the one with the piazza, if you remember it. It does seem a pity thus to destroy property, but if it is for the public good, eh bien! At any rate, we have not anything to say in the matter.

Just six months earlier, on April 15, and several yards out of the right of this view, Gus had a narrow escape from a Federal shell:

> ...Just at the corner of Tradd & the Bay, as I was going to step on one end of a cellar door, a shell fell on the other end, not three feet away from me, & burst down in the cellar, covering me with dirt & smoke but leaving me unharmed. Had it burst on level ground It would have killed me. One piece knocked the pipe out of my mouth & so close did it come that I could feel the wind. This is just a little closer than I care to have them come again.
>
> ...It is wonderful the little loss of life by the shelling.

One year after the war, this scene had changed dramatically. The *Courier* reported, on April 26, 1866:

> VANDERHORST'S WHARF nearly ever since the occupation of the city by the Union troops, has been doing a splendid business, foreign and coastwise. The buildings have all been repaired and the counting rooms all taken and filled with merchants over a year. A very neat and handsome building for a wharf office has been erected on the spot of the old Scale House, and in the place of the large two ten-inch Columbiad Battery erected by the Confederates. The earth used in the construction of the battery has nearly all disappeared. A large part of it was given away by the owners, and a considerable quantity carried away in vessels as ballast. It has been taken by both foreign and domestic vessels, and distributed in Europe and the North. The wharf is owned by ELIAS VANDERHORST, son of Governor VANDERHORST. It is the only wharf in the city which has not changed ownership, having been kept in the VANDERHORST family since its construction.

Today this scene has changed drastically. The land in front of the wharf has been filled out into the Cooper River for over sixty yards, and almost all of its wharf buildings are gone. The site is now a playground, but

some fifty yards of its cobblestone street survives-one of only seven cobblestone streets preserved today in Charleston.

H-5

Shelled house near Tyler Cotton Press, carte-de-visite, William E. James, April 14 or 15, 1865. **(Cal Packard)**

Locating these war-worn buildings was my most difficult challenge, and Mr. James' pen caption, "Charleston," on the front was of little help. This dramatic view shows a shell hole through the third floor of the corner house. The shell hole indicates a west side of the street. Balcony shadows indicate a mid-morning view. Four-story buildings are rare on the peninsula and none survive on a corner lot that also have a neighboring brick house with a setback. A retouched board sign, spiked to the stuccoed brick wall reads COTTON PRESS. The 1860 city directory and the 1861 Census list only five cotton presses in town.

1. Charleston Cotton Press   *65 Church Street*
This was on the west side of Church, four doors south of St. Michael's Alley. It burned in 1864, along with the brick homes of William Newnan at 67, John H. Grotheer's at 71, and Isaac Levy's home at 73. Levy's house was on the southwest corner of St. Michael's Alley. These destroyed buildings were not available for Mr. James' camera in 1865.

2. Calhoun Cotton Press   *89 Church Street*
James Copes' Calhoun Press is also on the west side, four doors south of Chalmers Street, Wm. Hamm's at 91, Mrs. Eliz. Gitsinger's at 93, Diedrich Wm. Ohlandt at 95, and Archibald McKenzie's on the corner at 97. The 1861 Census lists Mr. Ohlandt's as wood. As the photo shows the setback building to be brick, this cannot be the site.

3. Palmetto Cotton Press   *Dry Dock Wharf*
Before secession it was the Union Wharf. The 1861 Census describes Dry Dock Wharf, "Is on East side of the City, formerly Williams' Wharf, first Wharf above the Market." They list it on the north side of the wharf, between the shops of Thomas Trout and Patrick Gafney. Concord Street is on the east end of Dry Dock Wharf, and there were no old, substantial brick buildings on that street, so this cannot be the site.

4. Ship's Cotton Press   3 Anson Street
John Von Hollen's cotton press complex occupied the whole east side of Anson, from North Market Street to Hayne Street. There were no three-and-four story balconied brick houses on Anson at Hayne. This also cannot be the site. That block is now a parking lot.

5. Tyler Cotton Press   9 Longitude Lane
    Mr. A. R. Mitchell's Tyler Press filled most of the south side of narrow Longitude Lane. If his sign board advertised his office building, or an entry down an alley, this is the most likely location for Mr. James' subject. This area escaped most city fires, and by 1860 it was still lined with 18th and early 19th century brick buildings.

    After 1884, all old structures north and south of Longitude Lane, on East Bay, were gone. The 1884 Sanborn Fire Insurance map for that year shows a large cotton complex here, with a description: "12 cotton press tylers pat." A second look at this image reveals a "T" on the sign board, if you are looking for it. This is the most likely location for this image.[4]

    The 1860 City Directory and the 1861 Census list Alexander R. Mitchell's office in the left building, #41-45 East Bay. He shared it with Henry Lewith's "clothing boots & shoes" store. Eibe Struss rented the four-story #47 for his "grocery and barroom." Across Longitude Lane at #49 was Pinkus Pinkushon's clothing store.

H-5. Shell-damaged house and the Tyler Cotton Press.

H-5, Modern

H-6. Damaged building at the corner of East Bay and Elliott streets.

H-6

East Bay & Elliott, stereo, William E. James, April 14, 1865.   (Author's collection)

Gus remarked on November 25, 1863, that it was one of the "worst hurts I saw...the house N. Corner Elliott & East Bay which has quite a hole in it...." A shell had crashed through the right (east) slope of the roof, blowing out its opposite slope. Graber & Thode rented 99 East Bay, where Henrich Graber and Charles Thode sold "clothing, boots, shoes, &c"[5]

I have observed, on my explorations of Civil War shell-damaged Charleston buildings, that plunging Federal heavy artillery shells continue to travel one floor below penetration before its impact-fuze can detonate the shell. Usually the shell explodes in the top floor after passing through the roof or attic. All windows in this top floor are blown out or nearly so. Third floor intact win-

H-6, Modern

dows are scarce, and the second floor has several broken or shuttered windows.

Not surprisingly, the building looks abandoned. The shopkeeper's sign over the doors has been removed, and there is nothing to identify the site but wood street signs—Elliott St. and East Bay spiked to the corner.

Mr. James unknowingly agreed with Gus' appraisal. He set up his stereo camera across the street, exposed one plate, and took it back to Brooklyn for printing. He made no effort to advertise his Charleston views, but simply pasted his images onto cream-colored cardboard, and penciled on the back: "Ed. C./Charleston/April 14th 1865," to record which customer would get this print (see other James stereos B-16 and I-21).

Graber & Thode's ruins were later replaced with the printing and lithography shop of Evans & Cogswell. That successful business continued in trade until the late 1980s, advertising on their trucks: "We print everything except money, and we did that in 1864!" The renovated building is now an upscale condominium.

The corner brick building to the left survives. George Barnard used its balcony to photograph image H-7, his large plate of Federal sailors in front of the Post Office. After the 1886 earthquake, this building was repaired, brick stuccoed over, and its balcony removed either from earthquake damage or by an antique collector.

H-7

Exchange & Post Office, glass plate, George Barnard. (West Point)

Built in 1771 as the Exchange and Custom House for the royal government, this building has been a center of activity since colonial days. The U.S. Post Office moved here in 1818. Alfred Huger, Charleston's postmaster since 1835, fought secession, but when South Carolina seceded he loyally followed his state out of the Union and was asked by Governor Pickens to be postmaster of the Independent Republic of South Carolina. South Carolina joined the new Confederacy on February 4, 1861, but Huger remained a U.S. postmaster until mid-1861. Washington wished to retain some Federal services and Federal influence in the South as long as possible.

Major Robert Anderson carried on his Fort Sumter correspondence with the War Department in Washington through this office. He continued to send a weekly boat for fresh provisions and mail until the Confederate Secretary of War cut him off at the end of March.[6] U.S. stamps still carried mail until May 31, 1861, when the Confederates took over, more than six weeks after Anderson was shelled out of Fort Sumter. Huger became Confederate postmaster for Charleston on May 13, 1861.[7] Huger then closed his books with Washington, deposited his monies in a local bank, and commenced his Confederate services the next day.

Confederate Postmaster-General John Reagan raised the single-letter rate from three cents to five cents (later to ten cents) as part of an attempt to make his Post Office Department operate at a profit. In this he was successful—the only time in our united or disunited states that this has happened.

Less successful was Reagan's attempt to furnish his department with stamps. United States stamps were no longer valid for postage in the South. There were few large printing plants in the South, and Confederate postage stamps were more than five months in coming. Postmasters were told to collect the money in coin or make do. A good bid from the American Bank Note Company in New York was promising, but deemed unreliable. The first Confederate stamp, a pretty 5-cent green lithographed with the face of Jefferson Davis, was finally issued on October 16, but supplies for this second-largest Confederate city did not arrive until December.

Postmaster Huger could not wait. He was to collect postage in coin, but inflation quickly drove coins out of circulation. He went to a local lithographer and had his own stamps printed—an attractive blue stamp reading Charleston S. C./5 cts./Postage Paid, charging five dollars for a sheet of eighty stamps. The difference paid for his printing. This Charleston stamp could send a letter for 500 miles into the Confederacy. Today this Postmaster Provisional commands a high price at philatelic auctions.

Blockade runners paid their custom duty here, and for a while, their mail was censored here. Emma Holmes and Gus picked up their mail here until August 26, 1863, when shelling drove Mr. Huger to move his post office to the southeast corner of King and Ann (J-3). Later he moved again. This time to the northeast corner of Ashley and Cannon. By most accounts, Alfred Huger ran an efficient post office in this second largest of Confederate cities. He had to move twice to avoid shelling, handle a tremendous amount of soldier mail, and print his own provisional stamps when Richmond was unable to provide them. His last Confederate mail departed Charleston on the railroad to Florence, on the day of evacuation.

After the war, Federal authorities hounded Huger for his final postal receipts that he had not sent to Washington. He defended himself, saying the North had confiscated assets from rebellious states, and the Confederate

H-7. Exchange and Post Office.

government in return confiscated Northern assets held in the South—including his postal accounts.

George Barnard photographed five U.S. Navy sailors and a local boy at the corner of Exchange and East Bay, in front of the shelled and empty post office. He set up

H-7, Modern

his camera on the iron balcony over Henry Thees' barroom, on the southwest corner of Elliott and East Bay shown in H-6.[8] Cobblestone pavements were removed from East Bay and Broad during the war for fortification fill. That balcony is lost, perhaps by the 1886 earthquake or to an antique collector. With Mrs. Fay Solomon's permission I matched the scene from their second floor (presently 107 East Bay). I worried that their Persian, Happy, would climb out onto my back while I was leaning out their window with my camera.

Just to the south of the post office, below Exchange Street, are the East Bay offices of three brokers and auctioneers: E. Devineau (60, but still bearing an old painted number, 52), Alonzo White (58), P. J. Porcher & Son (56). A Federal shell appears to have blown out the tile roof and south end of John A. Lalane's "tobacco, snuff & segar" store at 54 (old 46), though Barnard managed to keep most of that damage out of his negative.

I claim this to be shell damage with much reluctance, for this may be only the shadow from a much taller building to the south, across Elliott Street. I have been unable to learn the height of that building to the south, as it was removed long ago.

The south side and part of the west end of Lalane's store have been replaced. The different brick work and mortar indicates this may also be repairs to the shell damage. If this is indeed repairs to a shell hole it is one of only two places where evidence of Federal shell damage is readily seen today.

The other is Subway Sandwiches and Salad shop, at 184 East Bay; a shell exploded south of this brick structure, peppering its south wall with iron fragments.

Caution must be used in researching Charleston street addresses. Prior to the 1886 earthquake, houses were renumbered frequently. Tax books and city directories should also be consulted. Obsolete painted house numbers could remain for years. The *1859 Tax Book*, which shows cross streets and blue-penciled addresses burned in the 1861 fire, has these four addresses below the Exchange and Post Office:

52 Est. Michell
50 A. J. White
48 George Gibbon
54 Est. Mrs. Mary Myers

The *Census of Charleston, 1861*, has the houses renumbered, as was often done:

Owners	Occupants
#60 Est. John Michel	E. Devineau
#58 Alonzo J. White	A. J. White & Son.
#56 George Gibbon	P. J. Porcher & Baya
#54 Estate Mary Myers	John A. Lalaue [sic]

The 1860 *City Directory* advertises:

E. Devineau:	"Broker and Auctioneer, also Havana Agency For R. H. L., #52 East Bay" (pg. 30)
White, Alonzo J.:	"broker, auctioneer, & Com. agt., 27 Broad
J. Porcher:	"Will attend to the Purchase and Sale of Real Estate, Negroes, Stocks, Bonds, Furniture &c, # 25 Broad" (pg. 46)
John A. Lalane:	"tobacconist"

H-8

Offices of Treasury Agent and Quarter Master, Charleston, S. C., stereo, Brady & Co., also published by Anthony as stereo #3435, May 8, 1865.   (N. A.)

When Brady's operator set his tripod in Broad Street, he photographed an eagle that had spread its wings in the pediment of the Bank of Charleston since 1832. The bank was evacuated during the shelling, to get out of range. Their deserted office was taken over by the Freedman's Bureau in March 1865. Souvenir hunters from the *Oceanus* described the scene on April 14 and 15:

> The Bank of Charleston is much less injured and ravaged (than the State Bank of the State of Charleston, across the street, to the left and out of the camera's view). Originally it was a much finer structure. The marble-topped desks and counters remain, and are occupied by our officers, who make the bank a business depot. A gentlemanly official, lighting a candle, conducted our party into the vault, a room about 10 by 15 feet, lined on three sides, with pigeon holes, and carpeted now with worthless paper rubbish. The "Director's Room," handsomely frescoed and furnished, was in the possession of a U. S. Officer. The rooms upon the second floor were piled knee-deep with old bank accounts, notes, bills of exchange, papers of every description, and of the least possible intrinsic value. Here the mania for "relics" ran high. Dozens of curiosity-hunters were bending over them on hands and knees, untying old yellow and dusty bundles, selecting ancient and curious documents, and duly bestowing them in the voluminous depths of coat pockets, or carrying them off tenderly under the arm. Occasionally could be heard, "ah! Here's a prize! Only look! 1730, 1776," etc.
>
> Enough of these valuable acquisitions were brought home to comfortably stock No. 25 Ann St. (in New York).

At extreme right is the closed *Mercury* office. Its editor, Robert Barnwell Rhett, Jr. was one of the leading advocates of secession. By June 1864 the *Mercury* moved to 484 King Street to escape the shelling. In 1865 their printing machinery and paper were put into a box car to escape Sherman's army, but this train was burned by the invaders. Broad Street here is sand, in this 1865 view. Cobblestones of this end of Broad were taken up to build Confederate fortifications. Those stones were used to create an island battery of four guns upon a harbor sand bar to be named Fort Ripley.

H-8. Offices of the Treasury agent and Quartermaster.

A series of three nearly identical images was sold by
E. & H. T. Anthony & Co., New York, from "Negative by
M. B. Brady, New York," and this is the best of the lot.
Anthony & Co. was the largest photographic dealer during the war years, and Brady often marketed his views
through them. Brady's wartime images were not made by
Brady himself but by one of his employees. There is little
evidence Mathew Brady was ever in Charleston. His
name is famous in Civil War photography, as "Photo by
Brady", but he had poor eyesight by the war years. He
was no longer able to focus a ground glass upon his subject. He had a well-paid "operator" do this technical
work. Since Brady owned the business, hired & fired, and
paid the bills, he owned the negatives, and could rightly
claim the work to be a "Photo by Brady."

In April 1865, Brady was busy in Virginia, photographing the aftermath of Lee's surrender to Grant. He
and his operators recorded on glass plates the newly captured Richmond and Petersburg, the victorious armies and

H-8, Modern

generals, including Grant, and indeed Robert E. Lee himself. Brady has detailed his story of boldly sending an introduction to the recently defeated and depressed Lee, requesting a sitting based on previous acquaintance. Lee agreed, and on April 16, Brady personally posed the General in a dignified manner.

Today, much survives of this scene in the busy financial district of Charleston. The *Mercury* buildings, and others to the corner, burned in the 1950s. The Bank of Charleston was the only bank in the state to recover after the war. It later became South Carolina National Bank, and was taken over by Wachovia in 1992; the continuity is still there. Today, anyone may take original bank notes—say a Bank of Charleston $10 bank note of 1857—up to their drive-in window and they are legally required to redeem them!

Wachovia now owns the whole block along Broad Street. The exteriors of the Bank of Charleston, the earthquake-damaged facade of the Fireman's Insurance Company, and the Charleston Insurance & Trust survive. Their interiors are renovated into one continuous building, but the decorative plaster ceiling cornice of the original bank lobby survives, as does as the full interior of the magnificent "Director's Room."

The porticoed brick Bank of the State of South Carolina on the northwest corner, Broad and State is gone, replaced by the People's Building in 1910-11. This was Charleston's first skyscraper and was celebrated as the beginning of progress along Broad Street. Many expected that skyscrapers would soon line the whole street.

Some felt otherwise, that old buildings should be saved. Reaction to the People's Building reinforced preservationists' dedication to form the Preservation Society scarcely a decade later, in 1920. Charleston's 1931 zoning ordinance created the first historical district in the country, though the whole of Broad Street west to Chisolm Street was not included until 1975.[9]

Using shadows along the top of the Charleston Insurance & Trust I estimate that this photo was taken on May 8, 1865, at 10:45 a.m. ±10 minutes.

H-9

Post Office, East Bay St. Charleston, S. C., showing the only Palmetto tree in the city, left half of a glass stereo plate, Brady & Co., published by Anthony, April, 1865. (L. C.)

Brady's operator was as much fascinated by the cast iron boxed palmetto tree as the ancient and abandoned post office building. The sighting of a palmetto tree

H-9. Post Office on East Bay Street.

within the city was rare then, as it is not a shade tree. South Carolina has been called the Palmetto State, because a successful Revolutionary War fort defending Charleston harbor in 1776 was built of palmetto log cribs separated by fifteen feet of sand. Palmetto is a fiber type of wood which does not splinter when hit by an artillery shell; projectiles pass through without destroying the logs and are stopped by sand.

Newspapers report many palmettos planted in the city about the time of secession, but apparently few survived. I have examined 141 photographs of 1860-65 Charleston, and this image has the only palmetto I have seen. Charleston photographer Charles Quinby published in the 1870s stereos of two formal garden views along the western part of the city, each highlighting a treasured palmetto as an exotic plant.

This particular palmetto may have been used as an advertisement. Behind that tree is a marvelous wrought-iron gas light that illuminates a shop sign:

PALMETTO
SHADES

It was hard to grow a palmetto tree in town, and this particular tree appeared in an *Illustrated London News* woodcut, drawn in 1853. That woodcut featured a slave auction, with frequent auctions held here, and advertised "on the north side of the Exchange." That two-foot high wood auction platform stood in front of the center window until complaints of traffic obstruction caused these auctions to be moved to the various auction houses throughout the city.

This view shows a dirt East Bay Street in 1865. Normally paved with cobblestones, this was one of Charleston's busiest streets, as it serviced all the eastern wharves of the city. It had to support most of Charleston's

heaviest wagons, pulled by four or six or more horses. The city fathers cobblestoned it to avoid a teamsters' quagmire following the slightest shower. Confederate Engineers gathered the cobbles from East Bay and several other streets in 1863-4 for fill to support harbor fortifications.

Dating was a challenge. Buildings to the right burned in the 1950s but if their replacements are the same height as the old, shadow-dating places the cameraman's visit the third week of April 1865, about 3:00 p.m. This date must be used with caution since other images supplied to Brady's firm appear to have been produced in late April or early May. Brady's man made at least three exposures the same day from the same camera location, differing only in movement of workmen, horses, carts, and roll-down doors of James E. Adger's commercial building. Mr. Adger was Gus' uncle, and one of the five wealthiest men in South Carolina in the years before the war. The 1790 commercial structure to the far left survives, completely reworked in this century.[10]

H-10

View of the Wharves, Charleston, S. C., near the Battery, left half of stereo, George Barnard, also published by Anthony as stereo #3093, 1865. (L. C.)

This is one of the more frustrating images for a modern photo-historian to work with. I have not been able to identify any of these ships, or to locate this wharf. The Cooper River waterfront has changed, and aside from the granite "bridge" of North Adger's Wharf (rebuilt about 1990 as part of the "Waterfront Park") all the old palmetto-cribbed wharfs have completely disappeared.

Wharfs "near the Battery" were Southern, South Commercial, North Commercial, Vanderhorst's, Adger's South and Adger's North, and Boyce's Wharf, until the post office is reached. The caption does explain enough to a prospective customer in, say, Rochester, N.Y., who has entered a local photographer's gallery to buy souvenirs of the Great Rebellion. She is perusing racks of recently-published stereo views, and Mr. Anthony has told in his caption, really all she needs to know to select her purchase.

What is remarkable is that one can see the waves in the water. In 1865, this is an almost impossible accom-

H-9, Modern

H-10. View of the wharves.

plishment. Operators then needed to leave their lens cap off for one to twenty seconds, depending on brightness of the light and darkness of the subject, to record a clear image onto their glass plate. It was nearly impossible to record gunfire or moving men, horses, wagons, trains, or ships. Aside from danger to the artist, movement made photographs of Civil War battles impossible.

One artist who did record Charleston shortly after its fall, and thereby within the focus of this book, was George Barnard. In 1860 he visited Cuba to make images to sell to Americans. Even then Cuba held a fascination to Americans, and some felt we should own it.

Keith F. Davis, in his masterful 1991 biography, *George N. Barnard, Photographer of Sherman's Campaign* explains how Barnard used the bright sun of Cuba, a high vantage point, an emulsion more sensitive than usual, and redevelopment of an underexposed plate. He claimed to have made an exposure of 1/40th of a second, and did produce unblurred stereos of moving ships and crashing waves, and of a column of marching Spanish soldiers. It was hard work for him, but his Cuban stereos sold well.[11]

Five years later Barnard, or someone as skilled as he made this view of a rocking rowboat and sailboat next to a barge. Chop on the water is clear. Nothing is blurred. Piles of coal fill the near wharf, and at least five schooners, ships, and steamships fill the background. This is the Cooper River, for the shallow Ashley does not allow deep-draft shipping. An occupying army and Yankee merchants have arrived to give this port more life than it had had in the previous four years.

H-11

Vendue Range, Charleston, glass plate, George Barnard, March 13, 1865.   (N. A.)

Barnard was ready for his first shot of the day: the handsome Collonade Range (sic)[12] along a line of auction houses. A dud 100-lb. shell lay less than fifteen feet in front of him.

H-11. Vendue Range looking west.

The heat of a Charleston summer usually caused Charleston business to grind nearly to a halt. Such business in July through September as was done, was usually in the early morning or late afternoon. From noon till three was time for a "Charleston Supper," the main meal of the day, followed by the *Mercury* or *Daily Courier* and a nap. The large German community enjoyed the *Deutsche Zeitung*. Then the industrious resumed work for another four hours. Few prospective buyers wanted to make purchases in a dark, stifling auction house. This colonnade provided relief for both auctioneer and buyer. It served as a shaded, open sales room for the several auctioneers, who could then use their small quarters exclusively for bookkeeping and storage. On sale days they brought their goods out and under the colonnade, where buyers could congregate and buy, all the time enjoying the shade and harbor breeze.

This colonnade was a plasterer's minor masterpiece. Shell damage and weathering show that the columns were brick, not stone. The columns and wood roof were covered with wood lath, then finished in plaster. Some columns were painted with different colors and false joints

to complete the effect. Repaired, this colonnade shaded auctioneers for another twenty years until the earthquake of 1886.[13]

At first glance, Vendue Range looks in fair shape, but the left building is a burned-out shell, and its neighbor has two tileless dormers and a shattered third. The high-pitch

H-11, Modern

roof brick building at the end of the block has several shattered windows. That building's two lower floors survive, but much remodeled. Visiting in 1989, when its second floor was an architect's office, I saw two shell holes through its ceiling beams.

Buildings on the south side are also in bad shape. Peter Brown's "tavern and boarding house"[14] is burned out. The roof of his neighbor, cotton merchant Philip Fogarty[15] is damaged. Next is Benjamin Lazarus' storehouse, unrented in 1861, which appears burnt-out in 1865. Brick rubble litters the wide sidewalk.

Using shadows from buildings, left of center, cast onto the street I estimate that the original photo was taken on March 13, 1865 at about 8:30 a.m.

H-12

Vendree [sic] Range, one of the principal business Streets, Charleston, S. C. The building on the left is where the first shell struck, George Barnard, also published by Anthony as stereo #3070, late March, 1865. (Jeffrey Krause)

Charleston papers reported that the first shell hit in Hayne Street[16] but in fact the early shells landed in a widely dispersed area over a half mile square, from Hasell to King to just below Broad. Shells randomly crashing into this wide area produced a terror, which is exactly what the Federals wished.

H-12. Vendue Range from the ferry slip.

H-12, Modern

Collonade Range held seven offices that were rented to merchants: Moses Goldsmith, who dealt in hides, wax, and wool before the war, commission merchant Joseph Thouron, another commission merchant named George Huncken, and John Burns.[20]

The artist emphasized war damage here. Three Federal shells found Collonade Range, smashing through one of the fluted Doric columns, and twice through the parapet. On the left, the camera includes Peter Brown's burnt-out tavern and boarding house for effect.

This area is in transition. A very successful Waterfront Park, with walks, trees, a fountain, and a pier extending out into the Cooper River is bringing visitors to what had been a derelict waterfront of burnt wharves. The Range lost its beautiful colonade after the 1886 earthquake and when the railroad was extended down through Vendue Range in the late 1880s.

In 1998 Harbor View Inn, at 2 Vendue Range, fills this northeast corner.

If the caption is correct, lime dealer[17] George W. Olney's white-washed warehouse was struck by one of the Swamp Angel's 100-pdr. Parrott shells on August 22 or 23, 1863. The Federal 8-inch gun burst on its second day of service while firing its 36th round.

This view was taken from the ferry slip[18] that serviced Mount Pleasant and Sullivan's Island. It is possible that this view was made by Barnard, but it is also possible that Barnard and other independent operators were traveling the city more or less together. They may have photographed scenes at the same time, but in their own manner to fill demands of each man's own employers.

This is also a morning exposure but possibly a week later than H-11. Though no buildings in this view survive to their original height, shadow angles suggest a date in late March, within fifteen minutes of 11 a.m. The near gaslight pole and twisted roofing tin are not noticeable, but some rocks in H-11 are still in the street.

H-13

Vendue Range, Charleston, S. C., left half of stereo, Anthony, 1865.   (L. C.)

This afternoon image was taken later than H-12, possibly in early April. The camera was set on the south side of the ferry slip to feature Collonade Range (sic), just to the west of John McKee's store house.[19]

H-14

Vendue Range, Charleston, S. C., looking east, from near the corner of East Bay St., stereo half, published by Anthony as stereo #3109, March, 1865.   (L. C.)

I have seen a caption in MOLLUS's Volume 86, page 4303, claiming this view was made "three days after evacuation." This claim of photographers' industry is impressive, but shadow-dating tells otherwise. News of the February 18 evacuation took a day to arrive at Hilton Head headquarters. Photographers there were not prepared to leave their established portrait business on Robber's Row, and pack up for a fast move to Charleston. Boston newspapers were first to publish the news on February 22, 1865. Several more days would pass before Northern photographers would prepare for their own trip south.

It is a late afternoon scene. While these buildings are gone, save two on the extreme left, shadows of present buildings that follow old footprints indicate it was taken about 4 p.m., around the last week of March or early in April. These two left buildings are presently numbered 18 and 16 Vendue Range. More correctly, their basic construction survives. Facades, roof line, and interior beams remain, but little of the interior. There is a fashion today for renovators to remove old plaster, leaving brick and

H-13. Vendue Range from the ferry slip.

H-14. Vendue Range looking east.

H-13, Modern

beams exposed. This practice saves money for the modern owner and looks "old timey." Victorian occupants would have been horrified to have to live and work in an unfinished interior. Recently, more renovators have taken care to preserve or repair original interiors.

These surviving two-story brick stores are just to the west of John Burns, the end-renter of Collonade Range. The first, 18 & 16, was rented by Nathaniel Hunt, an "auctioneer & com. boot & shoe merchant." His neighbor James Wm. Brown of 22, was as well a commission merchant.[21]

This is a desolate scene. On the right, only John H. Lange's bar room survives on the corner of Prioleau Street. His building lasted well into the twentieth century. Its walls were shored up with iron supports, for 1960s owners of that lot had hoped the old walls would be incorporated into a new structure. Late in the 1980s this whole block was cleared for construction of a large hotel. As of 2000, the block remains vacant.

H-14, Modern

Mr. Lange's neighbor across Prioleau Street, to his right, is gutted. It housed A. H. Abrahams & Son, auctioneer & commission merchants. The street is empty, the city ferry slip lies deserted, the Charleston Gas Company's posts have been stripped of their lamps. Its cobblestones are gone, to fill Confederate earthworks.

H-15

Fraser's Wharf, glass plate.   (N. A.)

Confederate engineers mounted their second 12.75" Blakely in a single-gun earthwork, built on Fraser, Trenholm & Co.'s wharf. In the background is the unfinished New Custom House. Fraser, Trenholm & Co. was the most successful blockade-running firm operating out of Charleston. With long-established offices in Liverpool, good international credit, and a sympathetic British government it became the defacto agency for the Confederacy in England. Their offices were located here, at North Central Wharf, at the foot of Cumberland Street. Before the war they could handle thousands of bales in a morning. By mid-1862, however, the blockade kept ships from France, Bremen, and the East Indies out of Charleston, and trade stagnated.

Money was still to be had in any market—good or bad. George Trenholm aggressively used his company's steamships to run cotton out through the blockade, and bring goods and guns in through any Southern port that offered a chance for a successful run. His steamer *Gibraltar* sailed into Wilmington, N. C., in a daring daylight run on August 18, 1863. Her cargo was two monster 12.75" Blakely rifled cannon, with carriages, shot and shell for them. Four days later the first of them arrived in Charleston on specially-fitted Northeastern Railroad rolling stock. This first gun was quickly and improperly field-tested at White Point Garden. It burst.

When the second gun arrived—it cost 5,000 British pounds plus shipping—Confederate ordnance men were much more careful. They test-fired her on skids, aiming down the Cooper River. On October 12, officers on the Federal monitor USS *Catskill* reported seeing a Rebel shot skip through the harbor entrance between Fort Sumter, and Battery Bee on Sullivans Island. Two more shells followed, having come from either the Calhoun Street Wharf or the Gas Company Wharf. Confederates had accomplished two things that

H-15. Fraser's Wharf and the unfinished New Custom House.

day. That the Blakely worked, and the Federals knew what waited for them if their Navy tried to penetrate Charleston Harbor.[22]

Confederate ordnance men chose Fraser's Wharf as a good site for the remaining Blakely. After the shelling commenced, Fraser & Trenholm moved operations upriver, out of range. Part of their nearly abandoned dock was filled in and strengthened, and the Blakely made operational. Deserters informed the Federals of this. On June 6, 1864, Gus reported on their counterbattery fire: "The Yankees are continuing their shelling of course. Today they are aiming at the big gun on Fraser's wharf, &

some very good shots they have made. The last shell burst on the wharf, but I don't think it would have hit the gun itself." The photographer worked his apparatus from Accommodation Wharf.

Today, the site of Fraser's Wharf has been extended with fill, nearly 100 feet into the Cooper River. The modern view, from the State Port's Authority offices, looks toward the completed New U. S. Custom House.

H-15, Modern

H-16

The ruins of the 600 lb. Blakely Gun, Frazer's Wharf, Charleston, S. C., exploded by the Rebels at the time of the evacuation, left half of stereo, Anthony #3088. (L. C.)

Retreating Confederate gunners burst this gun on February 17. Its muzzle tumbled out through the embrasure. This muzzle survives, taken to West Point, New York as a war trophy, and is displayed next to the breech of the Blakely gun from the battery at White Point.

H-17

Fraser's Wharf Blakely Gun, miscaptioned as "Interior view of Ft. Moultrie, Charleston, S. C., Apr. 1865." Brady-Handy Coll. (L. C.)

Confederate heavy artillery was usually mounted on wood carriages and chassis. The only Charleston guns mounted on iron were those that came with the two imported British-built Blakelys. Both were intentionally burst during the Evacuation. Their ruined gun chambers look confusingly alike, but after the destruction, both sides of the White Point's Blakely remained upright. One side of the Fraser's Wharf chassis lay flat on the ground.

Today, the Blakely's site is under a five-story parking garage, possibly the ugliest garage in Charleston.

H-18

Fraser's Wharf Blakely Gun. (N. A.)

Behind the burst Blakely's fallen chassis, pieces of her gun tube, elevating screw, and carriage litter the foreground. Two heavy shells and wooden ammunition crates have been "posed" in this view. Planking that had lined the lower part of the gun pit, still visible in the White Point's gun chamber, are gone, possibly for firewood. In the rear, beyond the embrasure, are masts of a schooner tied up, across the boat slip, to Accommodation Wharf.

To the right, out of the picture, rises the gun's earth bombproof.

H-16 (top), H-17 (center), & H-18. Ruins of Blakely gun at Fraser's Wharf.

H-19

New Custom House, glass plate.   (N. A.)

Work began on a new United States Custom House at Bay Street and Market Street in 1849. International trade had grown so much that the customs office needed its own building—a grand edifice in days when customs duties financed the Federal government. For $370,000, Washington planned to include a splendid dome and porticoes on all four sides. Federal construction stopped in 1861. Its roof had been finished and the incomplete work was then used by the Confederate Navy as offices.

Visitors from the *Oceanus* were impressed with the unfinished work in 1865.

> The splendid marble Custom House,...though standing on the margin of the harbor, escaped the iron missiles with but little damage. It is now being stored with the confiscated cotton which is rapidly arriving.[23]

H-19. New Custom House.

H-19, Modern

Congress authorized resumption of work in 1867, and work was finished in 1879. What began with planned costs of $370,000 wound up with no dome, no north or south porticos, poor acoustics, and a total cost nearly eight times the first estimate. Finally, the officers left their home in the Exchange Building where they had been housed since 1771. This handsome building continues today as the Customs Department for the Port of Charleston.

H-20. Laurens Street Battery.

H-20

Laurens Street Battery, glass plate, Spring 1865.   **(N. A.)**

This one-gun battery with an earth-covered magazine holds a 10-inch Columbiad. It was built on a palmetto-log wharf at the east end of Laurens Street, between Concord and Wharf streets, and protected part of the Cooper River. Just behind the gun in the two-story stucco building with the double row of dovecotes is an entry hole from a Federal shell. This area is outside of the effective range of the Union artillery, but it was still in "annoying range," showing how high up the Cooper River the terror of these enemy shells extended.

Evacuating Confederates disabled this gun by removing its elevating machinery. A gun could not safely be fired with its muzzle at such a high elevation. Probably it was also spiked and part of the wood carriage chopped up, as was done at several other forts in the harbor.

When the photographer visited, life here had pretty much returned to normal. Two or more schooners are tied up at the dock, and smoke rises between the stack and clapboard building.

This area has completely changed. All period buildings disappeared when the waterfront was filled some 100 yards to the east, with port expansion, and with projects

H-20, Modern

of the 1930s Works Progress Administration. I feel the battery's location was just to the front of White Stack Towing's modern two story brick office at the end of Laurens Street and just east of Concord. Dockside Condominiums, partly boarded up for a hurricane, rises in the background.[24] As this book goes to press, White Stack's office is being replaced by Laurens Place Condominiums.

H-21

Calhoun Street Battery, glass plate, Spring 1865.   (N. A.)

On the east end of Calhoun Street, this is one of six earthworks protecting the west bank of the Cooper River from a breakthrough of Federal navy past Fort Sumter into Charleston Harbor. It boasted a single 8" rifled and banded gun. In the background to the north is the Northeastern Railroad trestle servicing the Charleston City Gas Works. Gas was generated by coal, and brought in by rail.

servation balloon. It was launched from a lot at George and St. Philip streets. The Count later became famous as a designer of German rigid frame airships.[26]

The modern view was taken from Dockside Condominium, looking north. Calhoun Street ends in the center, near the Charleston Aquarium's construction trailer and site. In the background are some of the original gas works buildings. The waterfront here has changed completely, filled in some 100 yards to the east. I believe the battery's site to be under a driveway or parking lot for the new Fort Sumter boat dock.

H-21. Calhoun Street Battery.

This gas works provided lifting power to Charleston's only Confederate silk balloon. It was to be used by the Signal Corps as an observation balloon. It worked well, but the cost of filling the bag was so great that the Signal Corps decided they could observe nearly as well from the steeple of St. Michael's Church.[25]

Yankee shells occasionally reached this far up the waterfront. The gas holder at this plant was struck by an 8" shell, which tore a hole through the cover but did not explode. It was found by workmen when the holder was replaced in 1893. Charleston was to see one more balloon during this war, but during the Federal occupation. In 1865, Count Ferdinand von Zeppelin, military attache to the Union Army, used Charleston gas to inflate his ob-

H-21, Modern

H-22

Half-Moon Battery, glass plate.   (N. A.)

Gus was impressed by the number of heavy guns sent to Charleston for its defense. He reported a new rifled gun just received from Selma, Alabama, freighted in on a South Carolina Railroad flatcar: "They have mounted a splendid triple-banded Brooks rifle gun at Half Moon Battery, in addition to some other guns. The Yankees won't get into Charleston in a hurry but may shell it from Morris Island."[27]

This was the uppermost Confederate battery on the west bank of the Cooper River, at the southwest corner of Columbus Street and East Bay. While the occupying Federals quickly dismantled most town batteries, this earthwork remained, and shows up in the 1872 *Birds-eye View of Charleston*.

At the center of the photo, still standing today, is the cupola of the Faber House on East Bay Street. This was built by Joshua John Ward and his brother, both Georgetown rice planters. Surviving also, at the extreme right, is a two-chimney frame corner store at Drake and Amherst, though propped up and with but one chimney.

H-22. Half-Moon Battery.

H-22, Modern

The preservation ethic is spreading to this area, the Upper East Side, and a serious effort is being made to save this specific building. Action to preserve these once-common types of buildings, neglected in favor of more stately homes, is underway.

The Half-Moon Battery's site is now a parking lot. Save for the Faber House and the corner grocery on Drake and Amherst, all other houses and the battery in this view have not survived. I matched the view, by climbing to the roof of the Charleston Cotton Mill, later called the Old Tobacco Factory. It has been renovated into the Port City Center on East Bay.

MEETING STREET

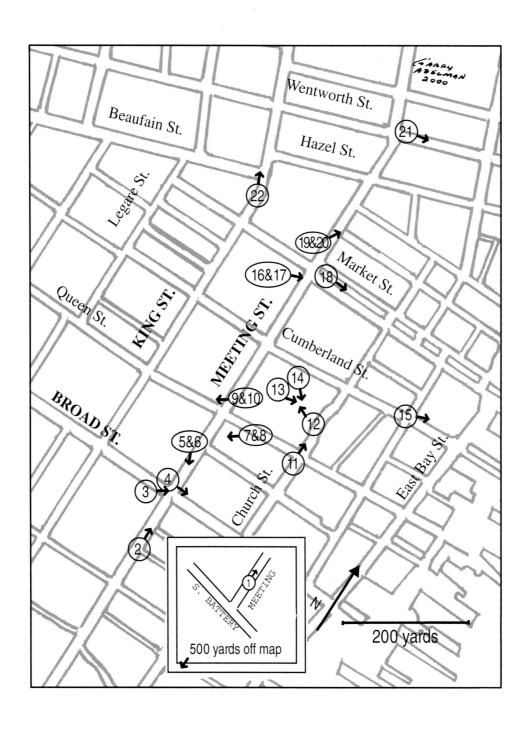

I-1

Meeting St. with barricade, Rev. Thomas Smyth's house on right, glass plate, April, 1865.   **(N. A.)**

The view is to the north, up Meeting Street, with St. Michael's Church visible in the center. Gus Smythe's family home is on the right at 12 Meeting Street (now 18 Meeting). His father was minister to the Second Presbyterian Church, at Meeting and Charlotte (see J-7). This area has always been upper-class residential with little heavy traffic, so a cobblestone pavement was hardly needed in the 1800s. This absence of clattering hoofs and iron tires was appreciated by residents retiring to bed.

Up the street is a ditch dug across the road, with an earth breastwork behind. Both had been partially removed when this view was made. Worried about a Federal landing on White Point Garden, Confederates planned to rally at this earthwork, burn the houses on both sides to provide a field of fire, and hold off the attackers. If necessary, the plan was to hold again at Broad Street. To his Aunt Janey Adger, Gus wrote on November 18, 1862, that "[Beauregard]...told Col. L. M. Keitt...that he intended to fight Charleston street by street and not surrender it. This came straight from Keitt & may be so."

It was to be so. He wrote to his mother on Sept. 2, 1863, "They have thrown up a heavy embankment just opposite Lightwood Alley [now Atlantic Street] as the first parallel; the second to be built at Broad St. & so on thro' the town. The town is to be burnt in divisions in this way, & then fought street by street."

Shelling commenced on August 29, 1863, and panicked civilians fled the city. Many returned when the shells proved to be few in number and did little damage. Renewed shelling from more Federal guns drove much of the population uptown to get out of range. Gus' family evacuated to Summerton, 60 miles by rail north to Kingstree, then some 30 miles west on dirt roads. But Gus was in the Army and had to stay. He eventually got used to the shelling. Gus wrote lively letters to his family who had evacuated. Letters have survived to his mother, Aunt Janey Adger, sister Sarah Annie, and to his fiancee Louisa McCord ("Miss Lou"). To his mother, on December 10, 1863, Gus wrote:

Last night just as I was going to bed about 10 p.m. they commenced shelling again. I heard two come and then went to sleep and did not hear any others, though they threw about ten. Again about 3 a.m. they opened up and threw some five or six; but I did not wake in time to hear them. I did not wake until early 7 a.m. o'clock, and that was too late. I am so used to shells that they don't keep my eyes open at night-time easily.

Nearby houses were hit, but 12 was unscathed for a time. Gus continued to enjoy the garden:

The garden is in fine condition. The Pride of the Woods [wisteria] is in full bloom, or rather bud, but will be in bloom in a day or two. It is going to bloom all around the balcony and will be beautiful. The rose-trees are all budding and will be magnificent if the shells don't spoil it all. *To Mother, 12/20/63*

[Our big dog] Don is still in the yard & is a great protection. All of the soldiers are afraid of him & none of them venture to go in the yard. This is fortunate for our pumps & pipes, nearly every yard in our neighborhood has been rifled. *To Mother, 2/14/64*

Barker's lot [next door, to the south], is ruined. They are hard at work [for earth to build the works on the battery], opened a gate into Church St. through the wall, and have already made a considerable hole. They have dug it up some 5 ft. & now it is all muddy & full of water... It seems such a pity that it should be so ruined. [The new owner, George] Williams will have a hard job to fix it up again. It is all the better for us tho' for it will insure us having the open lot [and view to the south] so much longer. They are still digging at it. *To Mother, 3/20/64*

Terror from the shelling caused the lower peninsula to be evacuated, and eventually only Confederate soldiers and some teamsters remained. Some lawless soldiers began looting empty dwellings:

Our own soldiers are doing us more damage than the shells. I should much prefer a shell to go thro' the house than to let them do so. *To Sarah Annie, 4/9/64*

They just roam at will now through the whole lower portion of the city. Our house & Mr. Middleton's [1 Meeting] are the only two in Meeting St. below Broad which have not been entered. This we owe in a great measure to Don. I have another now, [his brother Adger's fine bull dog,] Flora by name, & do not think any soldier will venture in just now. They are worth their food over & over again. Not much meat do they get however, principally hominy. They have done three times the damage to the city that the shells have done. This a shame. *To Mother, 4/15/64*

The soldiers stole lead pipe, copper kitchen boilers, lead from the bathing tubs and pantry, pumps from cisterns, and brass gas fixtures. This scrap they sold to the ordnance offices, getting as much as $1 per pound for bronze from chandeliers.

Radishes for breakfast & music by the shells.... The peach trees are full of fruit, grape vines putting out finely, & everything about the yard look-

Gen. B.[eauregard] has gone to North Carolina & we are to have Gen. Sam Jones. *To Mother, 4/22/64*

[A] shell struck the pavement in front of our gate, knocking off a small piece of the wall. It tore up a big hole, but I have all the flags gathered up & put inside, so as to mend it sometime or other. Two that hit Mrs. Howard's passed right over our house as it is in a direct line. So you see it is not safe. *To Mother, 5/1/64*

I-1. Meeting Street looking North.

ing well. The soldiers have not been in here yet, so the house is not ruined as are many others. ...you would be surprised to see what a domestic man I have become. I hardly ever go out at night, but stay here at home, writing, reading or singing. Very often a friend or two drop in & we so end the evening pleasantly. Edgerton plays on the piano & I on the violin together. The Yanks have been shelling all morning, throwing the shells well into the City, & nearly all of them bursting. They shell now nearly every day, but generally many of them fall short [into the Cooper River]. One fell on the Battery the other day & several down town, but No. 12 has not yet been struck; long may it wave.

I-1, Modern

The shells have been dropping all round our house the last day or two. They come popping round the house, sometimes shaking it till you can feel it tremble when they burst near at hand. *To Mother, 5/15/64*

I am not alone. Benti Middleton...is here also. He is now stationed in town & will mess with me. This will be pleasant company for me. He furnishes his share of provisions, of course, so we shall get along finely. *To Mother, 5/19/64*

It has been such a lovely Sunday. This afternoon sitting out here a little while on the piazza, the remembrance of old times was so strong; when we used to assemble for evening church, loose Don, bolt the gate, & then all go off. Those were happy times. I wonder if we shall ever see such again! The Yankees have not appreciated the day however, for shells have been flying thick & fast, & most of them very near our house. In fact for the past week nearly all of them have fallen in this part of town, below Broad St. Very many have fallen between this & 36 [the James Adger House, now 48; offices and classrooms of the First Baptist School], in the street, some twenty I think... Today one fell in Barker's lot, just in one corner & burst, throwing pieces of brick, &c. into our piazza, & several whole brick into the garden, breaking off two or three small branches of the big peach tree, & knocking off some of the peaches. It fell not 10 yards from the wall. I was lying down in the house, & at first supposed the house had been struck... There have been several others quite close, but I do not know exactly where they went as I was unable to go out & see. This is pretty close shooting, & as there is no telling when one may drop into our house, it makes living here especially now when staying in the house all the time, quite exciting....

Still, as always, I have no idea that our house will be struck. As Adger says, Father prays too hard for it, & I do believe there is something in it, for nearly every other house round here has either been hit, or has received a shell in its yard....

The gas won't light to-night, but I am fortunate in—Shell just fallen in Church St. back of us—in having a candle or two yet....

One has just passed over the house & burst in the square opposite. Hope none will come tumbling into the room to-night. *To Mother, 5/22/64*

An incident not found in any of Gus' surviving letters, was recorded in 1911 by his granddaughter's husband, John Bennett.

The cousins in the squad...made their quarters at old No. 12, Meeting Street...in the butler's quarters over the cow's stable.... On one occasion as the household of young men sat at table, eating, in the dining-room of [old] No. 12, a Federal shell broke through the house-wall, penetrated the floor and fetched up in the cellar. So familiar were all with the nature of shells and shell fire, bomb-explosion, and the like, that no one left his seat, or left off eating the food before him; as each one knew that if the shell was to explode at all the explosion would be instantaneous; and not a man would have an instant's reprieve from immediate death; that if the shell did not explode at once, the likelihood was that it would not explode at all; in which case the best thing to do was just to go on doing what they were busy about, and finish their breakfast.[1]

Did I tell you of the shell which came into the yard about ten days ago? It fell just by the side of the drain opposite Old Philip's door, but only made a hole in the ground which I have had filled up since. All the damage it did was to frighten Philip & the dogs a little. The shell that came in the house did not even break a pane of glass which is very fortunate. Had it burst the damage done in this line in the study would have been very great....

We have got off very fortunately so far, especially as they deducted from the valuation of the house made for taxation, of about of $1000., on account of its being struck.... I have got the shell here. *To Mother, 6/27/64*

After some little difficulty I have succeeded in getting our roof mended. It was rather hard to find a slater, but I did, & he has been there & stopped it up very well, but at the cost of $15. This is as reasonable as could be expected from the high price of all the material necessary. *To Mother, 7/8/64*

Two fell in the street exactly in front of our house, between us & Mr. Roper. One of these I had dug up, & as it is a large one, a 100 pdr., have put it by the small one which came in the house, as mementoes.... There is almost more danger from the fragments than from the shells themselves. Tuesday several fell in our yard, one even coming into the house, & into this room. They fly very far. One burst in the lower end of Water St., & a fragment was picked up by the Guard house. [some 450 yards distant!] *To Aunt Janey, 8/4/64*

No law down in this part of town now. Assaults every night or so. The other night they robbed a man here, just at our door, & another night pulled our Courier off his horse, robbed him, & then put him on again & sent him off. It is horrible; the lawless state of old Charleston, formerly so orderly. No shelling tho'. *To Aunt Janey, 1/23/65*

May have to evacuate, but not at all so decided. Government needs the port, & will strain every nerve to keep it open & hold it. So far as the city itself is concerned, I am much more sanguine. ...No, No, Mother, we are not whipped yet! And by March 4th the old Pope, or some nation may want to say something. Hope on! Hope ever! This the best way.

You have asked me what I shall do if Charleston is given up.... Of course I leave, & most probably, nay certainly almost, with the Corps. It will be needed in the field, & tho' it will be reduced a good deal, I am marked down as one of the last to be sent back [to my old unit, Co. A, 25th S. C. Infantry]; only in case they break it up. Already some 11 have been returned, as the junction of the [Savannah Signal] Corps with ours, renders it rather large. *To Mother, 2/9/65*

I am afraid Charleston is doomed.... We are expecting orders to leave to-morrow, or even to-night. Dear old Charleston. My heart is very sad. To leave her now to these wretches after she has so long withstood their assault. Indeed, indeed, it is a bitter cup to drink....

I have arranged for our gardener, a Scotchman, to live at our house. This has been a relief to me, for it is hard to think of the despoiling of our homes....

The Yanks are shelling away at a great rate. One shell has just burst close by. They might as well save their ammunition.... But everything is ready to move.... *To Miss Lou, 2/14/65*

This letter to his fiancée, in Columbia, S. C. was delivered with difficulty by the Confederate Post Office Department. When Sherman captured Orangeburg on February 12, he cut the usual mail route on the South Carolina Railroad. Postmaster Huger had to redirect his Columbia mail through Florence, which was now the only way out of Charleston.

This letter may have been in the last Confederate mail from Charleston to get through to the state capital, which fell to Sherman on February 17.

Shadows from Gus' south roof overhang suggest an April date. His west wall shadow on the brick sidewalk times it to around noon.

I-2

Meeting St., near Broad, Charleston, S. C., looking north, St. Michael's church in the middle distance, glass plate, also published by Anthony as stereo.   **(L. C.)**

Meeting Street was not paved south of Broad. It became a quiet, largely residential street lined with mansions all the way down to White Point Garden. Wide brick sidewalks were shaded with trees that had been planted shortly before the war.

St. Michael's clock informs the pedestrian the time is 10 a.m., and the leaved-out trees indicate a day in late April or early May. Her bells are silent. The 18th century peal was refugeed to Columbia for safekeeping, and there burnt by Sherman's army. Remains of these bronze bells were shipped to England for recasting. Whitechapel Foundry had retained the molds.

The steeple appears to be dark-possibly painted black, supporting a story that the Federal gunners wouldn't be able to sight their guns on it. However, extensive repairs after 1989's Hurricane Hugo revealed this black paint to be only its third layer of paint. As the steeple was finished in 1756, the legend of the black paint may date to 1780 when British gunners sighted upon this steeple from across the Ashley River. The idea of this being the third layer of paint after 24 years of weathering, is supportable.

A portico was added in the 1820s to South Carolina Society Hall, to the right. This was, and is, a gentlemen's club formed in 1737 by Huguenot immigrants. They finished their present meeting hall in 1804. In the pediment of the portico is a large wood carving with the word "Posteritati," above a hand that is planting an oak sapling over the stump of a fallen oak. This woodwork is original to the 1820s portico and symbolizes their charity toward education. Since their founding they have sent needy boys to school.

Much of this building's maintenance is paid by rental for wedding and private receptions.

I-2. St. Michael's church on Meeting Street.

I-2, Modern

I-3

State House & City Hall, glass plate, March 27, 1865.   (L. C.)

Charleston's ca. 1800 City Hall received four shells that overshot St Michael's Church. The Charleston *Courier* on August 1866 reported it newly repaired and renovated: "The first shell struck the Northeast wing demolishing the Clerk's office. It was the second shell fired upon the renewal of the bombardment after the answer of Gen. Gillmore to General Beauregard's protest."

The clerk, W. H. Smith, was in his office, completing passports for two ladies who wished to leave the city. The *Courier* said Smith "...made a very narrow escape by a precipitate retreat down the flight of stairs into the hall below. Two more shells struck this wing, and a fourth entered the Council Chamber."

After General Quincy Gillmore's first bombardment, Beauregard sent a scathing letter denouncing the shelling of a sleeping city filled with helpless women and children, "against the rules of civilized warfare." Gillmore stopped for a period, but only because his 200-pdr. Parrott rifle had burst on its 36th round. In August 1863, he had only one battery location that could reach the city and that was the Swamp Angel that had been mounted with heroic effort in the marsh behind Morris Island.

Two holes caused by Federal artillery are visible in the photograph, one in the lintel near the corner of the first floor that burst in the basement, taking out the sheriff's office. Another lopped off the roof balustrade near the pediment. The *Courier* continued:

> After the Council moved to the Orphan House, the City Hall was ransacked by the gangs of plunderers and the thieves who at that time infested the Lower Wards. ...a large portion of the furniture of the Mayor's office, and of the Council Chamber, [went to] General Hatch's Headquarters, and was restored by General Devins.

In spite of the bombardment, when President Davis visited Charleston in November 1863, the city gave him a grand procession down Meeting Street to City Hall. State and Confederate flags hung from hotels and private residences. The *Mercury* reported on November 3:

> From the City Hall to the Court House a garland of laurels had been extended, with a banner in the center, bearing the following inscription: "The Ladies of the Soldiers' Relief Association welcome President Davis to Charleston." On arrival of the procession at the City Hall, President Davis alighted from the carriage amid the cheers of the citizens, and was introduced [by] Mayor MacBeth.

The mayor warmly welcomed President Davis, who addressed a crowd from City Hall's steps. He said it would be better to leave Charleston as a heap of ruins than "prey for Yankee spoils," but that the city would never be taken. He also said the citizens should "trust to our commanding general," but otherwise snubbed General Beauregard who was stoutly defending Charleston, and felt he should have gotten far more praise. The two just did not get along.

Addressing the crowd, he reminded them, "It is by united effort...that our success is to be achieved.... He who would attempt to promote his own personal ends...is not worthy of the Confederate liberty for which we are fighting." Davis enjoyed the reception for him held inside the City Hall. During the week he spent in Charleston, inspecting forts and reviewing the troops, his own morale was probably raised as much as the support he gave Charleston.

In March 1865, Federal soldiers lounge next to the basement, and their muskets are stacked in front of the stairs. To the left of Meeting Street is the Charleston District Court House also known as the State House. The state legislature met in Columbia, but there were duplicate state offices in Columbia and Charleston. Stone fenders protect freight wagons from knocking off the corner of the building. One shell hole is visible, next to the Federal sailor. The shell crashed in but did not explode, leaving a scar. This scene today has changed little but for the pavement, sidewalk, and streetlights.

The State House became Charleston County's courthouse, and was used simply as an ordinary public building for nearly two hundred years, receiving a renovation every quarter century or so. Little care was taken in the renovations to save any of the original building. Damage from Hurricane Hugo in 1989 caused the city fathers to appreciate its antiquity. Archaeology has revealed much of what the old 1752 structure was, and rebuilt in 1792. As this book goes to press, work has finally begun to return the building to its 1792 appearance, inside and out.

Removal of later stucco in 1998 revealed a repair patch that filled the shell hole seen in the 1865 view. That shell hole was repaired shortly after the war. Post-war brickwork filled in the back of the wall. Its street face was repaired to vividly show outlines of the old filled hole to passersby, to remind everyone of Charleston's determination to hold out through the bombardment. After the 1886 earthquake, the whole building was stuccoed with portland cement, which covered the scar.

With current restoration, that scar was exposed again, but the patch was slated to be replaced by new brickwork.

I-3. State House and City Hall.

That scar so sharply delineated the shell damage that with this photograph, it was immediately recognizable as a repaired shell hole. This was one of two buildings in town that show Federal shell damage visible from the street, and the most graphic. Mounting a campaign to preserve that patch, I gained support from numerous preservationists. The State House in Columbia was hit by Union shells in 1865 and today has stars by each strike in the marble wall. These are battle scars, honorably preserved. Charleston could do as well. But Charleston County Council voted to replace the patch of the 1860s. Their short-sighted reasoning was that it would not represent the Court House of 1792.

Using the position of the shadow of St. Michael's steeple, just out of view to the right, I date it to within 5 minutes of 11 a.m., around March 27, 1865.

I-3, Modern (1996)

I-4

Charleston, S. C. 1865. View looking east from the corner of Meeting Street and Broad Street. City Hall in the foreground used as a Provost Guard House. Glass plate, May 1865. (L. C.)

From these City Hall steps came the announcement that Lincoln had won the 1860 presidential election. Days later South Carolina seceded from the Union. On several occasions during the next six months a gun was fired in Broad Street, to announce the secession of yet another Southern state. But in City Hall, municipal life went on until the shelling emptied out this part of the city.

Here in 1865, Federal soldiers patrol a nearly empty Broad Street. It is May, fully-leafed locust trees[2] shade the street, and the shadow of St. Michael's steeple barely protrudes into the right margin. No blurred images of horses or wagons block the view of the Post Office three blocks away. On the corner a well-dressed little boy stares at the camera.

Signs of war remain. In the foreground a filled shell hole mars the Belgian block pavement intersection of Broad and Meeting. Broad Street's cobblestones have been pulled up all the way to Meeting Street to provide foundations for Confederate earthworks. *Oceanus* passengers, exploring the city after witnessing the re-raising of Major Anderson's flag at Fort Sumter in April, saw a changed City Hall:

I-4. View looking east from Meeting and Broad streets.

I-4, Modern

...The old City Hall we found to be the rendezvous of the regiments which are now on guard in the city. Muskets were stacked before it and within it; patrols walked measuredly back and forth, while the "boys" off duty were asleep upon the benches and floors within. This building was in the same general condition of those before described, everything indicating that the Rebels went out in haste and by flight.[3]

By July 1866, City Hall had been tidied up and reopened with Gen. W. W. Burns acting as Mayor.

Anthony published this same image as a stereo, but I have chosen to use the clearer Library of Congress glass plate.

I-5

City Hall and St. Michael's Church, glass plate, April 4, 1865. (N. A.)

St. Michael's clock reads 2:16 p.m. Double-checking the clock against the shadow along the doors of the west entry, it appears the clock was ten minutes slow that day. Using shadows on the roof, I date the photo to April 4, 1865. The 1761 steeple of St. Michael's Episcopal Church held the tallest platform in the city. The Confederate Signal Corps placed a telescope in the gallery to observe Federal troops on Morris and Folly Islands and

the blockading fleet; a telegraph line ran directly to headquarters. This was better than an observation balloon, and much cheaper to maintain.

Gus had a new assignment:

My very dear Mother,
I have just been ordered on duty in St. Michael's Steeple. ...*March 28, 1864*
...Here am I on my lofty perch, behind a big telescope, looking out for any movements of the Yankees which may be of sufficient importance to send up to Gen. Jordan (of Gen. P.G.T. Beauregard's staff)...My tour of duty to-night is from 1.30 A.M. to 9 A.M., & I have been on duty half the day. To-day however, I shall be off duty. ...The duty is pretty heavy as I am on every other day & half of every other night. The worst difficulty is the trouble of getting up here, for it is no joke climbing up 150 feet... Our place is in the upper piazza, above the clock. We have it boarded in, & bunks put in for us to sleep in, so that we are tolerably comfortable, except the wind which blows thro' the cracks of the boards at a great rate & there is always a wind up here.
I still eat at home & shall try to fix it to sleep there every other night, when I am not on duty. Our business up here is merely to keep a close eye on all movements of the enemy & report them to the Genl.... It is quite interesting to watch them, as we have a splendid glass. Now it is day break, & their vessels are moving about, & soldiers marching on Morris Is. at a great rate. *My very dear Mother, 3/31/64*

Federal artillerymen on Morris Island used this steeple as an aiming point. At a range just short of 4 1/2 miles, the most specific target they could hope to hit was a two block by two block area. Indeed they did not particularly want to hit this steeple, as it provided an excellent aiming point for the general city.

Still, the sighting of a puff of smoke from the Morris Island 100-pdr. Parrott rifled gun batteries,[4] seen by a Signal Corps man at his telescope, was unnerving. It meant a shell was on the way, and if the rising black dot appeared not to drift off to the right or left, he knew he was the target. A rope ladder hung on the outside of the steeple was supposed to offer a way of escape in case the staircase of the steeple were hit. A little black and tan terrier named Pic, gift of his fiancee' Louisa McCord, kept him company on his watches.[5] That rope ladder can be seen in the photographs, draped over the parapet at the foot of the steeple, and hanging down onto Broad Street. Gus kept up his lively correspondence.

I have got into the most responsible post in the Signal corps here & the most dangerous when they are shelling, for they avowedly make this steeple their mark when firing & have made some very close shots. To look down on them from here, all around the foot of the Steeple, in the grave yard, Streets, City Hall, Court House, Guard House, & houses, it seems, & is, miraculous that so far they have missed. I only hope they will continue to do so, for tho' there may be some "glory," there will be very little pleasure in tumbling down with the Steeple. Still the risk makes the excitement. *to Aunt Janey, 4/2/64*

You must not feel anxious about me up here, & never fear my falling down the stairs, tho' there are 170 of them: "High Life above Stairs" with a vengeance...Oh my, there goes that bell (10 o'clock), & such a cracking & shaking as this old steeple does get up whenever they ring, is a caution. The first time you experience it you feel certain that it is going to fall immediately. Now I have got rather used to it, but still it is not the most comfortable feeling I have ever had. It shakes so I can hardly write, so you may judge of the motion. Luckily I am not given to sea sickness. *My dear Mother, 4/7/64*

I cannot write very well up here in the Steeple, as I am very much interrupted by the constant lookout I have to keep.... Oh! How the wind does blow up here. It keeps up such a dreary whistling & moaning, really very pleasant about midnight.

...there is another Monitor outside, making seven in all. Now whether this means fight or not is beyond my ken; certainly if those vessels were not there, we could easily retake Morris Isl. *My dear Sarah Annie, 5/11/64*

The fog is so thick we can't see James Island. Still the Yanks keep up their shelling.... What wonders science has wrought, that thus persons can stay at four miles distance & hurl shells into a place they cannot see. Truly man is wonderful in his ingenuity.... They struck the Court House steps the other day. The shell must have gone over the steeple, or gone round it, for the steeple is in a direct line between Morris Isl. & the Court House. *My dear Mother, 5/12/64*

They have again begun on Sumter.... Friday & Saturday they were firing at it all day long, not only from the land batteries on Morris Isl. but also from two of their Monitors which came up near the Fort, & participated in the bombardment. It was a magnificent sight from The Steeple here, to look

at this fierce fight, tho' 'twas hardly a fight, for poor old Sumter could do nothing, going on below us. Sullivan's Isl. Opened on the Monitors & hit them several time, & yesterday all our batteries on James Isl. fired on Morris Isl. It was really grand. Notwithstanding all this to occupy them however, the indefatigable Yankees still found time to keep up their shelling of the City as steadily as usual. They can teach us a lesson in energy. During all this firing so far the only casualties have been two or three negroes slightly hurt by shells, the severest wound being the loss of a foot. This the effect of over 1000 shells. No serious damage done to the Fort. This will hardly pay. *My dear Mother, 5/15/64*

Two shells fell this morning at the corner of Broad & Meeting Sts. Nearly in the same spot, within 18-in. of it. *My Dear Mother, 5/22/64*

Another shell burst in the Guard house yard the other day. I was in the Steeple & at first thought it was struck. The next struck the house adjoining the Guard house & Set it on fire, but this was quickly put out by the guardsmen. *My dear Mother, 5/27/64*

They are using now a very heavy gun, & the roar of the shells as they fly on the path of destruction is really awful. One struck quite close to the Steeple this morning just before I left, in Broad St. between King & Meeting. It did make a terrible noise as it flew past the Steeple.... Strange that these shells never give me a moments thought now. I hear them coming & they all seem a matter of course, & I pay no attention to them at all. But then I have had some little experience now, & you remember the old adage, "Familiarity breeds contempt." Well, one of them will knock me over some day I expect & thus teach me the respect due them.... It is beautiful to see from my elevated position, these bombardments. The white smoke, puffing out in dense clouds from the batteries, then the flash & small speck of smoke, indicating the bursting shell, but which gradually expands & enlarges, until it is lost among the real nebulae. It is a sight worth seeing & one to be remembered, but seen too oft, why there the beauty ends. *Sarah Annie, 6/3/64*

Yesterday they aimed at the Steeple & the shell flew round here thick & fast. Thirteen fell between Queen St. & St. Michael's Alley yesterday after 12 M. Two of these struck the Hibernian Hall, one the Mills House, one the Court House, two fell here at the corner of Broad, two in the City Hall Square,

I-5. St. Michael's church.

& one in the Sunday School Union—the second that has been there. This one knocked out the whole front of the store, leaving it entirely exposed. It made more of a wreck than any one shell I have seen yet. There is quite a stock in the store, too. It is nearly miraculous that this Steeple has not yet been hit. *(to Gus' other sister) Sue, 6/6/64*

Well! The Yankees have succeeded at last in hitting St. Michael's Church. Not the Steeple, just at the base of it. The shell entered the South roof of the church on Tuesday, but did not burst nor do much damage.... I do not consider the charm as broken now even until the Steeple itself receives a scratch. *My dear Mother, 6/9/64*

I-5, Modern

I-6

City Hall and St. Michael's Church, glass plate, April 4, 1865.   (L. C.)

This view was taken also from the same tripod as I-5, but with a wide-angle lens. St. Michael's clock reads 2:30 p.m., fourteen minutes later than I-5. That allowed enough time for the photographer to install a different lens while his assistant processes the I-5 glass plate, and sensitize a new plate. The artistry of this pair of photographs is striking. The steeple is centered a bit off to the left, and Meeting Street diverges out to the right. Patches of light in the shadow of the building on the right, show it is burnt out and its windows and roof are missing. Gus wrote to his Mother on July 8, 1864:

The shells that are coming to us are the large ones, & they do make a pretty noise when they burst. Not very close to the Steeple however. The nearest have been in Chalmers St. ...There just when I was in a hurry some ladies must come up here & interrupt me. This is quite a lion now of the city, & every young lady who comes to town, must go up the Steeple. The view up here is beautiful, besides the interest one naturally takes in looking at the various batteries.

He wrote to her again on August 26, 1864:

None very near our house except fuze shells bursting in the air & throwing fragments near by. They have been aiming at the Steeple.... Yesterday two <u>fragments</u> from fuze shells stuck

I-6. St. Michael's church.

the Steeple below us, one in the morning & one in the afternoon, & two or three <u>fragments</u> struck the church. As they were only fragments, not much damage was done. Glad you got away before they commenced, as the pieces flew almost too near No. 12 to be pleasant.

But on October 16, 1864, he wrote to his sister, Sarah Annie:

I am sorry to tell you that St. Michael's Steeple has been struck at last, this morning at 10. o'clock, a shell entering & bursting in it. Fortunately it came in just by a window, so the wall is little injured, not at all of any account. I was not up here at the time. It came in considerable below where we reside, in the compartment below the clock, just where the works are, & fortunately also, not in the staircase, so that with the exception of tearing up the floor considerably, & making a great litter, there is no damage done, save the loss of the old prestige of the Steeple. It had escaped so long, I was in hopes it would have done so entirely. The shell just before that one entered the church, going thro' the S. E. Corner of the roof, but not bursting, & the one before that, struck the Court House. So you see it was pretty good shooting.

...This church, St. M.'s has had now two shells in it, besides one in the Steeple, & has been hit several times by fragments.

The real value of Charleston to the Confederacy was as a major blockade running port. For four years United States Navy gunboats sought to close this harbor. Gus wrote to his mother on the first of December, "Last night they had a regular 4th July down the harbor with blue lights, & red lights, sky rockets, & roman candles, & cannon shooting. Two Steamers ran in & were fired at, & the picket boats were sending up their fire works as signals."

Two blockade-runners came into Charleston harbor that night, *Kate Gregg* and *Laurel*, both completing successful runs from Nassau. Another steamer, *Syren,* ran out of Charleston that night, bound for Nassau and filled with bales of cotton. *Syren* was an incredibly successful blockade runner, making twelve successful runs in or out of Charleston late in 1864. Just two roundtrips were enough to turn a profit for her investors.[6] He shivered while penning a letter to his mother on December 23, 1864:

Oh it is very cold this morning. I am here all in a heap by my stove, while the wind whistles around.... Savannah has been evacuated, that seems certain.... Porter's fleet is off Wilmington, So that is where they will attack. We expected it here, but are ready for them.

Happy New Year to you Mother—

The new year has opened clear & cold. I was on duty all Saturday night, & saw the old Year out & the new one in. Oh but it was cold!... I am up in the Steeple this morning, but shall be relieved at 3 o'clock & then go home to a good dinner. Yes I have a turkey! A box came on Saturday from Mrs. McCord [his fiancee's mother].... With a turkey, ham, some sausages, cake, etc. on which with Ellen's pickles & some of your potatoes & rice I expect to enjoy a fine new year's dinner. All she sent was cooked, but I can warm it over & anyhow I hardly think I shall grumble. Your box also came just at the right time. Thanks for the socks. They are done beautifully.... All quiet outside.[7]

I-6, Modern

I-7

Hibernian Hall, Charleston, S. C. 1865, glass plate, March 28, 1865.   **(N. A.)**

I-8

Charleston, S. C. 1865 Hibernian Hall (Meeting Street), place of meeting after the burning of Secession Hall, glass plate, March 28, 1865.   **(L. C.)**

A stereo version was published by Anthony, N.Y. Both views were taken by the same operator, about March 28, 1865, at the same location from Queen Street. I shadow-dated by the portico's roof casting a morning shadow down onto its sheltered east wall. First, the time was determined by the morning eastern sun moving down toward the doorway lintel. This photographer exposed I-7 on a large glass plate around 9 a.m. and then changed to a stereoptican lens for stereo view I-8 at 9:18 a.m.(± two minutes.) Once the images' respective times were determined, the investigator tries to date them: as spring advances, the south (left, in these images) side of the portico's shadow moves to the left. Both images have identical "south-shadows," so they were indeed exposed on the same day.

These images preserve three landmarks: the Hall itself, the most graphic shell hole illustration, and General Robert E. Lee's hotel room, on the second floor, corner.

In Hibernian Hall's image, the operator preserved a view of one building prominent in the April 1860 Democratic National Convention, where the Democratic Party split over the question of slavery's expansion into newly-organized states. The delegates knew there would be a shortage of hotel rooms during the large convention. Indeed, delegates from some of the Northern and New England states steamed in with their

I-7. Hibernian Hall.

I-8. Hibernian Hall.

I-7 & 8, Modern

chartered three ships to sleep in, bringing along hundreds of barrels of liquor, beer, and some amiable females.

The Northwestern Delegation took over the Mills House Hotel, shown on the extreme right of the picture. Their overflow rented the Hibernian Hall, providing an upstairs dormitory of over sixty budget-priced beds. These delegates supported the nomination of Stephen Douglas. Douglas felt each state should choose for itself whether to permit slavery within its own boundaries.

Eighteen months later, much had changed. The Democratic Party split into three factions, each with its own presidential candidate. Lincoln's new Republican Party carried none of the slave-holding states but got more electoral votes than any of the Democratic candidates and thus won the presidency. Fort Sumter fell, but by November Lincoln's navy had captured Beaufort, S. C. The Yankees were now less than sixty miles from Charleston.

General Robert E. Lee arrived at the Northeastern Railroad station on November 6, 1861, to reorganize the South Carolina defenses. He rented the fine second-floor corner room seen in this photo. During the 1861 fire, Lee tried to supervise the fire fighting from this balcony.

By August 1863, Federal artillery was only four miles away, on Morris Island, and their shells began to terrorize Charleston. A shell crashed into the brick building that housed the bar-room for the Mills. It burst in the second floor, destroying the bar-room of the Mills. Arrival of this particular shell probably caused much more sadness than anger to the population.

This view shows the progress of a typical Federal shell into the city, and shows the process better than in any other Charleston view. This projectile was fired from Morris Island and descended toward the city at a steep angle, here crashing through the third floor street wall and exploding in the floor below. The image shows the penetration into the top floor, and the blow-out when it detonated in the second floor.

Shells fired into Charleston were usually the Parrott design. These were cylindrical in shape and pointed at one end. The base had a soft brass band. When fired, that band pressed into the guns' rifling, causing the shell to spin rather like a football, to be more stable in flight. Screwed into the front was an impact-type fuze that was to explode immediately when it hit something hard, but the shells traveled so fast that it usually penetrated down through one more floor before detonating. The Parrott shell was designed well. It was about 90% effective, and if the shell did not wobble or tumble in flight, it almost always burst. Ten pounds of gunpowder did not do damage compared to modern explosives. According to Gus' letters, it took about five Yankee shells to thoroughly destroy a building. One shell into the owners' parlor though, was usually enough to encourage him to evacuate.

The 1865 view was taken across vacant lots burned over in the 1861 fire. That rebuilt area required a modern view to be made from Meeting Street's eastern sidewalk. An earthquake destroyed the Hibernian's 1840 portico in 1886. Rebuilt to the original dimensions, the new portico throws the same shadows today. Today's shadows compare closely with the Hibernians' shadows of 1865 and today's shadow dating is comparable to that of 1865.

I-9

Mills House, glass plate, George Barnard, March 15-20, 1865. (N. A.)

Barnard shows the Mills House Hotel, apparently intact, but surrounded by ruins of the 1861 fire. It shows dramatically a hotel apparently completely surrounded by devastation. To dramatize the extent of the foreground ruins, a carriage box has been put loosely atop another carriage's running gear. The running gear and box do not fit: the step up to the box sticks through the running gear's wheels. Of more interest is a magnificent iron gate, that shows in such detail that it could be copied by a modern blacksmith. The image is dated using the shadows from the Mills' east wall's window cornices to about 11 a.m. The present cornices are cast from the Mills' originals.

I-10

The Mills House, with adjacent ruins, stereo, George Barnard,[8] also published by Anthony as stereo #3078, March 15-20, 1865. (L. C.)

Taken about twenty minutes after I-9, when the rising morning sun completely shades the Mills' facade. One of Barnard's models, seated in the foreground, wears a Confederate jacket and civilian cap. More interesting is the standing black man effectively emancipated barely one month before. He is a bucksawyer, with his portable sawhorse on his back resting on the tool of his trade, a bucksaw. One handle lies on his shoulder, the back of the blade against his back, the other handle below, and the tensioning rope in front of his body. He leans against the front wheels of the two-horse cart seen in I-9.[9]

Both images are powerful, implying the devastation of war. But the scene really shows damage solely caused by the fire of 1861. It also shows the result of heroic efforts of the hotel staff. They hung wet blankets out of the windows and had men on top to extinguish falling embers before they could catch on the roof.

Otis Mills claimed his new $200,000 hotel, opening in 1853, as "the finest hotel south of New York City." It offered a grand marble staircase, a cast iron balcony from Philadelphia, and steam heat in all the public rooms. Each floor had eight bathing rooms exclusively for the ladies,

I-9. The Mills House.

with warm shower baths. Bathing rooms for the gentlemen were on the first floor.[10] Separate from the ornate dining room was another for the children and their nannies. Its barber shop was run by Joseph Rainey, a free person of color.[11]

The Mills hosted many famous guests. Stephen Douglas stayed there in 1860 during the Democratic National Convention, and the South Carolina Secession Convention booked the whole hotel that December. On November 6, 1861, General Robert E. Lee arrived to take command of the Department of S. C., Georgia, and East Florida. He kept rooms at the Mills, on the southeast corner of the second floor.

On December 11, 1861, Lee returned with his staff to the Savannah Railroad depot at the Ashley River's south bank. After a tiring day inspecting defenses along the railroad, they looked forward to dinner at the Mills. While crossing the Ashley in a small boat, his Adjutant, Walter Taylor, noted a glow in the northeastern sky,[12] but with no concern. The vaunted volunteer fire companies of Charleston could easily handle any blaze. They proceeded to a delicious supper at the Mills. About eleven o'clock reports of the spreading fire compelled Lee and his staff to climb to the roof. Major A. L. Long of Lee's staff recorded:

More than one-third of the city appeared a sea of fire, shooting up columns of flame that seemed to mingle with the stars. From King Street eastward to the river, extending back more than a mile, stores and dwellings, churches and public buildings, were enveloped in one common blaze, which was marching steadily and rapidly across the city."[13]

Lee could see that the under-manned volunteer fire companies were overwhelmed, and there was little he could do. He had placed Brigadier General Roswell Ripley over the Charleston district and felt Ripley was fighting the disaster as well as anyone. Lee had the Mills' manager drape wet blankets out the windows, and place men on the roof to stamp out burning embers and shingles that might set the roof alight.

Finally, buildings across the street flamed up and it was time to leave. The general and his staff fled down a back staircase (there is a story he carried a little girl with him), flagged down an omnibus and accepted the hospitality of Charles Alston on East Battery.[14]

The Mills House survived, though the buildings on three sides perished. It stayed open, hosting more leaders such as Gen. P. G. T. Beauregard. Finally, shelling compelled the hotel to close in November 1863. Mr. Burckmeyer wrote to his wife in France on July 21, 1864,

I-10. The Mills House.

that the "Mills had eleven holes in it."[15] Accounts report up to thirteen shells striking the hotel. A close look at the image shows half the windows are shattered. By the end of the war, Otis Mills was broke. The barber of his hotel, Joseph Rainey, prospered and eventually served in the United States House of Representatives for nine years.

The Mills House struggled past the middle of the 20th century under the name of the St. John's Hotel. In 1968, local investors purchased the weary hotel, intending to restore her to her former glory. Their ambition is impressive, for in those days most visitors were still abandoning city-center hotels, and staying at outlying motels.

While still showing some magnificence, on inspection her brick's mortar was found to be crumbling. The investors stuck with their goal. After making measured drawings of much of the Mills, she was demolished. They kept the original cast-iron balcony and window cornices, and purchased chantiques for the public rooms. It was rebuilt as a modern seven-story hotel, and the front entry and reception rooms copy exactly Mr. Mills' grand design of 1853.

I-10, Modern

I-11

St. Philip's Episcopal Church, on Church St., glass plate. (N. A.)

Every building and fence in this photo has survived, save the one on the corner right of center. St. Philip's lost 36 members in Confederate service. Recent repairs to this 1838 church found some rafters above the plaster ceiling had been grazed by Federal shells but needed no modern reinforcement.

In autumn 1863, the rector, Rev. W. B. Howe, endeared himself to the community. While preaching one Sunday in his pulpit, a shell was heard to fall and explode in the western churchyard. The congregation sat until his sermon concluded in the regular manner. The next services were moved to the Church of St. Paul's [out of range, where they shared services with the] other refugee (episcopal) congregations...of St. Michael's and Grace Episcopal.[16]

Ten shells passed through St. Philip's. Its chancel was wrecked and its organ demolished.[17] Nearly all church bells in the city were given to the Confederacy—bell metal makes very good gun metal. St. Philip's bells were not replaced until 1976. Interior beams were shattered by plunging shells, but were reinforced. Those massive oak beams still support the plaster ceilings today.

To the right are the twin pinnacles of the 1845 Huguenot Church. A wartime story survives:

An elderly member wished to be buried in his feather bed. In time bed and all were entombed in the churchyard. During the War Between the States a shell burst it open and bed feathers went flying, and as they drifted to earth, spectators nearby referred to it as "huguenot snow."[18]

An Ohio regiment ransacked the area after the war, and two chandeliers and the communion silver disappeared. The 1847 Henry Erben tracker organ was taken down in pieces to the dock, to be shipped to the North. Some citizens prevailed upon some officers to give it back. Restored, today it is the oldest functioning church organ in the city. *Oceanus* tourists observed:

...The interior of the Church is sadly ruined. Two immense holes upon either side, just beneath the cornice, show where the destroyers entered. The chandeliers were struck and shivered, whole tiers of pews were torn up, and the walls frightfully scarred.... Happily, the marble tablets, with their inscriptions in French and English, have been spared. ...the tall trees still wave over mossy and

mouldering graves, ploughed by cannon shot, and slabs broken by the exploding shell.... A cow was browsing from the mounds of the graves.[19]

To the left is the lacy iron balcony of the 1855 Planter's Hotel. At that time it was one of the top four hotels in Charleston. To *Oceanus* tourists, it was,

...long since rendered uninhabitable. It was fairly riddled.... Mrs. Eliza Havens...teaches her little school. This woman...has lived in Charleston twenty years, and throughout the entire war, was a declared and unflinching unionist. She has three times been shelled out from her house...robbed of all her property—some $12,000—and reduced to actual beggary. We found her standing at the door of the Hotel, very meanly dressed.... She declares that the old flag has always been "her soul's delight," and that she often sang "The Star Spangled Banner" in the streets of Charleston.... A purse of $34 was raised for her-sufficient for present exigencies.[20]

Much of the old Planter's Hotel was saved in 1936 as a WPA project and renovated into the Dock Street Theater. An auditorium was built in the courtyard of the derelict hotel. Preserved was the original recessed porch with its brownstone columns. The theater entry uses the handsome old hotel lobby with its grand staircase rising to the reception room.

Occasionally, I have found buildings that still show interior evidence of the shelling. Federal shells approached Charleston from the southeast, so most of the penetrations are in the southeast slopes, or south or east walls. The most remarkable example can be barely seen past the corner of the Planter's Hotel, on Queen and Church Street. It is a two-story frame house, presently 137 Church Street. It was nearly gutted during renovations in the late 1980s. I climbed to the attic and saw an 8" round shell hole on one of the roofing boards on the east slope. The metal roof had been patched soon after the war, but the hole in the board looked as fresh as if the 100-lb shell had crashed through just the week before. I saw where this shell penetrated the attic floor boards and shattered a joist below. A reinforcing board was still scabbed to the damaged joist. The shell exploded in the second floor; the plaster [fortunately not the original plaster] had been removed, exposing the woodwork. I could go down the first floor and see the exposed second floor joists and floor boards. When the shell burst, fragments tore up some second floor boards. The underside of those replaced floor boards were easily seen.

I-11. St. Philip's Episcopal church.

I-14

Charleston, S. C. 1865. Grave of John C. Calhoun in front of St. Philip's church, glass plate, also published by Anthony as stereo. **(L. C.)**

I-14. Tomb of John C. Calhoun.

I-14, Modern

Much more revealing is this third stereo in locating Senator Calhoun's original gravesite. The camera looks to the east. Visible in the left background is St. Philip's south portico, and in front of the columns is the vault and monument to Anne and Benjamin Smith.

Lining up St. Philip's columns with the remaining pedestal to the Smith vault for the modern view, I verified that the senator had indeed been moved in 1884 back to his original gravesite, upon departure of the Federal occupation troops. A more remarkable discovery was a recently planted sapling, which is seen also in image I-12 and I-13. It survives today as a magnificent mature southern magnolia tree 7'10" in circumference.

I-15

Archibald McLeish's Vulcan Iron Works and other houses on Cumberland Street, Charleston, S. C. 1865, glass plate, April, 1865.

(L. C.)

Mr. McLeish's advertising sign is the most spectacular ironwork ever produced in Charleston. It boasts the work he could produce—a spoked iron wheel, anchor, plow, anvil, and projecting some 25 feet over Cumberland Street, a brass cannon. His business was brisk that spring. New prosperity from incoming Yankee greenbacks brought in a lot of deferred repair work. Awaiting his attention are wagons, a carriage,

I-15, Modern

Archibald McLeish's Vulcan Iron Works on Cumberland Street.

and on the right margin a large iron-hooped wood barrel. In the center are two large two-wheel carts that the Federals will use to remove captured Confederate heavy guns.

At the end of Cumberland can be seen part of the earthwork defending the Fraser's Wharf Blakely, seen in H-15. Next door to the Vulcan Iron Works is a three-story brick store with a faded sign "Wholesale Dry Goods." That spring it would be rented by a new firm, Wm. A. Bird & Co., dealers in whale oil.

Today a modern parking garage occupies Mr. McLeish's site. Bird lost his top two floors in the 1886 earthquake but rebuilt with almost the exact architecture. Had I not seen a post-earthquake photo, I would have remarked how well the prewar building has survived. It is now a popular restaurant site. Wm. A. Bird & Co. has moved to Morrison Drive, where they still have a thriving paint business.[22]

I-16

The old Market House, junction of Market and Meeting St., Charleston, S. C., left half of stereo, Anthony #3118, April 21-23, 1865.
(L. C.)

Finished in 1841, Market Hall was built to resemble a stone structure, but it is mostly brick covered with stucco, rusticated and scored to resemble stone. The stucco finish was painted to resemble stone, the false "joints" highlighted in white paint.

In the early colonial period, this was a creek to the Cooper River. Farmers beached their small boats along the banks to sell meat and produce to townsfolk. It was filled in after the Revolution. The Pinckney family gave the property to the city to "vend all sorts of butcher meats, poultry, game, fish, vegetables and provisions."[23] Eventually sheds were built from Meeting to the shore: the first for meats, next for "small meats," two for vegetables, and the last for fish. Slaves were never sold here.

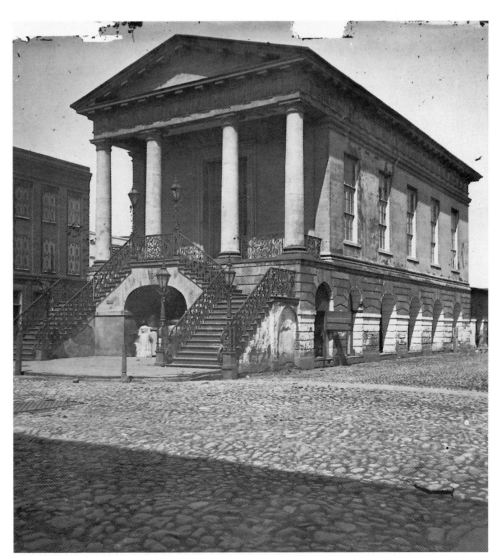

I-16. The old Market House.

I-16, Modern

The upstairs had offices for the Market, and a Hall rented out for meetings, dinners, and balls, with three splendid chandeliers. In 1861 the Palmetto Guard was honored here with a farewell reception on its way to the Confederate army in Virginia, where it fought at 1st Manassas as part of 2nd S.C. Regiment, Kershaw's Brigade. Its blue silk company flag was retired after that battle when Beauregard had all company flags replaced with a single regimental flag.

Palmetto Guard veterans returned here annually to toast their fallen comrades. The last two veterans met in 1917.[24] The silk flag was on continuous display here in the Confederate Museum until 1989 when Hurricane Hugo damaged the building. It is hoped that after the city finally repairs Market Hall, the Daughters of the Confederacy will be allowed to reestablish their extensive collection here.

Shadow dating suggests that this image was taken approximately 3:18 p.m. (± 2 minutes), April 21 to 23, 1865.

I-17

Old Market House, cor Meeting and Market St., Charleston, S. C., stereo from a "Negative by M. B. Brady, New-York," published by Anthony #3428, May 1, 1865. (L. C.)

Shadow dating of images I-16 and I-17 was accomplished by observing first the afternoon shadow creeping up the west wall under the portico to determine the time of day (3:40 p.m. ±1 minute). Then watching the shadow creeping down the south wall each day to determine the correct day (May 1, 1865 ±1 day). It was fortunate that both cameramen shot on sunny days with sharp shadows, and that the sun produced long shadows under the original portico and from the edge of the south roof. Image match-ups were helped by survival of original 1841 false "stone-block" lines inscribed in still-wet stucco, and the lines were highlighted with white lines to indicate false "cement" between the "stone-blocks." The paint has been touched up over the years but as of 1998 the original stucco under the portico survives.

From 1889 to 1989 Charleston Chapter 4 of the United Daughters of the Confederacy maintained here the finest collection of Confederate relics south of Richmond and east of Atlanta. They have the first Confederate flag that flew over Fort Sumter (Stars and Bars), the last (a 2nd National), eleven Confederate coats, and some relics of Gus and his younger brother Ellison. This city-owned building had roof damage from 1989 Hurricane Hugo. The city gave the Daughters two days to move out. Temporary quarters were found at 34 Pitt St., with promises that the Daughters could return after repairs. The Market House was neglected, and is the last public building to start repairs from that hurricane. Not until 1998 did serious repairs commence.

I-18

Interior of Market, carte-de-visite, Osborn's Gallery, Charleston, S. C. (Beaufort)

James Read wrote of this view in his carte-de-visite album of the beef market, under Market Hall: "Interior of Market house. The market is only open from [blank] a.m. and from [blank] p.m. Nothing is allowed in the building at any other time, which accounts for the appearance of the picture." Passengers of *Oceanus* observed on those same days, April 14 or 15:

> The long Market extending from Meeting street to the harbor gives evidence, at the upper end, of the revival of business. The stalls are rented by negroes and Germans for $1 per week, where they carry on the meat business in a small way, and making a bare livelihood. Very little money is in circulation yet. Confederate notes were bought by the bushel at a nominal price, and carried away as curiosities by our steamer's company.

I-17. Another view of the old Market House.

I-17, Modern

We found the price-list lower than in New York, though it must be confessed that the quality of the meat was also decidedly lower.

Sirloin steak sold for 25 cents a pound; Mutton from 20 to 25 cents; Veal, 25 cents; Butter, 65 cents; Lard, 30 cents; Cheese, 25 cents.

"In Federal money, we presume," we said.

"Certainly," replied the ebony salesman.

"But how much in Confederate currency?"

"Oh, sar, we better *gib* it to you, sar!"

Potatoes and green peas were abundant, and we were told that strawberries would be in market in a few days. Behind some of the stalls were well-dressed and handsome mulatto girls, having bouquets of choice flowers for sale. Advancing toward the river, the market became more and more deserted, and the stalls entirely empty.

I-18. The interior of the market.

I-18, Modern

Hanging overhead are masses of something that Karen Prewitt identifies as Spanish moss. One could reach up and pull it down to wrap purchases. Today, black flower vendors in front of St. Michael's Church still bind the stems of daffodils they have sold with this moss.

I-19

Charleston Hotel, Charleston, S. C., glass plate.   (L. C.)

One of the most notable hotels in the United States when built in 1839 at the corner of Meeting and Hayne Streets. During the 1860 Democratic National Convention it housed the radical secessionist delegates. In 1861 it was the favorite place for speeches, assemblies, and presentation of South Carolina and Confederate flags to regiments and militia companies.

On the Hayne Street wall is one of the new Fire Telegraph boxes. This newly invented electrical system was finished just before the war; much was expected of it, to quickly direct and concentrate the Volunteer Fire Companies to any fire. When the December fire broke out at the east end of Hasell Street by the waterfront, however, none of the fire boxes had been installed in that area. When this photograph was taken in 1865, wires to this box had been removed, possibly for reuse in Confederate Signal Corp telegraph lines, or to detonate mines.

The right-hand building shows where a falling Federal shell had plunged through a roof and two floors before blowing out its Meeting Street wall. Along the left sidewalk is a ladder wagon belonging to one of the Vol-

I-19. Charleston Hotel.

unteer Fire Companies—a heavy duty dray wagon with massive axles.[25] The Federal-controlled Charleston *Courier* reported on April 14, 1865:

Scenes At The Charleston Hotel
Official correspondence announcing the glorious news of the surrender of Lee's Army, was read to a dense crowd assembled at the Charleston Hotel and received with wild shouts & enthusiasm. The splendid bands of the 127th New York Volunteers and the 14th Maine were in attendance....

The drawing rooms and private parlors of the Hotel were thrown open by the generous host, Stetson, and refreshments liberally furnished.

Oceanus visitors of April 1865, reported:

...The "Charleston Hotel" was the only one open at that time, and was kept by Mr. J. P. Stetson, brother of the present proprietor of the Astor House, New York. It was crowded during our sojourn to overflowing, and its tables were said to be inviting.[26]

...Passing down Hayne street, we came to..."The Invalid's Commissary." Standing, sitting and lying around the entrances, were hundreds of poor freed-men and women, in every state of raggedness, waiting their turn to be served. Elbowing our way through...we entered the immense stores of Mr. George W. Williams...one of the aldermen of the city and chairman of the Subsistence

I-19, Modern

Committee,...[He] has devoted his whole time for the past two years to distributing food to the poor.

The [departing] Confederate authorities turned over to him all the [cotton and] stores owned by them, to distributed...to the poor of Charleston.

Since the occupation...three million pounds of...rice, grist, meal and salt, have been issued. ...Tickets are issued to needy families, two-thirds being colored.... Many millionaires...are reduced by the war, to want, penury and beggary.... The [chief] cashier of the Bank of Charleston, comes every day to his store, to get his peck of rice or meal.

...These supplies will soon be exhausted, and then what will become of this helpless and suffering people?[27]

W. E. James published a close-up carte of this hotel, not reproduced here as it shows little of the surroundings. Also not used is another Library of Congress plate, taken a few days later, which is darker, and does not show the shelled building.

I-20

Leonard Chapin, carriage dealer, detail of image I-19.

Around 1839 William Gayer built this brick building with a handsome Italianate facade. Located on "The Bend of Meeting," it could be seen for blocks away. Here his carriage works thrived until his death around 1858. The 1860 *City Directory* listed this building in Gayer's estate, with his widow living at "N. E. cor. Pitt & Wentworth."[28] In 1860, and for years after the war, Leonard Chapin, carriage dealer, operated his "Carriage Repository" from this landmark at Meeting at the Bend.[29]

Early this century when it was owned by a tire company, the front forty feet were removed for a driveway. In 1986, I learned that its new owner, Frank Brumley, wanted to rehabilitate the building into a bank. His architect, Chris Schmidt, suggested that they restore the facade to its former glory. Chris found a photograph of that corner building dated 1902, and

I-20. Leonard Chapin, carriage dealer.

I-20, Modern

planned to base the new bank building facade on that 1902 photo. No 19th century photo of Mr. Chapin's Carriage Repository (for that is what it was called in 1865) survives, but I examined the incredible detail of image I-19 (Charleston Hotel) and my friend Jim Nicholson enlarged the lower left corner. I offered the architects an 1865 view, showing it very much as it was when Mr. Gayer had it built. The architects were pleased, the owner was pleased, and I was gratified. They used much of its information for their reconstruction. The finished building, leased to the Bank of South Carolina, received several design awards for this reconstruction effort.

I-21

Lecture Room, Methodist Episcopal Church, right half of stereo, William E. James, April 14, 1865. **(Author's collection)**

This is the third of three stereo cards purchased at an antique photo show in Washington in 1987, along with B-16 and H-6, plus a view on the same card stock of the April 1865 re-raising of the U.S. flag over Ft. Sumter. They had no maker's marks or printed captions to identify the town, but all were marked in pencil to an "Ed. C."

B-16 was easily recognizable as Charleston's Circular Congregational Church, but H-6 took a good deal of investigation to place the site. On the reverse of this image, in pencil, is only:

Ed. C.
Charleston, S. C.
April 14, 1865

"Ed. C." is probably Edward Carey, co-author of *Trip of the Steamer Oceanus* and the only member of the Sumter Club that chartered the ship with those initials.

James' penciled note is helpful to identify this as a Charleston view, but is hardly conclusive, as I have seen many images misidentified even with printed captions.

Presence of a piazza told me this must, however, be a Charleston view. A piazza is a side porch, almost unique to this city. During the Charleston summers, which can be quite warm, they shade the house from the afternoon sun. Residents practically lived on their piazzas in the summer, taking meals there, reading, hosting visitors, and chatting with passersby. On hot nights they brought bed and mosquito bar onto the top piazza. The piazza was a standard Charleston architectural feature for 200 years, until the invention of air conditioning.

But where in Charleston is it? The location of the piazza is the clue. Piazzas usually face to the south or west, to shade the house from the summer afternoon sun. Therefore the view is likely to the north or east.

There is a four-column building in the center, probably a church, so I searched Frederick Ford's 1861 *Census of the City of Charleston*, by Evans & Cogswell. At 35 Wentworth Street, on the south side, was the "Lecture Room, Methodist Episcopal Church." This is presently St. Andrews Lutheran Church, and has been renumbered 43 Wentworth. The white brick house with the west piazza was 33 Wentworth, occupied by Gustavis Follin. A shell has blown out the whole gable end of this residence. Next to Mr. Follin's home is an outbuilding of Chapin's Carriage Repository. Across the street is the almost illegible sign of:

C. D. Franke   34
COACHMAKER

Franke manufactured heavy artillery carriages for the Confederate army, and remained in business into the 1950s at South Market and Church Streets.

While this is a full mile distant from White Point Garden, it is still within effective range of Yankee shells. On the left one of their projectiles has crashed through the flat roof and exploded in the top floor, blowing out the west wall. This is consistent with the fuzed Federal shells: an impact-fuze detonates the charge when the shell hits something, but the explosion

I-21. Lecture room, Methodist Episcopal Church.

is usually delayed until the falling shell has penetrated into the floor below. Brickbats still litter the sidewalk and cobblestone street, though this view was taken almost two months after the evacuation.

I-21, Modern

I-22

King Street, at The Bend, stereo, early March, 1865.   **(Author's collection)**

This fashionable shopping street for Charlestonians follows a prehistoric Indian path up the peninsula. Paved with cobblestones, with blue stone crosswalks, it held the city's finest retail shops.

This is likely the earliest "post-war" image of Charleston. Confederate troops evacuated the city on the evening of Feb. 17, 1865, and Federal troops from Morris Island occupied the city the next morning. A Northern photographer may have exposed his glass plate to this scene only two weeks later. It has been a challenge to date this image, as I have never seen it with a caption to be able to date it as prewar by a local artist, or as postwar by a Northern artist. Horse car tracks were not laid down on King Street until well after the war.

The view is to the north. Though the clock reads 10:35, shadow-dating places the exposure as very early in March, within five minutes of 11:55 a.m. I determined the

I-22. King Street.

I-22, Modern

time from shadows cast completely over the west side-walk, and shadows on top of the N. E. corner building. Its top shadows cast from the cornice under the parapet of the west wall shades down almost to the top of the third floor window cornice. An October date could be considered, but winter has not set in, for Charleston, that early.

More likely this is March, for it looks wintry. Trees are bare and everyone wears a coat. This area was in "Annoying Range" of Federal shells only a couple weeks earlier. Few pedestrians and fewer wagons indicate people are just starting to return to this recently-empty area. Traffic will be heavier in fall 1865 or March 1866. I determined the year to be 1865, by learning when the King Street merchants, here at "The Bend" were in business.

Advertising signs for only three of these businesses are readable. Siegling's Music House was on King at Beaufain from 1840 until the early 1970s, advertising themselves in later years as "America's oldest music

Enlarged detail of I-22 showing Quinby's sign.

house." That feat is the hope of every ambitious business-man, but Siegling's continuity does not help to date the image.

The second readable sign is William G. Whilden & Co., located on the west corner. The 1859 *Charleston Directory* lists him as a partner in Hayden & Whilden. This firm was successor to Charleston's most famous pre-war silversmith firm, Hayden, Gregg and Company. The 1860 *Directory* names them as Hayden & Whilden, 250 King, at the Drum Clock, corner of Hasell, and dealing in watches, clocks, jewelry, silver ware, military & fancy goods. They also sold fire insurance. Their partnership dissolved June 1, 1863, with Whilden in the Confederate Army. A. H. Hayden remained at the corner of King and Hasell. The 1866 *Directory* proclaims:

> Whilden, W. G. & Co., bankers and dealers in China, glass, and earthenware

A third sign is visible above Mr. Whilden's vertical corner sign:

> QUINBY & Co.
> ARTISTS

Charles J. Quinby, photographer, is first listed in the 1860 directory at "233 King (up stairs)." In 1861 he moved to 261 King, remaining there through 1867. He quickly became an important Charleston photographer, second only to George S. Cook, who was his business neighbor. Quinby's sign decorated King Street, but the caped coachman has stopped his carriage in front of Cook's carriage block. It is doubtful either artist was back at work so soon after the evacuation. Cook's family records indicate he did not return to Charleston until May 1865. I have not discovered when Quinby reopened his gallery, but he began a segar and tobacco store at his old location just days after the occupation began. Below Cook's gallery was J. R. Read's dry-goods store.

With Mr. Whilden open for business at the northwest corner of King and Beaufain, and a non-functioning drum clock at Hayden's presumably still-closed jewelry and silver shop on the northeast corner of King and Hasell, this view was probably produced very early in March 1865. Business is dull. Few wagons, people, and open shutters are visible.

The great-coated coachman, a bare-limbed tree, rolled-up awnings, and long shadows at midday all support a late winter day of early March.[30]

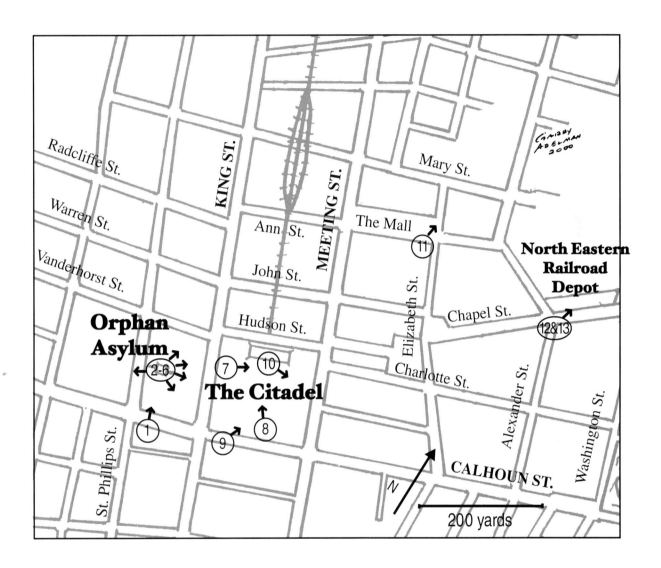

J-1

The Orphan Asylum. Charleston, S. C., glass plate. **(L. C.)**

In 1790 Charleston created the first municipal orphan asylum in America. It was enlarged and remodeled as a six story steam-heated structure in 1855. The largest building in Charleston, pride of the city, it was crowned with a 14-foot statue, *Charity*. A 1769 marble statue of William Pitt, who helped repeal the Stamp Act, graced the

yard. Children in the orphanage were schooled, and indentured to tradesmen or farmers. During the war they produced much of their own food and clothing, but eventually all 360 children plus the staff were evacuated to Orangeburg for safety.

City offices and the police department moved here from Broad Street to avoid the shells, but that hope faded when Federal artillery increased their range to beyond Calhoun Street. Gus wrote on September 2, 1864:

The Yankees are shelling continuously with fuze shell. Tuesday one went...in the Orphan

J-1. The Orphan Asylum.

House yard. There was great excitement up town, women running about with their babies, etc., & one colored woman killed.... They are much more dangerous than the other shells, as they burst in the air, & the fragments scattering all about, produce quite a wide scatteration among any crowd of people near by. The pavements all about the city are marked with the spots where they have fallen. Strange, that I have heard of no accidents & yet every shell must break into 10 or 12 pieces. It is miraculous.

When *Oceanus* visited in mid-April 1865, after the evacuation, their passengers noted, "...that the "Citadel" itself, together with the famous Orphan Asylum, is now used as a barrack for colored troops, who flock into our army at the rate of about one hundred per day.[1]"

The orphans returned after the war and remained until the whole complex was demolished in 1951 for a Sears, Roebuck store and parking lot. Sears moved out 30 years later. Today, the Orphan House bell is in North Charleston at Oak Grove, the institution's modern equivalent. Mr. Pitt's statue (minus one arm blown off by a British cannon ball and the other lost in the earthquake) and the remains of *Charity* reside in the Charleston Museum.

Northern photographers found the Orphan House a favorite subject. I have seen seven or more views taken of the Calhoun Street entrance or just inside its well-kept grounds. I chose this view for its clarity that shows Pitt's statue, *Charity*, atop the cupola, and the effects of a Federal shell that penetrated the portico. It blew out the south corner and damaged part of the pediment, shattering eight windows or more.

The following images reveal the imagination two or more photographers possessed, to climb to the cupola to record a panorama of Charleston's rooftops. This series records many parts of the city otherwise missed by cameras of the 1860s.

J-2

West part of city, toward Ashley River, north of Calhoun Street, albumin print, late March, 1865. (L. C.)

An operator, so far unidentified, climbed up to the Orphan House cupola one morning in late March to take J-2. On its western platform, looking west over the slate roof and three chimneys, toward the Ashley River, he

captured a rare view of Charleston's upper wards. Few mansions dot this part of the city, which was not filled and built until the 1820s. This area houses Charleston's middling sort, and many of its free persons of color.

The enlarged detail photo (J-2a) shows Duncan Street, which runs west only for one block from Coming to Pitt, perpendicular to the camera. Most buildings on that block survive. Just behind the houses on Pitt is Coming's Creek. It runs northeast from the Ashley River, and was filled in the 1880s. Another detail photo (J-2b) shows an industrial area on the Ashley River, and the single smokestack of a rice and lumber mill complex on Bennett's Mill Pond, which also served as the shipyard for a huge torpedo boat/ blockade runner seen in image E-4. Twin stacks of the West Point Rice Mill (E-5) lie just beyond.

Today, a large number of prewar homes and small stores survive in the middle ground. Detailed in J-2a is Duncan Street, seen perpendicular to the camera. It has survived almost in total. Most of Duncan was owned by free persons of color and/or occupied by them or slaves. Facing us, on the northwest corner of Duncan and Coming streets, is the steep shingle roof and one dormer of what was 99 and 101 Coming (now 107). This duplex was owned by John C. Wohlers, a grocer who lived across Duncan to the left. He rented them in 1861 to Martha Cochran, and Adeline Blaney. To their north, at 103, was then a vacant house owned by Beekman and Sophia McCall. It also survives.[2]

J-2. View from the cupola of the Orphan Asylum looking toward the Ashley River.

J-2a. Enlarged detail of the right half of J-2.

J-2a, Modern

J-2b. Enlarged detail of left half of J-2.

The 1987 view was taken from scaffolding while the new College of Charleston, St. Philip Street dormitory, was under construction. Fortunately the dormitory's north side lines up almost exactly with the Orphan House cupola, though not quite as high as its platform. It shows that a modern medical complex has taken over the west end of town and extended it over the Ashley River marshes. The medical complex has not been subject to strict historic zoning or height restrictions and Charleston's skyline suffers from it. On a positive note, today many more trees shade Charleston and its streets.

J-3

View from the Orphan House, north toward the Cooper River, albumen, March, 1865.   (L. C.)

The same photographer returned to the cupola in the afternoon to continue his series. From the east platform,

his camera captured a part of the city that boomed during the shelling. The Confederates were gone when this view was taken, and no more would the right-hand white building's flagpole fly a Confederate Stainless Banner. This was Aimar's Drug Store (1852-1978) on King Street at Vanderhorst. It also served as the 1st Georgia Hospital.

This section of town bustled. The busy King Street business and shopping district had compressed by half, into these upper wards. In early 1864 this area north of Calhoun was considered to be nearly out of range.

It was just one block from the busy freight sheds of the South Carolina Railroad. The three railroads were not connected. The Northeastern's station was only a quarter mile away to the east, but if anything was to connect between stations it had to be unloaded onto a freight wagon, driven to one of the other two stations, and reloaded into the competing road's boxcar. The Savannah Railroad stopped on the Ashley River's west bank, but in 1863 Confederates ran a connecting rail line across the "New Bridge," east on Spring Street, to connect with the SCRR and Northeastern rails.[3]

Army supply wagons rumbled through the streets with blockade-run army supplies from the Cooper River docks. Few trees graced streets in this part of town. On

J-3. View from the cupola of the Orphan Asylum looking toward the Cooper River.

J-3a. Enlarged detail of left portion of J-3.

J-3, Modern

summer afternoons, convalescent soldiers favored the west sidewalks to lounge in the shade. On the left of the enlarged detail photo (J-3a) is the Confederate Post Office on the southeast corner of King and Ann streets, moved here from Broad Street in August 1863 to escape Yankee gunnery.

The Post Office was busy but its neighborhood was becoming unsavory. Auctions were held at this corner. Even the bordellos along Beresford Street (today's Fulton Street) had relocated nearby.

One had to go in person to pick up or drop off mail, for there was no street delivery until after the war. A wartime story survives of a flustered lady of quality who had just returned from the Ann Street Post Office. The rudeness of idle men on the sidewalk had vexed her.

"O, dear me!" exclaimed Henrietta, throwing herself into the rocking chair, "I'll never go to the Post office again, to be looked out of countenance by all those men on the corner. It's so provoking. What can I do, Sarah Jane, to stop those awful men staring at me in the face?" "Do as I do," replied Sarah Jane, with a sly look—"show your ankle."[4]

Eventually Yankee guns increased their range. Gus wrote to his sister Susan Smyth on September 2:

My dear little Sister,

You see by the papers that the [Post] Office has been moved, & far enough this time, up to the corner of Ashley & Cannon Sts. The shells were falling too closely around the old stand, & the Officer could not bear the pressure.

The 1987 view of J-3, was also taken from the top of the dormitory, but several yards to the west of the 1865 vantage point, and a few yards lower. Along Vanderhorst Street in the foreground is Aimar's Drug Store (also the Georgia Hospital) and, two doors to the west, the two-story house of Attorney Charles Simonton. Both survive. When Gus Smythe was in the Washington Light Infantry early in the war, Simonton was his captain. In the background are the Cooper River bridges to Mount Pleasant.

J-4

View from the Orphan House, toward the Citadel and Cooper River, albumin print from a cracked glass plate, late March, 1865.

(L. C.)

Lighting indicates that the same photographer on the same afternoon, also from the east platform, moved his camera further to the east to capture the South Carolina Military Academy. Its west wing,[5] in the center, was demolished in 1886 for a new police station. King Street, running left to right, is visible behind the gate and board fence in the foreground. A new Federal gridiron flag flies from the pole inside the Citadel's quadrangle. The observatory, at the extreme right edge, housed a large telescope that disappeared

J-4. View from the cupola of the Orphan Asylum looking toward the Citadel.

J-4a. Enlarged detail of J-4.

during the war. This may have been the same strong tele-scope Gus used from St. Michael's steeple.

In the center of the enlarged detail (J-4a) is the old-est image of rice planter Joseph Manigault's distinctive Adamesque villa, boasting a two-story curved piazza on its west wall. Designed about 1803 by his brother Gabriel, the mansion was finished when this area was still out in the country. In 1852, carriage maker George Reynolds bought the house. In 1864, it was conveyed to John S. Riggs, president of the Charleston Street Railway, who died there in 1899.[6]

The 20th century's history of this building repre-sents the first successful community effort to save early Charleston architecture. It had become a tenement and was threatened with demolition. In 1920 it was bought by what is now the Preservation Society, founded by Susan Pringle Frost. Two years later, short of money to preserve the whole complex, they sold off the gar-den and gatehouse to Standard Oil for a gas station site. Starting in the 1930s, with the help of the city, the Garden Club, and more work from the Preservation Society, all of Mr. Manigault's mansion and its garden was eventually put under the successful management of the Charleston Museum.

J-5

Panoramic View of Charleston, S. C., from the top of Orphan Asylum, the Citadel forming the prominent object, left half of stereo, nega-tive made for Mathew Brady, late April or early May, 1865. (L. C.)

An operator in the employ of Mr. Brady ascended to the Orphan House east platform, as did the previous pho-tographers, but several weeks later. He used a wider angle lens than did the previous artist, and captured much more of the foreground. The Federal occupation had been go-ing on for over two months, but the near gardens show their owners still planted their own vegetables as a war-time economy.

Behind the Citadel is the tower of Second Presby-terian Church, Gus' father's ministry. Gus reported to his father, Rev. Thomas Smyth, when he was trying to concentrate while writing a letter on February 2, 1864 from atop St. Michael's tower: "Mr. Moffett's house,—another shell, one an hour—opposite our Church, has been struck; one went into John St. They fly all round town now, & I expect they will soon reach the upper

J-5. View from the cupola of the Orphan Asylum looking toward the Citadel.

J-5, Modern

portion of the old city. It is so queer to see all the business up there & all down town so dull."

> St. Michael' Steeple
> Oct. 14th, 1864

My dear Sarah Annie,

...Fields is wrong tho' about our church. I have not been able to get into it, but I saw Mr. [George] Cook this evening up here, & he told me about it. Only one shell has hit it, on the South side, near the East Corner. It entered, bursting as it did so, but doing very little damage inside. The wall tho', the South wall is very badly injured indeed, cracked up to the roof, & Mr. C. fears almost will tumble, that portion at least, above where the shell struck. A fragment of a shell also hit the roof, not hurting it much. This is all so far, & they are not shelling high up town now, as you see. Now all the high places have been hit.

In the 1987 view, Aimar's Drug Store is seen at the right of St. Matthew's German Lutheran Church, finished in 1872. To its right is the old Citadel's main building. The old Citadel complex was renovated 1996-7 into an Embassy Suites Hotel. Further to the right, and almost behind the Citadel is Second Presbyterian Church. Behind that church are the two bridges spanning the Cooper River. I had one hour to record these three modern views in 1987 before the dormitory's metal roof was installed.

J-6

Panoramic view of Charleston to the East, stereo, probably by a Brady operator, April-May, 1865, Brady-Handy Coll.   (L. C.)

I have never seen a contemporary print or stereo of this image, also taken atop the Orphan House tower. Afternoon shadows, leafy foreground trees, and the cameraman's vantage point atop the east platform indicate it was taken at the same day as image J-5 and by Mathew Brady's operator. In the foreground are Orphan House dormer rooftops. In the left middle ground are a woodpile at the edge of the Orphan's swept yard, and a dovecote attached to the neighbor's whitewashed brick outbuilding.

Just left of center is the three-story brick house with two chimneys and a stairwell window between the floors, of William Enston's corner store at King and Calhoun, now Jackson-Davenport Opticians. Calhoun runs west, to the center of the edge. King Street runs south, to the upper right. Much of King Street survives, despite being Charleston's main shopping street. While facades have been altered and interiors gutted in many instances, a remarkable number of early 19th century structures remain. Rooftops, rears, and upper floors of a great many King Street stores remain essentially intact.

Today, King Street is again a vibrant shopping district, drawing customers from the nearby College of Charleston and growing tourism. St. Philip's steeple is just visible at the extreme right.

A modern view is impossible. In place of the Orphan House and courtyard, is the huge 1960s Sears Roebuck building, now College of Charleston's Lightsey Conference Center, which runs to Calhoun Street's sidewalk. To its east is the twelve-story Francis Marion Hotel.

J-7

"The Citadel and the Southern Military Academy, Charleston, S. C. The remains of the concrete wall, built in the time of the Revolution in the foreground," stereo #3113, Anthony.

(L. C.)

The South Carolina Military Academy provided four generals and nineteen colonels to the Confederacy, and an education in this state college started a successful career for many sons of South Carolina.

J-6. Panoramic view of Charleston to the East.

On the evening of February 16, 1865, the Cadets evacuated their picket post on the lower end of James Island, near the Stono River. The next morning they reunited with the rest of the Cadet Battalion and the rest of Hardee's evacuated Charleston garrison. Their superintendent, Major Benjamin White, left a huge Confederate Second National Flag flying defiantly over the Citadel. When the Federal occupiers reached this part of town, Lt. Col. Bennett replaced that Rebel thing with a United States flag.

That Confederate banner was sent to Washington as a war souvenir and returned to South Carolina in 1905, despite yelps from Grand Army of the Republic members. It was held in the Confederate Relic Room, located in Co-

lumbia, until 1973 when it was returned to the Citadel. The 10' x 20' banner is on display in the Citadel museum entrance stairwell.

In the foreground are the remains of the Revolutionary War defenses across the Charleston peninsula. Victorious Federals decorated it in 1865 with a fence of thirty 650-lb. Blakely solid, cast-iron artillery shells brought from the batteries at Fraser's Wharf and White Point Garden. In 1883 they were replaced by an iron fence in an attempt to beautify the square. The Park Commissioners' books note a receipt of $50 that year, possibly representing the projectiles' scrap value.[7]

The steeple of Gus' church, the Second Presbyterian, is in the right rear. His father, Thomas Smyth, was pas-

J-7. The Citadel.

tor here from 1831 to 1873. Gus' younger brother Ellison Adger Smyth (1847-1942) was in the last fight in South Carolina. He was a cadet in the Arsenal, which was a preparatory school in Columbia. After one year of studies there, Arsenal Cadets transferred to the SCMA to continue their education.

On May 1, 1865, the Arsenal Cadets, in the field as Co. B, Battalion of State Cadets, were approaching Williamston, S. C. They paused for lunch by a farmhouse near Shiloh Church, on the White Plains Road. Their rear guard was attacked by Union horsemen, led by two Negroes armed with shotguns. Repeating Spencer carbines were met with the Cadets' Enfields, and the blue-coats faded away. Ellison recalled 60 years later, when he was a successful cotton mill industrialist in Anderson and Greenville:

J-7, Modern

> Only a few shots were exchanged. When the raiders retired but one man fell off his horse, and lay on the ground, and was picked up by a comrade and flung across the front of his saddle. We thought he was dead; but the whole affair lasted three or four minutes, though it seemed to us cadets a much longer time.[8]

This was the last recorded action east of the Mississippi River.[9]

J-8

The Citadel and Citadel Green, collodion print. (MOLLUS)

This parade ground used by the South Carolina Military Academy was really the property of the Charleston militia companies, and was used as a drill field for independent volunteer companies of artillery, cavalry, and infantry. These companies owned their own artillery and each man furnished his own horse.

The United States Army was small in the 1850s, and mainly in the West fighting Indians. Indeed, most citizens were suspicious of a large standing army controlled by a central government, and considered the expense unnecessary. State militias were made up of patriotic, able-bodied white males, who wore a handsome uniform unique to their company, voted for their own officers, marched in parades and welcomed dignitaries. For the cost of a uniform and time, and the opportunity to charm the ladies, men avoided taxes that would be spent on a standing army. The Lafayette Guards hosted General Lafayette when he visited in 1826, but their members had to be carefully coached in advance to be able to give commands in French.

Uniformed state units drilled once a month, and even the non-uniformed "beat" militia companies had to drill twice yearly. These units were social but guarded against the very real danger of foreign invasion and slave rebellion.

J-8. The Citadel and the Green.

J-8, Modern

Citadel Green, now called Marion Square,[10] is owned today by the two surviving militia units that predate the Civil War—the Washington Light Infantry, founded 1809, and the Sumter Guard, which dates from the War of 1812. Occupying U.S. Army and artillery units had a garrison here until 1879. The military college reopened in 1882 until it moved to a larger campus in 1922. The old buildings were then used as county offices until 1994. Recently these were renovated into a modern hotel and its outside walls survive as the Embassy Suites.

J-9

Baptist Church, Citadel Green, carte-de-visite, Osborn's Gallery, Wm. G. Read album.
(Beaufort)

Mr. Read had little to tell in his caption: "Baptist Church, on Meeting St. facing Citadel Green." The photographer, James Osborn, captured a fine view of the Citadel Square Church, taken from Calhoun Street. In the foreground is the handsome wooden fence and gate entry onto Citadel Green. While there are no useful shadows for dating, leafy trees indicate a summer view.

Baptists reached out to the upper wards of Charleston, where more of the working class and slaves lived. Finally fourteen Charlestonians built an awe-inspiring church to seat 1,000, and a 224-foot steeple that could be seen by ships at sea. A stained-glass rose window looked out over the Green. Citadel Cadets sat on one

balcony. Slave members of the congregation filled the balcony opposite, while white members sat in the middle pews.

Finished in 1856 at a cost of $72,000, the church still carried a debt of $20,000. Cornelius Burckmeyer retired that debt by promising personally to match donations dollar for dollar, and the debt was settled in one week. Deacon James Tupper, guiding light of the church, built a Sunday school for white and black children as part of the building. For some children this was the only schooling they received.

During the war the church carpet and pew cushions were given to the hospitals, the former for blankets and the latter for beds.[11]

In October 1864, the congregation moved. All Baptists moved uptown to escape the shelling, and Citadel Square was out of range until September when one Sunday just hours after the service, it was reported that, "the villains threw a shell into the Lecture Room of our Church, a fragment of which passed through the side of the

J-9. Baptist Church, Citidel Green.

J-9, Modern

room into the alcove behind the pulpit of the church and another shell exactly through the center of the steeple....[12]

Gus heard of this, and on September 28 he wrote:

...Citadel Green is a common resort. The Citadel Square Church was hit the other day, and very much damaged.... Every church below [the Second Presbyterian], except Zion Presbyterian—the large Colored Church on Calhoun, & Bethel have been hit...—Also that again to-day the Citadel Square Church was hit, & Zion very much damaged by one....

And on October 16, he wrote, "Did I tell you that a shell had gone thro' the Steeple of the Citadel Square Church, entirely thro' it, but only knocking out some bricks. Now all the high Steeples have been hit, & all the churches below ours." The combined congregations then moved north to safety to the old Third Baptist Church on Morris Street, until 1866.[13]

J-10

Citadel Square Baptist Church, carte-de-visite, William E. James, April 14 or 15, 1865. (Cal Packard)

Mr. James photographed the Citadel Square Church but thought it was Zion Church. He was producing pictures for the abolitionist *Oceanus* visitors, and he may have confused the Baptist church on Meeting Street for the equally huge Zion sanctuary, just one block away on Calhoun Street. He had noted in the Charleston *Courier*:

Mass Meeting

By request of Major General Saxton, the Colored People will assemble at Zion's Church on Saturday Morning April 15th at ten o'clock A.M., when the Hon. Henry Wilson, of Massachusetts, will address them.

Oceanus was due to sail Saturday at 10 o'clock, but "a universal desire to see more of the city, and attend the 'Freedmen's meeting,' at Zion's Church, secured a postponement of 5 o'clock p.m. The day was therefore at the disposal of the company." James had another whole day to make more views of the city, but in his haste to capture the Zion he caught the wrong church.

The Zion Presbyterian Church was finished in 1858 on Calhoun Street, just east of Meeting Street. Blacks constituted fully 2/3 of the congregation of over 1,500. Whites filled the balconies, with overflow into part of one side of the floor pews. In 1960 the sanctuary was demolished, and a Holiday Inn now fills the site. Zion's congregation moved and combined as Zion-Olivet on 134 Cannon Street.[14]

James set up his camera in front of the Citadel's sally port in 1865, recording Citadel Square Baptist. This view is presently blocked by huge shade trees along Meeting Street, so I moved to the left, nearly to Meeting Street, to obtain a modern view. The 224-foot steeple was blown down by a hurricane in 1885, and in 1886, an earthquake damaged the tower. Its shorter replacement was damaged in 1989 by Hurricane Hugo. The congregation has since restored the steeple to its original height of 224 feet.

It is unfortunate that James missed capturing the Zion's image that day. Two or three thousand people rejoiced at Citadel Green before they moved to Zion Presbyterian Church for more formal speeches. When one speaker, William Lloyd Garrison arrived, the crowd was

J-10. Citadel Square Baptist Church.

J-10, Modern

so excited that he was carried in on their shoulders to the speaker's stand. This was the same abolitionist Garrison, editor of *The Liberator*, who had been burned in effigy in Charleston thirty years before. Now he cried with happiness at the metamorphosis he witnessed.[15]

J-11

Ex-Governor William Aiken's home (48 Elizibeth St.), glass plate, Brady operator, May 1, 1865.

William Aiken, Jr. inherited this rental house from his father in 1831, and renovated it into a splendid mansion

for his new family. He was governor of South Carolina from 1844 to 1846 and for the rest of his life was addressed as "The Governor."

Gov. Aiken's fortune was largely as a rice planter. One plantation near Edisto Island called Jehosee, held 1,500 cultivated acres worked by some 700 slaves. He opposed secession but like most Carolinians, followed his state when it left the Union. He invested in Confederate bonds and donated food to the army.

President Jefferson Davis was his guest November 2-5, 1863. The *Mercury* reported:

> ...the President was escorted to the hospitable residence of Governor Aiken, where he will remain during his stay in our city. At about half-past 9 o'clock last night a number of citizens, accompanied by the band of the first South Carolina Artillery,...serenaded the President, who returned his thanks briefly, and taking occasion to express his hope that our beleaguered city would soon be

J-11. Ex-Governor William Aiken's house.

J-11, Modern

J-11, Modern detail

freed from its assailants, and peace be restored to our struggling country.[16]

The governor held a dinner for him. Mary Boykin Chesnut, who learned about the dinner from a Mr. Preston, reported Davis' reception:

> Governor Aiken's perfect old Carolina style of living delighted him. Those old gray haired darkies and their noiseless automatic service, the result of finished training—one does miss that sort of thing when away from home, where your own servants think for you; they know your ways and your wants; they save you from all responsibility even in matters of your own ease and well doing.[17]
>
> ...He left on Friday morning at 7.50. He was escorted to the Northeastern depot by Generals Beauregard, Gilmer, Jordan, Col. Alfred Rhett and his staff, and the Charleston Light Dragoons and Skinner's detachment of Dunnovant's regiment of cavalry. Great crowds cheered him at the depot and all along the line. He traveled in a new, handsome car, recently built at the Florence shops.[18]

Few shells invaded this district, so General Beauregard found the governor's residence comfortable and safe when he moved in after the Mills House closed in November 1863. While working here, he strengthened Charleston's defenses. He rebuilt Fort Sumter into a defensive stronghold and mounted three heavy guns in its right face. Those guns, in lower casemates that could not be reached by Federal artillery on Morris Island, controlled the harbor's mouth. His defenses, along with better British-built steamers, ushered a resurgence of Charleston as a major blockade-running port.

Beauregard also encouraged development of the *Hunley*, a submarine torpedo ram that blew off the stern of the blockader USS *Housatonic*. This was the first submarine to sink an enemy vessel, a feat not to be repeated until World War I. The general lived here until April 20, 1864, when he was transferred to active field service in Virginia and North Carolina.

Known today as the Aiken-Rhett House, it survived in the same family with much of its period wallpaper, fixtures, and contents until acquired by the Charleston Museum in 1975. There has been a concerted effort to preserve the house, its outbuildings and workyard intact and unrestored. Survival of the latter, in good original condition, is unique in Charleston. The Charleston Museum, and its present owner the Historic Charleston Foundation, have conserved the property rather than the all-too-common habit of renovation and loss of much of the original fabric of the house to an artificial standard.

This photograph is dated to May 1, 1865 by shadows cast below the front pediment, and timed to 12:37 pm (±5 minutes) by the near vertical shadow on the left corner of the house along the piazza's west parapet. When the deteriorated piazza was rebuilt in 1987 that west parapet, present in 1865, was not restored. The near-vertical shadow along the west end of the piazza still allowed accurate timing of the near noon sun.

A decorative iron fence enclosing Wragg Mall to the photo's left edge disappeared many years ago, but the brick coping and sidewalk survived until replaced around 1990 during an ill-advised total replacement of all brick in Wragg Mall.[19]

J-12

Ruins of the Wilmington Depot, glass plate, George Barnard, 1865.   (N. A.)

J-13

Ruins of the North Eastern R. R. Depot, where many lives were lost by explosion, Charleston, S. C., glass plate, also published by Anthony as stereo, 1865.   (L. C.)

An explosion here early in the morning of February 18, 1865, killed more than 150 people. A quantity of damaged gunpowder was stored at this depot at Chapel and Alexander streets, also known as the "Wilmington Depot," during the winter of 1865. After Sherman captured Savannah and cut the South Carolina Railroad at Branchville in early February, the North Eastern was the only rail route out of Charleston. On the night of the evacuation, fires were set to keep Confederate cotton and supplies out of the clutches of the hated Yankees.

Few firemen were left in town to control these blazes. Volunteer firemen who had been exempt from conscription, were now called into active duty. Their duty had been to fight fires first and only serve locally in the army. Now General Joseph Johnston needed all the forces he could mass to face Sherman. Charleston's 10,000-man garrison was sent, largely by the N. E. R. R., to Florence. These volunteer firemen were called out to go with them.

J-12. Ruins of the "Wilmington Depot."

After the last troop trains had pulled out of this station on their way to join Johnston and Beauregard, civil law started to crumble.

Fire companies run by free blacks remained, but there were more fires than they alone could control. They dragged their hand pumpers to several blazes and sucked water from cisterns to save a number of buildings. Looters began to grab what they could. Many streamed into the North Eastern Depot, which was now empty except for some citizens who were still hoping for one last train. George Barnard described the scene.

> ...The rebels had left behind in the depot a large quantity of powder in kegs and cartridges. A number of boys thought it fine sport to throw the cartridges among the burning bales of cotton in the immediate vicinity. The powder dropped along the way to the fires soon communicated to the powder in the depot, and a terrific explosion followed which left the depot in ruin and flames. Over a hundred and fifty are thought to have been burned to death, while about a hundred more were wounded by the explosion.[20]

This was the largest disaster of the evacuation, and in Charleston during the entire war. In eighteen months of shelling, Federal artillery had killed only about fifty soldiers and civilians.

Another stereo identical to J-13, but without any men in the foreground, was published by Soule. Its caption claimed "about 300 lives lost."

It is interesting to compare photographic techniques of the two cameramen. Barnard highlights the desolation

J-12, Modern

J-13. Ruins of the "Wilmington Depot."

with only two well-posed men in the foreground. The horizon is bare; through a forest of burned chimneys and arches, only one wrecked boxcar can be seen. The unidentified photographer of J-13 has several men posed indifferently in the foreground, one wearing a Confederate sack coat and another wearing a narrow-sleeved Federal cavalry shell jacket. A restaurant presently occupies the site, at 14 Chapel Street, between Drake and East Bay streets.

THE RACE COURSE & PRISON CAMP

K-1

Club House at the Race Course, left half of stereo #373, John P. Soule, March or April 1865. (Jeffrey Krause)

Organized in 1734 by prominent South Carolina planters, as the Carolina Jockey Club, they purchased in 1835 what became the Washington Race Course. The members spent lavishly to improve it and had Edward C. Jones, architect, design this lady's stand.[1]

Race Week was always in February. Crops were in, and ground had been prepared for the spring planting. Planters competed with each other in displays of wealth and refinement. Horses came from as far as Louisiana, Virginia, and Kentucky. Wealthy planters dominated the sport, but all classes, white and black, attended. The annual Jockey Club Ball, in 1817, was followed by an 11 p.m. dinner for 200. The Jockey Club Ball, and that of the St. Cecilia Society, were the social highlights of Race Week, as well as concerts and theatrical performances.

The last great race was in 1861, when Major Jack Cantey's thoroughbred mare Albine, trained from a losing streak by the Sinkler family slave Hercules, beat Planet in a four-mile heat at the track (seven minutes, 36 1/2 seconds). Hercules was as proud as Mr. Cantey, and asked the major to send for a hamper of champagne and he would pay for it. He wanted to treat the Major and the other gentlemen.[2]

In 1861 Washington Race Course was turned into a Confederate camp of instruction, and in 1864 it became a prison camp for Union soldiers. No barracks were provided for prisoners, and tentage was inadequate. Conditions have been compared to Andersonville. A former prisoner described it:

Although in itself a beautiful spot and surrounded by overhanging trees, which afforded a pleasant and delightful shade, the location of the prisoners was such in the center of the camp as to deprive them entirely of the luxury. The prison was without shelter, except such as might be con-

structed from garments and blankets.... The deadline was formed by the turning of a furrow...and at night scarcely indistinguishable by the prisoners. The usual terrible penalty for its invasion was not, however, omitted.[3]

The Sisters of Our Lady of Mercy visited daily here, too. Another prisoner, Sgt. Samuel M. Corthell, Co. K, 4th Mass. Cavalry, wrote:

They would let them come right in among the prisoners...and do all they could for us. But there were so many prisoners they could not attend to all. I have seen a Sister stand there with a loaf of bread in her hand and break it up almost into mouthfuls and divide it around so that all the hungry mouths she could get at could have some.

Another wrote:

Our dirt-begrimed, half-naked persons must have been revolting, yet no word or look from these kindly Sisters showed shrinking or disgust.... Their kindly address of "My poor child" fell pleasantly on the ear. No importunities could vex them.... I may have been prejudiced, at first, against these Sisters of Charity, but certainly their acts were truly Christian.[4]

The Sisters were nearly ruined from the War. Their orphanage had been moved twice, their convent damaged, their assets were near nil after the war. Seeking reparations from the Yankees, they lobbied Congress for $20,000 based on their help to Union prisoners in Charleston and the Shenandoah Valley. They eventually received $12,000—probably the only financial aid Washington ever gave to Confederate Charleston.[5]

An *Oceanus* passenger, Rev. J. L. Corning, correspondent to the *New York Sun* wrote when he visited Charleston in mid-April, 1865:

The old race-course,...was the great "prison-pen," where thousands of Union soldiers suffered.... On this accursed...spot, during a long and stormy winter, our brave captured boys lay hungry

K-1. Club House at the Race Course.

and shelterless. The ground for the space of five square acres is to-day covered with holes, into which the poor victims crawled like beasts of the forest, to hide themselves from the driving storms. Patches of earth, from six to eight feet square, are marked off, all over the dreary plain, by ditches dug around them, and upon these they lay through rainy days and nights, as the best protection that could be invented against the pouring floods.[6]

By 1865 the South Carolina Jockey Club was a shambles. Sherman's troops took thousands of horses, Albine among them. The club Madeira was hidden in the insane asylum in Columbia, but 714 bottles were sold twelve years later to pay off $3,000 of the Club's debts. The planter gentry was ruined and Race Week, as an event, never fully recovered. The club disbanded in 1900, turning over their assets of some $100,000 to the Charleston Library Society. Today the Jockey Club account interest still buys books for their library.[7]

The site of the race track is now Hampton Park. Mary Murray Boulevard follows the old Washington Course one mile oval. It is used daily by many Charlestonians as the most pleasant part of their commute to work.

K-2

Union graves near the Race Course Prison, glass plate. (L. C.)

More than sixty-five headboards are easily counted in this cemetery for Union prisoners. I have been unable to locate the site of the cemetery through examination of

K-2. Union graves near the Race Course prison.

the photograph. The area around the Race Course is now covered with suburbia of the 1890-1920s, and no wartime landmarks survive.

All recovered Union remains were reburied at Beaufort (S. C.) National Cemetery around 1868. It contains over 7,000 Union burials, but 4,018 of these remains are unidentified. No identified remains are specifically listed as recovered from the Charleston peninsula. They do have an old burial register listing 2,677 unknown remains recovered from 68 locations in coastal South Carolina and Georgia. Only one is on the Charleston peninsula—130 from Potter's Field. Apparently the headboards did not survive, were illegible, or recovery teams were careless with recording soldier's identities.

The site of Potter's Field, (the name is often used for cemeteries of the indigent) is now Johnson Hagood Stadium, named after a Confederate general and Citadel graduate. It stands less than 150 yards south of the old Washington Race Course. Confederates buried all their naval dead at Potter's Field, and it is logical that they buried the Union dead near there as well. Also, it was good for the Federals' spirits not to have a cemetery quickly filling up next to their prison.

Reverend Corning of the *Oceanus* described the Union soldiers' cemetery, indicating that the headboards either had no names, or the inscriptions were illegible:

...A plain board fence, on one side of this acaldema, encloses the burial-ground; and here, as they died, they were shoveled into the earth like dogs. Over two-hundred head-boards can be counted in the yard; but these only avail to keep up a semblance of decent respect for the name and memory of the departed. Identification is impossible....[8]

A friend of Rev. Corning was Rev. A. P. Putnam. Writing for the *Independent*, he described the Union cemetery, when he visited it at nightfall:

...three hundred in number, were borne a little distance to a rising ground, and were laid side by side in the earth, in several parallel rows,...the unknown graves of the martyrs, to the sacred cause of Union and Liberty. The wind sighed mournfully through the pine trees, that surrounded the little cemetery, which our own troops had recently enclosed by a neat fence, and I came away, feeling that it was one of the saddest scenes I had ever witnessed; and feeling too, how just had been the judgments of God, which had rained down destruction upon that rebellious and cruel city.[9]

Postscript

Emma Holmes survived the war's end in the Upcountry. She was teaching school ten miles from Camden, among the hills of the Wateree at Mrs. John B. Mickle's large farm. "Out of her eleven I am to have eight—six boys and two girls—at $100 a month and board."[1] When Sherman's army came through her area on February 24, 1865, they ransacked her house but took nothing from the one room where the ladies sat. However:

> Down on the plantation they burned the ginhouse & nearly 80 bales of cotton and...stole almost all the negroes' meat.... Two hundred bushels of corn, removed to a house far off, was burned.... The servants all acted admirably....[2]

> The likeness of Dora [Furman] & myself, taken by [George S.] Cook in days of "auld lang syne" & a memento of many happy hours, was found in the yard with the mark of a heel, where some Yankees had ground it under foot, crushing both ambrotype & outer glass of course into fragments—doubtless, with the Nero-like wish that Hydra headed secession might have been then & there crushed out. I have put it aside as a "relic of barbarity."[3]

Late in 1865, Emma returned to Charleston where she lived through Reconstruction, spending the rest of her life there, tutoring and teaching. She never married. Emma died in 1910 and is buried in St. Philip's churchyard. Her diary gives a rare, detailed glimpse of a well-bred and educated Charleston young lady.

Her diary, kept from 1861 to 1866, was edited by John F. Marszalek and published in 1979 by Louisiana State University Press.

Sergeant Augustine (Gus) Smythe evacuated with the army, fought at the battle of Bentonville, N.C., but later got separated from the 5th S. C. Cavalry with which he was serving—his 25th S. C. had been captured at Ft. Fisher, N. C. in February 1865. He was given up for dead. In May a very skinny Gus rode into his fiancee's yard in Columbia with two horses, and a pair of mules that he had exchanged for his watch.

He married Louisa R. McCord (his Miss Lou) on July 27, 1865, at Trinity Church, Columbia. She had to sell hens' eggs to earn enough money to buy a bolt of cloth so she could sew her own wedding dress.

The Smythes returned to No. 12 in the summer of 1865, to find their house, in spite of Augustine's care, and the presence of Robt. McNeil, in a very distressful state. During the occupation an Army surgeon had taken possession, stripped the house of all that was left, and sent it to the auction rooms, claiming that it had been abandoned. Adger and Augustine succeeded in buying some of it back. Everything else was gone.[4]

After trying to keep the McCord plantation going for two years, they returned to Charleston where Gus became a moderately successful lawyer and state senator. His fortune was made with his younger brother Ellison [Elly] in the development of the Pelzer Cotton Mills on the Saluda River.

Gus died in Charleston at age 72, respected and surrounded by relatives. His parents, brothers and sister, and his children are all buried in his father's Second Presbyterian churchyard. In the words of his granddaughter and saver of his letters, Susan Smythe Bennett, "He died June 1914 and never knew of the new war." Gus' letters have "rendered himself historic."

Gus, Louisa and their grandchildren in 1912.
(L to R) Louisa , Bryan Wright, Gus, John Bennett.

ENDNOTES

Introduction

1. Glen and Ryan & Gardner were no longer listed in the *1861 Directory*, but George Cook recorded selling chemicals and equipment to them in that year, in his Account Books.
2. *South Carolina Historical Society Magazine*, Volume 62, 27.
3. Augustine T. Smythe, Letters, collection of South Carolina Historical Society, 77 and 78. Hereafter cited as *Gus*.
4. Gus's descendant John Bennett said that Summerton Plantation was on Loring Mill Road, near Sumter, S. C.

Researching The Photographs

1. His most valuable study is Keith Davis' *George N. Barnard, Photographer of Sherman's Campaign* (Kansas City: Hallmark Cards, Inc., 1990).
2. Savannah *Daily Herald*, 4/15, 4/16, 5/12 & 6/13, 1865; Savannah Directories; and help from Georgia Historical Society. His obituary is in Savannah *Morning News*, 2/28/1911.
3. *American Journal of Photography*, May 15, 1865, 525.
4. *New York City Directory*, 1865-6.
5. Davis, 227.
6. "The Trip of the Streamer *Oceanus*," *The Union* (Steam Printing House, Brooklyn, NY, 1865), 31. Hereafter cited as *Oceanus*.
7. Conversation with Keith Davis.
8. The *Daguerreian Annual 1995*, 22, quoting Samuel C. Busey, *Early History of Daguerreotypy in the City of Washington, Records of the Columbia Historical Society*, 3 (1900) 81-95. Two letters from Seibert to Busey are reprinted on pages 92-95.
9. Gen. A. W. Greely, *List Of The Photographs And Photographic Negatives Relating To The War For The Union, now in the War Department Library* (Washington, 1897); Introduction, 10. A copy is in the National Archives Photo Division.
10. Greely, 18.
11. Washington Light Infantry Minute Books, in W. L. I. Archives, Charleston, S. C.
12. Fernslowe's *1867-8 Charleston City Directory*, 11 & 70.
13. *1872-3 Charleston City Directory*, 23 & 277.
14. *1855 Charleston City Directory*, 81.
15. *1859 Charleston City Directory*, 60 & 159.
16. George S. Cook account books in Library of Congress.
17. *1867-8 Charleston City Directory*, 11 & 12.
18. *1860 Charleston City Directory*, 116.
19. *The Private Mary Chesnut, The Unpublished Civil War Diaries*. C. Vann Woodward and Elizabeth Muhlenfeld, eds. (NY: Oxford Univ. Press, 1989), 38 & 39. Regretfully, her diaries seldom give the address where she stays.
20. Chesnut, 50.
21. Charleston *Daily Courier*, 2/23/65.
22. National Archives and Records Administration, "Union Provost Marshall's File of Papers Relating to Individuals & Citizens," File "Charles J. Quinby, M-345 (10-26-60)." Hereafter cited as NARA.
23. Charleston City Archives, Charleston Land Records, Vol. U-15, 51.
24. *Ibid.*, Vol. L-16, 99.

A. Pre-war Charleston

1. Mary Sparkman, *Through a Turnstile into Yesteryear* (Charleston: Walker, Evans & Cogswell, 1966), 1-3.
2. John F. Marszalek, ed., *The Diary of Miss Emma Holmes, 1861-1865* (Baton Rouge: Louisiana State University Press, 1979), 79.
3. Priestly M. Coker III, *Charleston's Maritime Heritage 1670-1865* (Charleston: CokerCraft Press, 1987), 256-62.
4. One more signed later, on December 28: Artemas T. Darby, winner of a contested election in St. Mathews. Charles H. Lesser, *Relic of the Lost Cause—The Story of S. C.'s Ordnance of Secession* (Columbia: State Department of Archives & History, 1990).
5. Davis, 186-187. Davis, in this monumental work on Barnard, has worked out the succession of property owners through Charleston tax and property records.
6. Thanks to Juanita Leisch and Les Jensen for comments on clothing for images A-9 and A-10.
7. Robert Stockton to the author, 5/3/98.
8. George Gilbert, *Photography—The Early Years* (New York: Harper & Rowe, 1980) 132-6.
9. Gilbert, 75-77.
10. Thanks again to Les Jensen for clothing details.
11. *1861 Census of Charleston*.
12. Carriage type identified by Dan Hydrick.
13. *1860 Charleston City Directory*, 20.
14. Jeff Lea identified this type of saddle for me.
15. Information from Dan Hydrick.
16. *1861 Census of Charleston*, 147.
17. *1860 Charleston City Directory*, 46.

B. Aftermath Of The 1861 Fire

1. Holmes, 107. These are entries in Miss Emma's diary when she caught up with her entries on December 16.
2. *Ibid.*, 107.
3. *Ibid.*, 106.
4. *Ibid.*, 107.
5. Davis, 90, image #97.
6. Identities and locations of historic buildings were from the *1861 Census* and the *1859 Charleston City Tax Record*.
7. Jonathan H. Poston, *The Buildings of Charleston: A Guide to the City's Architecture* (Columbia: University of South Carolina Press, 1997), 403. Hereafter cited as "Buildings."
8. For this image, the *1859 Charleston City Tax Records*, *1860 Charleston City Directory*, the *1861 Census*, and the 1871 City tax book were used, as well as conversations with the late Mr. Birlant.
9. Holmes, 108.
10. *1861 Census*, 61.
11. Holmes, 107.
12. Thanks to Faye Halfacre, Secretary of the Circular Congregational Church.
13. South Carolina Historical Society image #39-6-3.
14. Holmes, 111-112. Robert Stockton says the Circular actually had Corinthian columns.
15. St. John's Lutheran Church records.
16. Sister M. Anne Francis Campbell, O. L. M. "Bishop England's Sisterhood, 1829-1929, the First Hundred Years," 99. Ph.D dissertation, St. Louis University, St. Louis, Mo. 1969.
17. *Ibid.*, 100; *Charleston Catholic Miscellany*, 12/14/1861, 4.
18. Joseph Ioor Waring, M.D., *In Roper Hospital—A Brief History* (Charleston: Nelson's Southern Printing Co., n.d.) copy in Charleston Library Society.

cent revenue stamp (Bank Check, in orange, Scott Catalogue R-6, pencil-canceled), indicating this stereo image was sold before August 1, 1866, when the war-time revenue tax on photographs was discontinued. Jeffrey Krause, Gardiner, N. Y., has an identical stereo with the same information in manuscript, but no revenue tax stamp. The 2-cent stamp taxed photographs selling for less than 25 cents, 3-cents for those selling for 26-50 cents, and 5 cents on those selling for 50 cents to one dollar. This information is from Wm. C. Darrah *Cartes de Visite in Nineteenth Century Photography*, (1981) 87.

23. Rogers, *Charleston In The Age Of The Pinckneys.*
24. Jonathan Poston, *The Buildings of Charleston* (Columbia: USC Press, 1997) 395-6.
25. Wagon type identified by Dan Hydrick.
26. *Oceanus*, 124.
27. *Ibid.*, 124-7.
28. *1861 Charleston City Directory*, 51 & 69; Also *1875-75 Charleston City Directory*, 86.
29. *1860 Charleston City Directory*, 19. Chapin's listed in the "Omissions" page, and for the first time in a Charleston directory as: "Chapin, Leonard, carriage manufacturer, 142 Meeting St."
30. Information on this image from the City directories at SCHS, Charleston, S. C.; personal conversations with Milby Burton, Director of Charleston Museum, and with Robert Stockton, and Hayden & Gregg, a Charleston Museum pamphlet.

J. Orphan House & Area

1. *Oceanus*, pg. 120
2. Randolph F. Martz, architect & historian, who has lived at 107 Coming since 1971.
3. Sparkman, 7. It was called the "New Bridge" when it was built in 1854. Later bridges, including the present 1926 World War I Memorial bridge, were until mid-century called "The New Bridge."
4. Charleston *Daily Courier*, March 30, 1864.
5. Conversation with Robert Stockton: The near wing of the SCMA later became the City Guard House; it was the police station from 1887 to 1905.
6. Anne Fox, curator of Manigault House.
7. C. R. Horres, Jr., "Charleston's Civil War 'Monster Guns,' The Blakely Rifles," (*South Carolina Historical Magazine*, Vol. 97, No. 2, April 1996, 124-138.
8. Adger-Smyth-Flynn Family mss. South Caroliniana Library, Columbia, S. C.

9. Gary R. Baker, *Cadets in Gray* (Columbia: Palmetto Bookworks, 1989) 180-183.
10. Sparkman, 9.
11 Burckmeyer Letters 2/26/64
12. *Ibid.*, 9/14/64
13. Conversations with Peter Wilkerson, Historian of Citadel Square Baptist Church.
14. Lois Averetta Simms, *History of Zion, Olivet, and Zion-Olivet Churches, 1850-1985.*
15. Bernard E. Powers, Jr., *Free Blacks in Antebellum and Civil War Charleston* (Fayetteville: Univ. of Arkansas Press, 1994), 70-71.
16. Nov. 3, 1864.
17. C. Vann Woodward, ed., *Mary Chesnut's Civil War*, (New Haven: Yale Univ. Press) 488.
18. *Mercury*, Nov. 12, 1863.
19. Renee Marshall of Historic Charleston Foundation gave needed details about the Aiken-Rhett house.
20. George Barnard, *Photographic Views of Sherman's Campaign* (N. Y.: Wynkoop & Hallenbeck) 29 & 30. Reprint. (Dover Press: 1977).

K. The Race Course & Prison Camp

1. Stockton to the author 1/18/00, Edward C. Tones designed the ladies stand in the 1850s.
2. Prof. Randy J. Sparks, "Gentlemen's Sport: Horse Racing in Antebellum Charleston," *South Carolina Historical Magazine*, 93 (1992), 15-30.
3. Campbell, 132.
4. U.S. Congress, House of Representatives, "The treatment of Prisoners of War by the Rebel Authorities during the War of Rebellion," (40th Congress, 3rd Session, Report 45, Serial #1391, 1869) 195-6.
5. Campbell.
6. *Oceanus*, 130-131.
7. Sparks, 29 & 30.
8. *Oceanus*, 131-2.
9. *Ibid.*, 133-4.

Postscript

1. Holmes, 388 & 390.
2. Holmes, 400-401.
3. *Ibid.*, 404.
4. Mrs. Bennett's notes in Gus Smythe's files in SCHS, 207.

Bibliography

Books

Boatner, Mark M., III. *The Civil War Dictionary*. New York: David McKay Co., 1959

Burton, E. Milby. *Siege of Charleston*. Columbia: University of South Carolina Press, 1970

Campbell, Sister M. Anne Francis, O L. M. *Bishop England's Sisterhood, 1829-1929, The First Hundred Years*. Her Ph.D Dissertation, St. Louis university, St. Louis, 1969.

Coker, Priestly C., III *Charleston's Maritime Heritage 1670-1865*. Charleston: CokerCraft Press, 1987

Davis, Keith. *George N. Barnard- Photographer of Sherman's Campaign*. Kansas City: Hallmark Cards, 1970

Davis, Wm. C, ed. *Images of The War*. (10 Volumes), by National Historical Society. Doubleday, 1981.

Davis, Wm. C. and Wm. Frassanito. *Touched By Fire. "A Project of the National Historical Society"*. 2 vols. Boston: Little, Brown, & Co., 1985.

Davis, William C., ed. *Images of War: 1861-1865* (Ten Volumes), by National Historical Society, Garden City, N.Y.: Doubleday, 1981

Darrah, William C. *Cartes de Visite*. Gettysburg: W. C. Darrah, 1981.

Daguerreian Annual- 1995

Finckel, Kenneth, and Susan Oyama. *Philadelphia, Then And Now*. Published in cooperation with the Library Company of Philadelphia, New York: Dover Publications, Inc., 1988.

Frassanito, William. *Antietam: The Photographic Legacy of America's Bloodiest Day*. New York: Scribner, 1978.
Early Photography of Gettysburg. Gettysburg, Pa.: Thomas Pub. Co., 1995.
Gettysburg: A Journey In Time. New York: Scribner, 1975
Grant And Lee- The Virginia Campaigns, 1864-1865. New York: Scribner, 1983.

French, J. Clement and Edward Carey. *Trip of the Steamer Oceanus to Fort Sumter and Charleston*. Brooklyn: The Union Steam Printing House, 1865.

Gardner, Alexander. *Gardner's Photographic Sketchbook of the Civil War*. Reprint by Dover, 1959.

Gilbert, George. *Photography: The Early Years*. New York: Harper & Row, 1980.

Hall, Isaac. *History of the Ninety-Seventh New York Volunteers*. Reprint by Butternut & Blue, 1991.

Hoober, James. *Cities Under The Gun: Images of Nashville and Chattanooga*. Nashville: Rutledge Hill Press, 1986

Horan, James D. *Mathew Brady, Historian With A Camera*. New York: Bonanza, 1955

Horan, James. D. *Timothy O'Sullivan - America's Forgotten Photographer*. New York: Bonanza Press, 1966.

Jordan, Ervin L., Jr. *Black Confederates and Afro-Yankees in Civil War Virginia*. Charlottesville: University Press of Virginia, 1995.

Kaplan, Milton. *A Century of Photographs 1846-1946*. Washington: Library of Congress, 1980

Katz, Mark. *Witness To An Era- The Life And Photographs of Alexander Gardner*. Viking Press, 1991

Kelbaugh, Ross J. *Introduction to Civil War Photography*. Gettysburg: Thomas Publications, 1991.

Marszalek, John F., ed. *Diary of Miss Emma Holmes, 1861-1866*. Baton Rouge: Louisiana State University Press, 1979.

Miller, Francis T., ed. *Photographic History Of The Civil War.*(10 Volumes) Review of Reviews, 1912.

Newhall, Beaumont. *The Daguerreotype In America*. New York: Dover, 1976

New York in the War of the Rebellion, 1861-1865. Albany: J. R. Lynn Co., 1912.

Oliver, Andrew. *Portraits of John Quincy Adams and His Wife*. Cambridge: Harvard University Press, 1970.

Poston, Jonathan. *The Buildings Of Charleston*. Columbia: University of South Carolina, 1997.

Powers, Bernard E., Jr. *Black Charlestonians: A Social History, 1822-1865*. Fayetteville: University of Arkansas Press, 1994.

The Private Mary Chesnut. Oxford: Woodward & Muhlenfeld, 1984.

Ramsay, Jack C., Jr. *Photographer . . . Under Fire*. Minneapolis: Bolger Publications, 1994.

Ravanel, Mrs. St. Julien. *Charleston, The Place And The People*. New York: MacMillan, 1912. (reprinted Easly, S. C.: Southern Historical Press, 1972)

Relic of A Lost Cause- The Story of S. C.'s Ordnance of Secession. Columbia: State Dept. of Archives & History, 1990.

Ripley, Warren. *Artillery and Ammunition of the Civil War*. New York: Van Nostrand Reinhold Co., 1970.

Ripley, Warren. *Siege Train*. Columbia: University of South Carolina Press, 1986.

Ripley, Warren. *The Battery*. Charleston: Evening Post Publishing Co., 1977.

Rosen, Robert. *Confederate Charleston: An Illustrated History Of The City And The People During The Civil War*. Columbia, S. C.: Univ. of S. C. Press, 1994.

Rosengarten, Dale [also by Martha Zierden, Kimberly Grimes, Ziyadah Owusu, Elizabeth Alston, Will Williams III]. *Between The Tracks*. Charleston: Charleston Museum, 1987.

Russell, Andrew J. *Russell's Civil War Photographs.*. Revised edition-New York: Dover Publications, Inc., 1982.

Smith, Margaret D. and Mary L. Tucker. *Photography In New Orleans- The Early Years 1840-1865.* Baton Rouge and London: Louisiana State University Press, 1982.

Smythe, Augustine Thomas. *Letter files of Adger/Smyth/Smythe/Bennett Family.* Unpublished letters held at the South Carolina Historical Society, Charleston, S.C.

Sullivan, Constance, ed. *Landscapes Of The Civil War - Newly Discovered Photographs From The Medford Historical Society.* New York: Alfred A. Knopf, 1995.

Sparkman, Mary A. *Through A Turnstile into Yesteryear.* Charleston: Walker, Evans and Cogswell, 1966.

Still, William N., Jr. *Iron Afloat.* Columbia: University of South Carolina Press, 1985.

Tower, R. Lockwood, ed. *Walter Herron Taylor, Lee's Adjutant.* Columbia, U. S. C. Press, 1995

Van Woodward, C., ed. *Mary Chesnut's Civil War.* New Haven: Yale Univ. Press, 1981

U. S. Government. *U. S. Census of 1850.*

U. S. Government. *The War Of The Rebellion: A Compilation of the Official Records of the Union And Confederate Armies. (also . . . Navies)* Washington: Government Printing Office, 1890.

Ward, Geoffrey, Ken Burns, & Ric Burns. *The Civil War. An Illustrated History.* New York: Alfred A. Knopf, 1990.

Waring, Joseph Ioor, M. D. *In Roper Hospital-A Brief History.* Charleston: Nelson's Southern Printing Co., no date.

Washington Light Infantry. *unpublished Minute Books.* Charleston, S. C.

Williams, T. Harry. *P. G. T. Beauregard, Napoleon In Gray.* Baton Rouge: Louisiana State University Press, 1955 (reprint 1975)

Newspapers

Charleston Daily Courier. Charleston County Library
Charleston Mercury. Charleston County Library
Frank Leslie's Illustrated Newspaper
Pittsburgh Dispatch
British Journal of Photography
American Journal of Photography
Savannah Daily Herald

Address changes determined by:

1855.   Gazlay, David M. *1855 Charleston City and General Business Directory,* Charleston: James, Williams & Getsinger, 1855.

1859   Means & Turnbull. *Charleston Business Directory,.* Charleston: Walker, Evans & Co. 1859.

1859   1859 Charleston City Tax Books, presently at Mesne Conveyance, Charleston

1860   Fernslew, W. Eugene. *[1860] Directory of the City of Charleston.* Savannah: John M. Couper & Co., 1860.

1861   *Census of the City of Charleston, S. C. For the Year 1861.* Charleston: Evans & Cogswell, 1861.

1867:   *Charleston City Directory [1867-8]*

1871:   *1871 City Tax Book,* at Charleston City Archives' Land Records.

1875   Haddock, T. M. & J. E. Baker *Charleston City Directory, 1875-6.* Charleston: Walker, Evans & Cogswell, 1875.

In this volume, Address Citations will be by <u>year</u> of publication, not by author's name.

ABOUT THE AUTHOR

Jack Thomson has been studying Confederate Charleston for over twenty years. Born in Miami, Florida, he was a U.S. Army Motion Picture Photographer in the 69th Signal Company in Germany. He received his bachelor's degree in business management at Florida State University in 1966. Living in Charleston since 1968, he worked in insurance while using his free time learning the lore of the "Holy City." Not all of Charleston's history is on dry land; Jack used scuba gear for three years to salvage artifacts from two sunken blockade runners *Georgiana* and *Mary Bowers*. He founded an American Revolutionary War reenactment unit, the 2nd South Carolina Regiment of Foot (1975-82) and has written about the Revolution for the S.C. school systems. He is married to Mary Peters both Presbyterians, they live in an 1882 house across the street from Charleston's 1787 Unitarian Church and the 1818 St. John's Lutheran Church.

In 1986 he began Civil War Walking Tours of Charleston and has led countless visitors around America's most historic city. His tour uses his extensive collection of Civil War images to show how much of 1865 Charleston has survived into the 21st century